Arthur Penrhyn Stanley

Westminster Sermons

Arthur Penrhyn Stanley

Westminster Sermons

ISBN/EAN: 9783743353916

Manufactured in Europe, USA, Canada, Australia, Japa

Cover: Foto ©Lupo / pixelio.de

Manufactured and distributed by brebook publishing software (www.brebook.com)

Arthur Penrhyn Stanley

Westminster Sermons

WESTMINSTER SERMONS

Sermons on Special Occasions

PREACHED IN WESTMINSTER ABBEY

BY

ARTHUR PENRHYN STANLEY, D.D.

LATE DEAN OF WESTMINSTER

NEW YORK

CHARLES SCRIBNER'S SONS

1882

PUBLISHERS' NOTE.

THESE Sermons have been collected and are now
published in accordance with the wish of Dean Stanley.
They are given as delivered, with the correction of
obvious errors. Some of them have been already
printed in periodicals and separately.

EASTER, 1882.

CONTENTS.

ON THE ABBEY.

PAGE

A REASONABLE, HOLY, AND LIVING SACRIFICE. (On the Dean's Installation) 1

DEDICATION OF WESTMINSTER ABBEY. (The 800th Anniversary) 18

THE CORONATION OF WILLIAM THE CONQUEROR, AND ITS CONSEQUENCES 39

THE ALTAR OF WESTMINSTER ABBEY . . . 50

THE RELIGIOUS ASPECT OF SCULPTURE . . . 66

ON ROYAL AND NATIONAL EVENTS.

A THREEFOLD CALL 75

THE NATIONAL THANKSGIVING :—

   I. DEATH AND LIFE 83

   II. THE TRUMPET OF PATMOS 92

   III. THE DAY OF THANKSGIVING . . . 102

ENGLAND AND INDIA 114

THE RETURN OF THE TRAVELLER . . . 128

FUNERAL SERMONS.

	PAGE
LORD PALMERSTON	138
CHARLES DICKENS	149
SCIENCE AND RELIGION. (Sir John Herschel) . .	162
THE RELIGIOUS ASPECT OF HISTORY. (Mr. Grote) .	179
FREDERICK DENISON MAURICE	191
THE MISSION OF THE TRAVELLER. (Dr. Livingstone)	197
CHARLES KINGSLEY	214
THE RELIGIOUS ASPECT OF GEOLOGY. (Sir Charles Lyell)	230
THE RELIGIOUS USE OF WISDOM. (Bishop Thirlwall)	246
THE RELIGIOUS ASPECT OF GOTHIC ARCHITECTURE. (Sir Gilbert Scott)	260
THE LATE PRINCESS ALICE	273
AN INDIAN STATESMAN. (Lord Lawrence) . . .	280
THOMAS CARLYLE	296
THE DAYS OF OLD. (Rev. Lord John Thynne) . .	307
THE EARL OF BEACONSFIELD	319

MISCELLANEOUS SUBJECTS.

CHRISTIAN FRATERNITY	330
DIVERSITY IN UNITY	340
THE CLOSE OF THE MISSION SERVICES ON ST. ANDREW'S DAY, 1879	356
THE DISTRESS OF PARIS	363

PAGE

THE CHRISTIAN RULE OF SPEECH. (American Independence) 374

THE CRUSADE OF CHARITY 384

THE GREEK MASSACRE 399

A REASONABLE, HOLY, AND LIVING SACRIFICE.

January 10, 1864, the day following the Dean's Installation.[1]

I beseech you therefore, brethren, by the mercies of God, that ye present your bodies a living sacrifice, holy, acceptable unto God, which is your reasonable service. — ROMANS xii. 1.

WHEN Christianity dethroned the previous religions of the world, it immediately did that which proved its sovereign right to the position which it claimed. It took the names, the institutions, the ideas which it found, and gave them a new and better meaning; or even if it destroyed them, it immediately planted a corresponding idea or institution in their place. It "took away" that which was old and ready to vanish, in order that it might "establish" that which will endure for ever and ever.

Of a thousand instances which might be given of this upward, soaring tendency, this transfiguration of earthly things by a new and heavenly light, none is more remarkable than its treatment of Sacrifice. Sacrifice, so universal in the old religions, both Jewish and Pagan, has in its ancient sense been rejected by Christianity altogether. There is now no Christian sect or church where God is worshipped by the slaughter of dumb

---

[1] This sermon has been published by the author as a first step towards the fulfilment of the prayer offered up in the Abbey on the day of his installation, "that those things which he hath promised, and which his duty requires, he may faithfully perform, to the praise and glory of the name of God, and the enlargement of His Church."

1

animals or of human victims. But in a higher sense
Christianity is, above all other religions ever known, a
Religion of Sacrifice. It is a Religion founded on the
greatest of all sacrifices, the Sacrifice of the Incarnation,[1] culminating in the Sacrifice on Calvary.[2] It is a
religion of which the whole continuance in the world
depends on continual sacrifice — the sacrifice (such is
the new meaning which the New Testament has poured
into the old word) of the heart and mind in grateful
praise and thanksgiving,[3] the sacrifice of good deeds,[4]
and broken hearts and contrite spirits,[5] the sacrifice of
the whole man in the dedication of himself to God.[6]

The very word as we use it in common parlance has
risen into this higher and nobler signification; the
earthly, Levitical, outward element has melted away.
The Prophetical, spiritual element, so strange and new
in the 50th and 51st Psalms, when David contrasted the
flesh of bulls and the blood of goats with the offering
of a right conversation and the sacrifice of a troubled
spirit,[7] became fixed by the Apostle St. Paul in the
permanent forms of Christian worship, in the ordinary
language of Christendom.

"I beseech you," — so he speaks to us in the Epistle of
this morning, — " by the mercies of God, that ye present
your bodies a living sacrifice, holy, acceptable unto God,
which is your reasonable service." That is to say, " I
beseech you, by all that God has done for you in creation and in redemption, in nature and in grace, that
ye offer to Him *your own bodies*, not the bodies of any
other victims or offerings, but your own, your own
beings, your own human forms; a *living* sacrifice — not

[1] John xvii. 19 ; Eph. v. 2 ; Heb. x. 7, 8, 10 ; Rom. viii. 32 ; 2 Cor. v. 21.
[2] Heb. ix. 28, xiii. 12.   [3] Heb. xiii. 15 ; Rom. xv. 16.
[4] Heb. xiii. 16 ; Ps. l. 23.   [5] Ps. li. 17.
[6] Ps. l. 23 ; 1 Pet. ii. 5 ; Rom. xii. 1 ; Phil. ii. 17.   [7] Ps. l, 13, li. 16, 17.

dead victims, falling lifeless on the ground under the sacrificer's flashing knife, but instinct with life and energy; *holy and acceptable unto God* — not less holy and acceptable because it is a moral and spiritual, and not a ceremonial holiness; your *reasonable service* — a worship, a service, not of irrational creatures, of bulls and goats, of flowers and fruits, but of reasonable human beings, worthy of the God who planted reason and conscience within us.

This is the true Christian sacrifice which should pervade all our worship and all our life, the breathing incense of all our prayers, all our actions. It is no metaphor, no figure of speech. It is the substance, the reality, which has taken the place of those older sacrifices which were but types and shadows of the true Sacrifice, as in the case of our Divine Redeemer, so, in a lower sense, in the case of His servants.

Let us trace the full meaning of these words.

There have been moments in the life of many a Christian man when this sacrificial act must have been true to the very letter. In the early ages of persecution, when Christians gave up their bodies to the sword, the stake, the cross, the wild beasts, for the sake of Christ, they must have felt that they were indeed presenting themselves to be "holy, reasonable, and living" victims in the cause of God and of truth. Soldiers, too, on the eve of some great battle, must, if they reasoned at all, have felt that they were sacrificing themselves in the literal sense of the Apostle's words. On the day when our armies landed on the shores of the Crimea, this very chapter was read to one of the advancing troops by one of the officers in command; and we and they may have truly felt how that was indeed a *living* sacrifice, a sacrifice of body, life, and limb, of the best blood of England's sons; *holy*, because it was made at the call of duty; *reasonable*, because it was not the devotion of brute courage or wild superstition, but of calm, loyal, reasoning obedience.

But not only in these greater occasions, but in the less exciting though still eventful days of our ordinary lives, we can enter into every word of the Apostle's appeal. We many of us feel its whole meaning, when in the Sacrament of the Lord's Supper, in that remarkable self-dedication which once formed the very central portion of the consecration prayer,[1] and which still forms the culminating point of the whole service, we use these very words, and "*present to God ourselves, our souls and bodies, to be a reasonable, holy, and lively sacrifice to Him.*" We feel it with an especial force in the beginning of the new year, when new hopes and new resolutions rise within us, and when we determine, it may be with many an effort and many a pang, to enter on a new course of life, and, like the early Christians, bind ourselves as by a sacramental oath or pledge to the renewed service of our Heavenly Master. We feel it still more, if there be any amongst us who are entering not only on a new year, but on a new crisis, a new career, a new position, which to be worthily fulfilled requires, in the most literal sense, the sacrifice of all our energies to this one purpose. And if, as in the case of him who now addresses you, this entrance on his new career, this admission to his new office is expressed in solemn words, handed down from former times, and solemnly spoken within these sacred walls, how naturally does the text of this day convey the feelings with which he would now appear for the first time before this congregation to devote himself to the work to which he has been called! Antique and peculiar as those words may be, fresh from the fiery struggles of

[1] **First Liturgy of King Edward VI.**

the age of our Royal Foundress, yet they rise by the force and elevation of their expressions so far beyond the occasion which gave them birth, and so singularly adapt themselves to the sacrificial and sacramental pledge in which all Christians are invited by the Apostle and by our own Church to join, that I may well unite both forms together, and combine for your instruction and my own the universal truth and the particular case, the Apostolic injunction and the Royal oath, by which you as Christian people, I as a Christian teacher, present ourselves on this day as a reasonable, holy, and living sacrifice to our All-wise and All-merciful Father — you, on the new year, which lies before you filled with its unknown trials, pleasures, and duties; I, on the new office which, in the sight of God, demands the same sacrifice and requires the same encouragement that belongs to every office and ministry in the Christian Church everywhere.

Let us, then, take the characteristics of this sacrifice as they are expressed by the Apostle, as they are put forth by the Church of England in its most solemn Service, as they fall in with the peculiar claims of this great Collegiate Church.

REASONABLE — HOLY — LIVING.

I. First, "A *reasonable sacrifice*." That is to say, a sacrifice, a dedication, not of mere impulse, fancy, affection, but of our reason, our understanding, our intellect; a sacrifice in which our reason takes full part, in which our understandings go along with our spirits, in which our minds go along with our hearts. How is this to be done? The sacrifice of our *reason*, the *reasonable* service, which the God of reason and of truth requires from us is, first and foremost, the sacrifice to Truth. Not to authority, not to freedom, not to popularity, not to fear, but to Truth.

It is, no doubt, a hard sacrifice which is thus required. Long inveterate custom, cherished phrases bound up with some of our best affections, the indolent respect of persons or acquiescence in common usage, these are what Truth again and again compels us to surrender. But this is precisely the sacrifice which God demands from us at His altar, this is precisely the sacrifice which in our solemn act of self-dedication we declare that we are ready to offer. *Vera consuetis semper antehabiturum* — that "we will always prefer Truth to Custom," that we will give to Truth not the second or the third, but the first place; that antiquity, novelty, prejudice, fashion, must give way before the claims of Truth wherever it be found. Dear, no doubt, is tradition; dear is the long familiar recollection; dear and most sacred in its own place and measure is venerable antiquity on the one hand or bold originality on the other; but dearer than any of these things, dearer and higher in human things, dearer and higher yet in things divine, is Truth, the duty of seeking and speaking the Truth in love, in the unshaken faith that Truth is great and will in the end prevail. And may He, whose name is Truth, be with our humblest efforts to teach the truth, and honor the truth. here and everywhere !

And close upon this pledge, in Christian teaching, there follows another like unto it. We declare that "we will always prefer the written to the unwritten," *scripta non scriptis;* that "the Word of God," as it appears in the Bible, is above all human opinions whatsoever. This, too, is a sacrifice often hard to make. To search the Scriptures thoroughly, to resign ourselves to their real original meaning, to make out the true sense of Prophet, Psalmist, and Apostle, and not force our opinions upon them, this is a task which may involve many a struggle hard to flesh and blood, many a sacrifice of time and thought, and ease, unknown to those who tread in the smoother walks of literature, or science, or practical life. But it is a sacrifice to which some at least in every generation are called; and the object is one which is worth the sacrifice to every Christian man, to every Christian teacher, who cares for the progress of the human race, who cares for the welfare of Christendom.

The Bible. Doubtless it contains many "things hard to be understood," many things "which the unlearned and unstable may wrest to their own destruction." But take it with all its difficulties — take it with all the imperfections of the human agencies by which it has come down to us, and it is still true that at least in the great field of Theology no more reasonable service can be offered up by man to God in this generation than the study of the Scriptures. "Thy word is tried to the uttermost," tried by the honest investigations of science, tried by the undue claims made upon it, tried by the misunderstanding of its enemies, tried by the misunderstanding and exaggeration of its friends; and yet, in spite of all, "Thy servant loveth it,"[1] because he knows that there is nothing else like it in the world, nothing else which will so well repay all the trouble, anxiety, and misapprehension which its study involves. Its value has increased, not diminished, with the lapse of ages. It is even more important than in former times to be able to go back from modern controversies to the fountain of our faith, pure and undefiled, in the hills from which it springs. It is still the Book of books, not to one nation only but to all mankind. It is still the guide both of the learned and of the ignorant. Through its vast variety of style and character, light and shade, parable and history, song and prose, sorrow-

---

[1] Ps. cxix. 140.

ful and joyful, profound and simple, it is more than
ever the best means of bringing together the educated,
the half-educated, the uneducated; the inquirer, the
waverer, the believer, the misbeliever; if not in one
communion of discipline and worship, at least in one
communion of thought and feeling. It is still "the
witness in all ages of the higher things in the heart of
man, the inspired source of truth, the way to the better
life." It contains treasures of wisdom, of justice, of
tenderness, of toleration, of freedom, which have never
yet been exhausted. It stands on a height above all
the human speculations which have gathered round it.
Ancient Creeds, modern Confessions of Theology, have
their own place and value, but in form, in substance, in
spirit, they are immeasurably below the Bible; they are
not to be named for a moment in comparison of the living voice of God, as it speaks to us through the living
acts and utterances of patriarch and king, lawgiver and
judge, priest and soldier, psalmist and prophet, through
all the manifold "sundry times," through all the infinitely "divers manners" in which He inspired the
teachers of His chosen people, until "in these last
days He has spoken to us" once for all "in" the Person of Jesus Christ "His Son." To bring out the true
meaning of each part of the Sacred Scriptures in its
due proportions; to interpret the Bible, not by our own
fancies concerning it, but by what it says of itself;
"rightly to divide the word of truth" by distinguishing
between the essential and the unessential, between the
eternal and the temporal, between the letter and the
spirit; to strive to put an end (if I may use the words
of one of my most distinguished predecessors) to "the
unnatural war between faith and reason, between human science and Divine;"[1] to confute the manifold

[1] Horsley's *Sermons*, vol. iii. p. 175.

and opposite errors which arise contrary to the plain, simple, Divine wisdom of the Bible; to confute them by every means in our power, but above all by the surest of all means, by candor, by moderation, by patient and comprehensive study, always making the best and not the worst of those who oppose us, constantly seeing truth even in the midst of error, making the best refutation of error, not by attacking what is false, but by fully stating what is true — this is the noble sacrifice, this is the reasonable service which the Christian teacher in the Church of England, and in this great Abbey, is pledged to offer to Him who seeks for His true worshippers those who worship Him in spirit and in truth.

II. Secondly, the sacrifice must be HOLY. Ah! to what a world beyond ourselves does this word carry us! how near to the Great White Throne! how far away from ourselves, and this miserable, selfish, sinful world! How easy to feel its meaning, how difficult to explain it! how far more difficult to apply it! A life, a worship, separate, consecrated from the low, envious, uncharitable, narrow, impure influences which dry up our better thoughts; a life set on higher aims, a life which has within it something at least which recalls the world to the sense of the saintly, the heroic, the heavenly, the divine! Where shall this holiness be sought? How shall we figure it to ourselves? There are many answers which might be given. But I fall back on two which are furnished in our own solemn pledge, that we "will draw our rule of life from the Word of God," and that "we will embrace with our whole souls the true religion of Christ." Weigh well the force of both these expressions. They are the same in meaning as those in which the whole aim of religious teaching has been well summed up — "To live in the spirit of the Bible, and to love the Lord Jesus Christ."

"The rule of life to be drawn from the Scriptures." I have spoken of the Bible as the fountain and the bulwark of Truth. Let me now speak of it as the fountain and the bulwark of Holiness. There is indeed a holiness in the Bible which speaks for itself. The spirit which breathes through it is indeed the spirit of the saints, the spirit of heroes, because it is the spirit of all holiness and of all goodness. To live in the spirit of the Bible, to live in that exalted atmosphere which nursed the faith of Abraham, and the unselfishness of Moses, and the courage of Joshua, and the devotion of David, and the hope of Isaiah, and the energy of Paul, and the love of John — this is better than any rule however careful, than any form however exact, which scholastic ingenuity or ascetic piety has ever devised.

Take even a single Psalm. Read over in your household the 15th or the 101st Psalm; read over to yourselves the 51st, which was sung in this morning's service. Or take even a single text — a single verse from the 13th chapter of the 1st Epistle to the Corinthians, or from the Sermon on the Mount; act upon it throughout a single week, make it the rule of a single family; what a holy sacrifice, salted with the salt of God's special grace, would then be offered up! What a difference would it make in the happiness, the usefulness, the dignity, the greatness of the whole neighborhood, of the whole institution, of which we form a part!

And yet further, if we ascend from the Bible to Him of whom the Bible speaks, what a lifting up of our hearts above the toil, and dust, and turmoil, and controversies, and doubts of the world, if we could with a full sense, or any thing like a full sense of the meaning of those majestic words, declare "that we embraced with our whole souls the true religion of *Christ!*" Of Christ, and of no one else; the religion, not even of His best-

beloved servants, or of His greatest and wisest and oldest Churches, but of Himself; the religion of Christ, as
He Himself has taught it to us, and showed it to us, in
the Four Gospels — in His words, in His works, in His
mind, in His Spirit, in Himself. Do not disparage the
teaching of the Apostles: it is full of instruction for all
future times. Do not disparage the teaching of any of
the Churches which they founded: each Church in each
age has rendered its own peculiar service to the cause
of goodness. But even the collective wisdom of all
the Churches has not in religious matters reached up
to the wisdom of the Apostles, who lived in the presence
and in the spirit of Christ; and even the Apostles point
not to themselves, but to Him, as the Founder of their
faith, as the Source of their spiritual life. Ask spiritual
counsel, O my brethren, from all these quarters, but ask
it especially from Him who, if our belief concerning
Him be true in any degree, must be above every other
religious teacher that has ever appeared on the earth.
Ask, in every perplexity, in every dispute that crosses
our religious life, ask what He would have said, what
He would have done. Ask not of Him questions of
times or seasons, or questions of this world's knowledge
and power, which he refuses to answer; but ask of Him
the questions how we are to please God, how we are to
serve our brethren, how we are to deal with sin, how we
are to deal with error, how we are to deal with our
opponents, how we are to deal with our own follies, and
passions, and sins; and assuredly we shall receive an
answer, not of this world, nor of this age, nor of the will
of man, nor of days long past, nor of any sect or party
or church, but the answer of the Eternal Mind of God
Himself, the answer of the Ancient of Days, the same
yesterday, to-day, and forever.

In the true, original, catholic, evangelical Religion of

Jesus Christ, and in this alone, all the divided religions of Christendom find their union, their repose, their support. Find out what He was and what He is — what He is and what He is not. Find out His mind, His character, His will; and in His greatness we shall rise above our littlenesses, in His strength we shall lose our weakness, in His peace we shall forget our discords.

O that we might be strengthened, every one of us, to make this holiest of all sacrifices to the holiest and greatest of all causes! O that Christendom might be drawn more and more, year by year, to its true Lord and Master! O that we might rise, ever so faintly, into that loftiest of all the aspirations of the sweetest psalmist of England and the English Church : —

> Weary of all this wordy strife,
> These notions, forms, and modes and names,
> To Thee, the Way, the Truth, the Life,
> Whose love my simple heart inflames —
> Divinely taught, at last I fly
> With Thee and Thine to live and die ![1]

III. " To live or die ! " This brings me to the last characteristic of the Christian sacrifice — not only " reasonable," and " holy," but " LIVING." There have been those who have offered to God a reasonable and a holy sacrifice, but a *dead* sacrifice — a sacrifice cold, hard, philosophic, reasonable, without warmth, without sympathy, without action; a sacrifice holy, devoted, but shut up within books, shut up within walls, the dry bones of religion without its animating spirit, the imitation of Christ in thought and feeling, not in life and action. Such sacrifices may be in their measure acceptable to Him who knows our manifold weaknesses. But

---

[1] Charles Wesley, *Hymn on Catholic Love.*

they are not the highest and best sacrifices, they are not those in which He most delights. No, our sacrifices must not be like the dead carcases of the ancient victims, thrown away to perish or to be burned; they must be living, moving, walking, speaking, acting in the face of day; living, vigorous, active bodies, living, cheerful, energetic souls. We know what we mean by saying that a child or a man is "full of life." That is (as long as God grants us health, and strength, and spirits) what our sacrifice of ourselves should be — "full of life." Not desponding, sickly, pining, morbid, morose; not gloomy, chilling, cold, forbidding; not languid, lazy, indolent, inactive; but full of life, and warmth, and energy; cheerful and making others cheerful, gay and making others gay, happy and making others happy, contented and making others contented, at ease and putting others at ease, active and making others active, doing good and making others do good, by our living, lively, lifelike, vivid vitality — filling every corner of our own souls and bodies, filling every corner of the circle and the institution in which we move, with the fresh life-blood of a warm, genial, kindly, Christian heart. Doubtless this, too, requires a sacrifice; it requires us to give up our own comfort, our own ease, our own firesides, our own dear solitude, our own favorite absorbing pursuits, our shyness, our reserve, our pride, our selfishness. But for this, too, there is a cause, there is a reward. That solemn pledge of duty which calls us to our *reasonable* and to our *holy* sacrifice, calls us also to the *living* active service of our neighbors, of our Church, of our country, to the living faithful service of the great institution of which so many of us in this place are members. To protect its interests, to guard its privileges, to extend its usefulness, is the vow which needs, or ought to need, no out-

ward words to express it in any who is summoned to
fill any place, from the humblest to the highest, in this
sacred building. To breathe a soul even into these
dead stones, to draw out the marvellous tale which lies
imprisoned within each wall, and tower, and arch, and
relic of this most august of English sanctuaries; to
make each sepulchre give up again to life its illustrious
dead for the glory of God and for the instruction of us
who tread these famous floors; to feel within ourselves
a new life inspired by the grandeur, the beauty, the
hoary crown and the length of days, beneath which our
lot is cast; to throw new life and meaning into the
words of our Services, into the truths of our Creeds,
into the very sounds of our hymns and anthems — this
indeed would be to become " living stones,[1] a spiritual
house, an holy priesthood, to offer up spiritual sacrifices
acceptable to God by Jesus Christ."

And not only from the dead outward structure, or
from the outward sounds and words, but from the living souls and spirits who live and move among and
around these ancient sepulchres and mighty walls shall
our living sacrifice be found.

What a fresh stream of youthful interest for so many
generations has been poured through our aged cloisters
and our venerable precincts by the illustrious School,
which unites us in them to the two greatest Colleges
of our two great seats of learning! What a refuge for
calm learning, for eager search after truth, for advance
of the landmarks of knowledge, is still supplied by this
sacred spot, — as in earlier ages rescued from amidst
the waste of waters and the tangled thickets of the
wilderness, so now rescued from the ever-advancing
roar of this vast city, from the thorny paths of passion
and faction; a temple where serener thoughts may be

---

[1] 1 Pet. ii. 5.

breathed and higher interests served, above the waves and storms of this troublesome and shifting world!

What a flood of spiritual life should stream from this the very heart of England's heart, to enlighten, purify, animate, the ignorant, the suffering, the young, the helpless, the oppressed, the desolate! What a returning stream of life should flow back from them to awaken our silence, to stir up our seclusion, to respond to our services, to profit by our instructions!

And as we look forward to the future, can we forbear with grateful hearts to reflect what an encouragement, what a stimulus to all who come after, has been already furnished by the changes effected through the activity and the self-denial of those who have gone before! How widely of later years have our doors been opened by the just confidence which has removed the barrier that shut out the sight of our historic walls from those who would most benefit by the sight of them! What a new glory has been thrown around even this glorious church, by the rule of the wise and good and gentle Head now to be withdrawn from us; under whose auspices the silence of our majestic nave has, after a slumber of three hundred years, been again broken by the trampling feet of vast congregations, by the welcome sounds of prayer and praise, by the eloquent voices of the goodly company of preachers! What a renewed energy of all good works, what an inroad of the living word of God into the dense circles of vice and ignorance which surround our precincts, by the zeal and munificence of those who have cared for the wants of our vast parishes; where within thirty years churches have been trebled and quadrupled, clergy raised from six to twenty-eight, school-children from three hundred to three thousand! What living sacrifices may have been already, and may yet still be, snatched out of the dead masses that enclose us right and left, by that adventurous movement for the spiritual aid of Westminster,[1] which was first begun by one of our own number, who threw himself with all the fervor and generosity of his nature into the work of rousing the neighborhood to a sense of the need! What a revolution, directly or indirectly, was effected by that single effort; a blessing not only to them that received and to those that are passed away, but to him that gave and to those that will come after; what a new crown of honor to the great Abbey, which for nineteen years he has thus faithfully served!

O may we all be roused by these and like mercies to renewed efforts for the future! O may we all unite in the living work, of whatever kind it be, to which by our own special gifts we may be called! Too vast, too various to be discharged by any single hand or any single mind, it belongs to all alike, for each to take that part which he can best perform. "Whatsoever — whatsoever it be that thy hand, thine own hand, findeth to do, do it with all thy might." Each has his own peculiar call. "We are," as the Apostle says, in the words following on my text, "many members in one body, but all members have not the same office." Let each make use of the other's gifts, to supply that which lacketh in himself, let each supply with all his force that which he alone can give; so shall our sacrifice be indeed the sacrifice of one living united whole, the more united, the more living, because made up of divers and opposite parts. And above all, let the one Divine gift be there which is to every Christian sacrifice what the fire from Heaven was to the sacrifices of old, the one living fire which gives warmth and light to every part — the

---

[1] The Westminster Spiritual Aid Fund, started in 1846 by the exertions of the Rev. Christopher Wordsworth, D.D., then Canon of Westminster, now Bishop of Lincoln.

fire, the life, of all Christian graces; that supreme grace of Charity which "bears all things, hopes all things, believes all things, endures all things," "without which whosoever liveth is counted dead in the sight of God," with which whosoever has even the very humblest measure of faith and hope, may have the blessed assurance that he has passed from death to life, if only he love the brethren.

In and through that Divine Charity, that Divine Life and Death of Charity, of which all earthly charity is the faint and humble likeness, we therefore now present unto Thee O Lord, ourselves, body, soul, and spirit, to be unto Thee, "a reasonable, holy, and living sacrifice;" and although through our manifold sins and weaknesses we are unworthy to offe unto Thee any sacrifice, yet we beseech Thee to accept this our bounden duty and service; not weighing our merits, but pardoning our offences; through Jesus Christ our Lord, by whom and with whom, in the unity of the Holy Ghost, all honor and glory be unto Thee, O Father Almighty, world without end.

DEDICATION OF WESTMINSTER ABBEY.

December 28, 1865 (the Feast of the Holy Innocents), being the eight hundredth anniversary of the foundation of the Abbey by King Edward the Confessor.

It was . . . the Feast of the Dedication, and it was winter. And Jesus walked in the Temple in Solomon's porch. — JOHN x. 22, 23.

EVERY word in this text seems to breathe a peculiar savor. It exemplifies a trait in our Lord's life, not common, not belonging to the essence of His Divine mission, not bearing on the general edification of Christendom, but still deeply connected with some of the best feelings of the human. heart, and a help to the upward course even of the saints of God. It is the sense of a great historic past; an attachment to local memories; the recollection of famous anniversaries; the delight in the names of the mighty dead.

"It was the Feast of the Dedication." It was the festival, not of the first foundation and consecration of the Temple, but of that reconsecration of it by Judas Maccabæus, when he and all the host "saw the sanctuary desolate, and the altar profaned, and the gates burned up, and shrubs growing in the court as in a forest, or in one of the mountains," and amidst the sound of "trumpet and songs, and citherns, and harps and cymbals," [1] the new altar was dedicated. "It was winter;" the words recall the very time of the year when this joyful celebration took place, on the five-and-

---

[1] 1 Maccab. iv. 38, 40, 52, 54, 55, 58.

twentieth day of the ninth month, — that is, of our month of December, — on the same day on which, three years before, the heathen had profaned it; in the same inclement season, of which we read in the book of Ezra,[1] how the wintry sleet so depressed the people, that they sat trembling and cowering "for the great rain" and cold; yet still, in spite of it, "there was very great gladness among the people," "worshipping and praising God, who had given them good success, and put away the reproach of the heathen."

On such an anniversary as this — not one of the greatest in their history, not sanctioned by the Law or the Prophets, full only of that strong religious and national feeling which belongs to the memory of every such event in every history — "Jesus," we are told, "was in Jerusalem, and walked in the Temple in Solomon's porch." He blessed it by His presence. The joy which broke through the gloom of that wintry season He condescended to make His joy. He walked to and fro in the courts and cloisters of the Temple hallowed by those ancient recollections of patriotism and devotion. He lingered in that splendid portico which closed the eastern side of the Temple courts, and which was called after the great king who, long before the dedication of Judas Maccabæus, had consecrated the whole place, and whose glory awakened a thrill of emotion, if we may so say, perceptible in the words of the Redeemer, whenever He named the name of Solomon.

On such an anniversary as this, we, too, are gathered together in a building, if less famous, and in some respects less sacred, yet of far grander dimensions, numbering far longer years, and bound up with events hardly less stirring than that in which "Jesus walked;" underneath a porch, and roof, and walls, which, in part,

---

[1] Ezra, x. 9–13.

even in name,[1] still more in the regal magnificence
which it has witnessed from age to age, recalls, by a not
unworthy association, the art, and the power, and the
glory of the kings of Judah.

Eight hundred years have passed since on this day
was completed the dedication of the Abbey, which, like
that Jewish Temple, was purified, and adorned, and
consecrated in the place of the ruin and desolation
which had well-nigh swept away the vestiges of older
times.

We know not what may have existed before in the
days of Offa or Edgar, or the doubtful Sebert, or the
still more doubtful Lucius, amidst the bristling thickets
and the stagnant channels of the Isle of Thorns,[2] beside
the swollen current of the dark and stormy river, in
the savage solitudes, parted by many a rushing stream,
and many a broad green field, from the Roman or British fortress on the adjacent hills of London. On that
earlier antiquity we need not dwell. We need on this
day only go back in thought to that Innocents' Day,
eight centuries ago, when the act was completed which
fixed the destiny of this building and of this spot for
all future time.

There is something in the simple words of the Saxon
Chronicle describing this event which almost seems
like a faint echo of the words of the text. "At Midwinter King Edward came to Westminster, and had the
Minster there consecrated which he had himself built
to the honor of God, and S. Peter, and all God's
saints." It was at Christmas time, — when, as usual in
that age, the Court assembled in the adjoining Palace
of Westminster, — that the long-desired dedication was

[1] The Northern Porch, the great entrance to the Abbey, is known by
the name of Solomon's Porch.
[2] Thorn-Ey.

to be accomplished. The King had been for years possessed with the thought. Like David in the Psalm of
this morning's service, he " could not suffer his eyes to
sleep nor the temples of his head to take any rest, until
he had found out a place " [1] for the great sanctuary
which was henceforth to be the centre of his kingdom.

On Christmas Day, according to custom, he appeared
in state wearing his royal crown ; but on Christmas
night his strength, prematurely exhausted, gave way.
The mortal illness, long expected, set in. He struggled
through the three next days, and, though when the
Festival of the Holy Innocents arrived he was already
too weak to take any active part in the ceremony, yet
he aroused himself on that day, to sign the Charter of
the Foundation ; and at his orders, the Queen, with all
the magnates of the kingdom, gathered within the
walls, now venerable from age, then fresh from the
workmen's tools, to give to them the first consecration,
the first which, according to the belief of that time, the
spot had ever received from mortal hands. By that
effort, the enfeebled frame and overstrained spirit of
the King was worn out. On the evening of Innocents'
Day, he sank into a deadly stupor. One sudden and
startling rally took place on the eighth day of his illness, on the fifth of January. The recollections of the
teachers of his youth, the dim forebodings of approaching disaster and change, found vent in a few strange,
hardly coherent, sentences that burst from his lips.
Then followed a calm, during which, with words, very
variously reported, respecting the Queen, the succession, and the hope that he was passing " from a land
of death to a land of life," in the chamber which long
afterwards bore his name in the Palace of Westminster,
he breathed his last.

[1] Ps. cxxxii. 3.

A horror, it is described, as of great darkness, filled the whole island; with him it seemed as if the happiness, the liberty, the strength of the English people had vanished away.[1] So dark were the forebodings, so urgent the dangers which appeared to press, that on the very next day, while Duke Harold was crowned in the old cathedral of St. Paul's, the dead King was buried within the newly-finished Abbey, — the first of the hundreds who have been since laid there round his own honored grave.

My brethren, this is not the time or place to enlarge on the historical or antiquarian interest of this remarkable event; to describe how far the present fabric corresponds with that erected by Edward;[2] to show where we can still lay our hands on stones which witnessed that scene; what changes it has since undergone, what has been done, and what still needs to be done, to complete and carry on the work on this day dedicated forever to God. But there are reflections which it suggests, such as can be offered nowhere else so fitly as on this occasion, and from this place.

---

[1] *Life of the Confessor* by Ailred of Rievaulx.

[2] For the Abbey, as built by the Confessor, see the representation in the Bayeux Tapestry, and the Latin description in the time of Henry I., and the French poem in the time of Henry III., published in Mr. Luard's Collection (pp. 90, 244, 417), with Mr. Scott's comments, in the *Gleanings of Westminster Abbey*, p. 3, 4. The Abbey, as we now see it, was for the most part rebuilt by King Henry III. (1220 to 1269) out of regard to the memory of the Confessor, and continued by subsequent sovereigns down to the reign of George II. But, though re-constructed on a more magnificent scale than the Church of King Edward, it covers, as is believed, the same ground; and there are still vestiges of the original building to be seen in the Pyx Chapel, in the passage leading from the Great to the Little Cloisters, and perhaps in some portions of the walls of the ancient Dormitory and Refectory, and of the Crypt under the Chapter-house. The Founder was originally buried before the High Altar, but his remains were ultimately removed to the present Shrine in 1269 by King Henry III. The original Church of Sebert or of Edgar stood at the western end of the present Abbey.

I. First, then, the celebration of this anniversary, connected as it is with the whole growth of the Abbey and all its glories, out of the act and deed, out of the life and death and grave of such an one as was our Founder, is a tribute to the undying power of that simple childlike goodness which this Festival of the Innocents of itself commemorates, and which is the one permanent and distinguishing feature of the traditional character of Edward the Confessor.

Let us see exactly what that character was. On the one hand, if we look at the details of his history, it is hardly possible to imagine a figure more unlike, more incongruous to our own time than was the quaint, irresolute, guileless King, who alone of all the canonized English saints rests undisturbed in his ancient shrine. We know him well, as he is described to us by his contemporaries. We see that grave, gentle figure, old even as a child, moving slowly along with downcast eyes. We recognize him at a distance by the singular appearance of his full, flushed, rose-red face, contrasted with the milky whiteness of his waving hair and beard. As we draw nearer, we hear those startling peals of strange unearthly laughter,[1] which broke through his usual silence; we see those thin pale hands, those long transparent fingers, with which, as it was believed at the time, and for many generations afterwards, he had the power of stroking away the diseases of his subjects. We are astonished, as we look into his outer manner of life, at finding a prince whose time is equally divided between devotional exercises and the passionate pursuit of hunting; when not in church, spending day after day with his hawks, or cheering on his hounds. We find, as we penetrate into his inner life, a childishness of

[1] As in the stories of his visions of the Danish king and of the Seven Sleepers.

thought and action, which at times turned into harsh disregard of those to whom he was most nearly bound, and at times into the most fanciful extravagances. We discover, if we examine into the actual grounds of his titles of Confessor and Saint, that they belong to the fierce struggles between Saxon and Dane, to the worldly policy of Norman rulers, to the lingering regrets of Saxon subjects — most interesting and touching to the English historian, but to the general heart and mind of Christendom of slight moment and of small account. In these respects the gulf of eight centuries between us and him is indeed impassable. His opinions, his practices, his prevailing motives, even in the act of this foundation, are such as in our own times, not only not in England, but in no part of Christian Europe, would be shared by any educated teacher or any educated ruler.

I dwell on these differences, because they serve to bring out more clearly the true lesson which is taught by his life and death; namely, that through, and across, and in spite of those immeasurable divergences, we yet can recognize an innocent childlike faith, which was the secret cause of the charm exercised by him over his countrymen then, which may flourish still in our altered age, and has always an appointed place in the economy of God's ever-moving world.

This Church — so we hear it said sometimes with a cynical sneer, sometimes with a timorous scruple — has admitted within its walls many who have been great without being good; wise, without being simple; noble, with a nobleness not heavenly or saintly, but of the earth earthly, of the world worldly, of the wisdom of the children of this world. Meanly and lightly do they conceive of the greatness and goodness of God who would complain of this wide recognition of all His gifts to man. Yet still it is a counterbalancing reflection, full of weighty truth, that the central tomb, round which all these warriors and poets and statesmen repose, contains the ashes of one who, weak and erring in many respects, as they were, rests his claims to interment here, not on any act or deed which could rank him amongst the great ones of the earth, but on the artless piety, the guileless faith of those early days. He towards whose dust was attracted the fierce Norman,[1] and the proud Plantagenet, and the grasping Tudor, and the fickle Stuart — the stern Edwards, the frivolous Richard, the conquering Henry, the worldly-wise Elizabeth, with her unfortunate sister, and still more unfortunate rival, the pedant James with his ill-starred descendants, and, even from remoter circles, the Independent Oliver, the Dutch William, and the Hanoverian George — was one whose humble graces were within the reach of every man, woman, and child, in every time, if we rightly separate the perishable form from the immortal substance. His goodness and piety were according to the light and means of his age. We, if we would follow in his footsteps, must be good and pious according to the light and means, not of his age, but of ours, not of the eleventh century, but of the nineteenth. The self devotion, the charity of those ancient times need not, must not, shall not die. In order to live, and flourish, and abound, it must take the forms, and use the means, and value the light of those eight hundred years, which God's mercy has added to the world's experience since the Confessor passed away. Still it is his goodness which is here enshrined — whatever shade or whatever light rest upon it — and which we, under forms however altered, must continue and in-

---

[1] The Norman kings were not buried, but were the first to be crowned, in the Abbey.

crease. It is to his faith in the unseen world, amidst whatever ignorance and darkness, that we owe this complex structure. He spoke the word, and it was transformed into stone; and even in some of its most peculiar features, the institution still perpetuates the thought of its first Founder. "Through faith," we may well say, "he has stopped the mouth of Time, quenched the violence of enemies, escaped the edge of the sword, out of weakness been made strong." [1]

II. And this brings me to the second point, of which the day invites us to think. Not only, as I have just said, have eight centuries rolled by, each bringing its accumulated stores of thought, and wealth, and experience to our country, but the very event of which we are now celebrating the anniversary, was itself the beginning of a new order of things which has continued ever since.

The year in which the Abbey was dedicated, was not only the last year of King Edward the Confessor, but it was the eve of the Conquest, the year preceding the greatest change which, with one exception, this Church and nation have witnessed since the days when this spot was first reclaimed from its thorny thickets, in the dim and distant age of our earliest conversion to the Christian Faith. Christmas Day, 1065, was the last which ever saw an Anglo-Saxon king bearing the English Crown. The first coronation which these halls witnessed was that by which, on Christmas Day, 1066, the Norman Conqueror effected his stormy seizure of the throne and realm of England. And of this vast change, the simple-hearted Founder of the Abbey was, consciously or unconsciously, himself the chief inaugurator. Saxon as he was by birth, yet by education he was a Norman. Almost at the moment of his death he wa-

[1] Heb. xi. 33, 34.

vered between a Saxon or a Norman successor.   He had imbibed the first elements of that Norman, Southern, French, Italian civilization, which was to quicken the dull and stagnant blood of our Anglo-Saxon ancestors.

This Abbey, the great work of his life, the last relic which the royal house of Cedric bequeathed to England, was itself the shadow cast before of the coming event, a portent of the mighty future.   Few changes have ever been so sudden and so significant as that by which, in the place of the humble wooden or wattled churches of the Anglo-Saxon period, arose the massive buildings of the Norman style.   The solid pillars, the rounded arches, the lofty roof, the cruciform shape, — all these were new and strange to a degree which we can now hardly conceive; and of this new style and shape and dimensions, the Abbey of the Confessor was the first signal example.   When Harold stood by the side of his brother Gurth and his sister Edith, on the day of the dedication, and signed his name with theirs as witness to the charter of the Abbey, he might have seen that he was signing his own doom, and preparing for his own destruction.   The ponderous arches in yonder cloisters, under which the Saxon nobles passed with awe-struck wonder, to the huge edifice that, with its triple towers and sculptured stones and storied windows, overtopped all the homely tenements far and near, might have told them that the days of their power were numbered, and that the avenging, the civilizing, the stimulating hand of another and a mightier race had been there at work, which would change the whole face of their language, their manners, their church, and their commonwealth.

And yet more, the Abbey itself was, as it were, a new centre for a new political and religious world.   The

"Old Minster," [1] as the Cathedral of Winchester was called, in which the Saxon kings had for centuries been crowned and buried, was now to be exchanged for this "New Minster," depending for its fame on the future generations which were to be gathered within it. It was, we may say, founded not only in faith, but in hope — in the hope that England had yet a glorious career to run; that the line of her sovereigns would not be dried up even when the race of Alfred had ceased to reign; that the troubles which the King, as it was believed, saw in prophetic visions darkening the whole horizon of Europe, would pass away, and that a brighter day was yet in store, than he or any living man in the gloom of that disastrous winter, in the rudeness of that boisterous age, could venture to anticipate. We have seen how that hope has been more than fulfilled; how the Abbey has been renovated, enlarged, glorified, by dynasty after dynasty; how, even if at times disfigured and neglected, it has kept its hold, with a tenacity unequalled by any other building, on the reverence of the whole English people; how its precincts have witnessed not only the solemn inauguration of each successive stage of the English monarchy, but the parallel rise and growth of English constitutional liberty; how it has been the refuge, both in life and death, of princes who had no other place to lay their heads. We see how, in the change of the Reformation, greater, as I have said, even than the Norman Conquest, it still survived the shock; how it has since enrolled amongst its ministers many "wise and eloquent in their instructions, honored in their generation," and lent its shelter to the famous School, which has bound the memory of so many illustrious names by the links of earliest affection to these

[1] Possibly, however, as distinguished from the "New Monastery," built by Alfred at Winchester.

venerable courts: how underneath its shade have been
held assemblies not only to discuss some of the most
momentous questions interesting the Church of England,[1] but also to compile and send forth the only Confession of Faith which was ever sanctioned by law for
the whole island,[2] and which, though bearing the name
of " Westminster," is still the established formulary of
the Presbyterian Church of Scotland. We know how
its pavement or its walls embrace memorials from every
rank and profession and opinion; trophies of chivalry,
ancient and modern; of poetic invention, sublime or
tender, grave or gay; of science in its loftiest speculations or its homeliest applications; of those who have
wrought immortal deeds, and those who have recorded
them in immortal words; of those who have relieved
the sufferings, or upheld the hopes, or purified the stains
of our common humanity. We know how in " this temple of silence and reconciliation " are found in a strange
but instructive union many renowned in their own day,
and forgotten in ours, with others once neglected, but
by a late justice receiving their meed of honor; sovereigns and statesmen, divided in all but in death and in
hope of a common resurrection; the ornaments of other
communions, Roman, Puritan, Nonconformist, beside
the uncompromising prelates of our own; the doubting
sceptic hard by the enthusiastic believer; the smoking
flax beside the blazing lamp, the bruised reed beside the
sturdy tree.

Such has been the growth and the development of the

---

[1] Within the Abbey the important though disastrous acts of the Convocation of 1640; in the Jerusalem Chamber, the approval of the Litur-
gical changes of 1662, by Convocation, and the discussion of the further
changes of 1689 by the Royal Commission.

[2] The doctrinal Articles of the Westminster Confession of Faith were
sanctioned by the English Parliament in 1647, and the whole Confession
by the Scottish Parliament in 1648.

seed planted here by our Founder. We do well to think of it. The Abbey, so considered, is a standing monument and witness of the peculiar formation of our English institutions, of our own duty towards them both as Englishmen and as Christians. The Norman Church erected by the Saxon King; the new future springing out of the dying past; the expansion of the first idea of an institution founded for a special and merely temporary object into uses co-extensive with the interests of the whole commonwealth through all its stages — how striking an example is this of the blessed continuity by which in England the new has been ever intertwined with the old; liberty thriven side by side with precedent; Church and State been inextricably interwoven one with the other; opposing parties both in Church and State co-existing, neutralizing, counteracting, completing each other, neither by the other entirely subdued, each by the other endured, if not honored!

Oh what an exhortation to hopefulness, to forbearance, to comprehensive charity! Fear not, though troubles brood thick around us; they cannot be darker than those which clouded the prospects of our country, when the last hope of England seemed to be buried in the grave of her last hereditary Saxon king. Fear not, though old things seem ever passing away, and all things seem to become new. The change cannot be vaster than when this new edifice sprang up on the ruins of the old, and the rustic solidity of the Saxon gave way before the fiery energy and fresh life of the adventurers from beyond the sea. Fear not to build up the waste places, and put a new sense and a new force into old words and old institutions; or to employ the resources of the present to carry out the duties and the principles of the past. There cannot be any difference more wide,

any incongruity more irreconcilable than there was
between the humble hovels that stood here amidst the
island thickets, and the new building that was to rise
in its place and gather within its walls the greatness of
a new empire. The vicissitudes and ramifications of
the architecture, the worship, the uses of this building,
are likenesses of that true "enlargement" of the Church
of God and of the Church of England, which is a chief
duty of every one who takes office in this place, so as
to embrace within its sympathy (I use the words of a
living [1] statesman), "every true instinct and need of
man, regardful of the just titles of every faculty of his
nature, apt to associate with and make its own all,
under whatever name, which goes to enrich and enlarge
the patrimony of the race." Here, at least, all Englishmen may forget their differences, and feel for the moment as one family gathered round the same Christmas
hearth. Underneath this roof, each one, of whatever
church, or sect, or party, will find the echoes of some
memories dear to himself alone, — some which are dear
to all alike — all of them blending, more or less, with
that manifold yet harmonious "voice from heaven"
which is as "the voice of many waters" of the distant
sea of ages past, or as "the voice of a great thunder"
pealing through the convulsions which have shaken
nations and churches, or as "the voice of harpers harp-
ing on their harps a new," a nobler "song" of Truth
and Love, "before the Throne," and "before the Elders"
of ancient days, and "before the Four Living Creatures"
of God's boundless universe.[2]

III. From this thought we pass at once to the direct
object of the foundation of this august edifice. I speak
not of those curious legends, and dreams, and visions,

---

[1] Address of Mr. Gladstone to the University of Edinburgh.
[2] Rev. iv. 2. The Epistle of the Day.

and vows, which wrought the Confessor's mind to the act of dedicating this Church, which now only concern us, as showing in how perishable, yet for the time how solid a vesture great ideas have clothed themselves. They shall perish, but these shall endure. For, underneath all these imaginations, there was the fixed intention, which has never died out of these walls amidst their many changes, that this magnificent pile was to be the house where Christian souls might meet to hold converse with their Maker. Whatever it has since become — of royal, or heroic, or historic, or artistic — it would have ceased to be, if it had not been, over and above these and much more than these, a place dedicated forever to the worship of Almighty God.

This, it is true, is the purpose which it shares in common with the humblest church or chapel in the kingdom. But, at least, to us who here carry on that worship, the dignity, the perpetuity, of our office is brought home with double force by the reflection that on it, as on a thin, at times almost invisible thread, has hung every other interest which from generation to generation has accumulated round us. Break that thread, and the whole building becomes an unmeaning labyrinth. Extinguish that sacred fire, and the arched vaults and soaring pillars would assume the sickly hue of a cold artificial Valhalla, and "the rows of warriors and the walks of kings" would be transformed into the conventional galleries of a lifeless museum.

You who have worshipped here week by week, year by year; to whom these stones speak not of any secular or ecclesiastical grandeur, but of the silent nurture of your individual souls, of rest to the weary and heavy-laden in its holy services, of dear recollections of departed friends, sons, brothers, parents, partners in life's struggle, that with you have here learned to know and

value the secrets of heaven and the blessings of earth:
— They who in former times, few and scanty it may be,
or in much ignorance, sought God beside mediæval
shrine or relic; or, in after days, caught here the impassioned words of Baxter and Owen; or through
succeeding generations have drunk in the calm and
strengthening prayers of our own Liturgy, in the ever-
recurring cycle of the Christian year: — By these, and
such as these, one may almost say, through all the
changes of language and government, this giant fabric
has been sustained, when worldly ecclesiastics or grasping statesmen would have let it pass away.

> From many a "secret" nook, unthought of there,
> Rises for that proud "Church" their "still" prevailing prayer;

and its Founder's intention has been carried on by many
a one who never thought of him, as he could never have
dreamed of them.

And you, young and old, who take part in our services day by day — you, too, who love to lend your
voices to add to them new grace and force — join hand
in hand, and heart to heart, with those who in times
gone by, within these walls, "found out those musical
tunes" which we to-day sing over their graves, to make
the worship worthy of the place, as the place is worthy
of the worship.

It was the hope of the Founder, it was the belief of
his age, that on this spot was literally planted a ladder
on which angels might be seen ascending and descend-
ing from the courts of heaven. Fond dream! we say;
yet surely not altogether fond if we can accept and fulfil
the brief words in which the most majestic of English
divines has described the nature of Christian worship.
"What," he says, "is the assembling of the Church to
learn but the receiving of angels descended from above?

what to pray, but the sending of angels upward? His heavenly inspirations and our holy desires are as so many angels of intercourse and commerce between God and us. As teaching bringeth us to know that God is our Supreme Truth, so prayer testifieth that we acknowledge Him Our Sovereign Good." [1]

And is this, too, a fond dream? — a hope too lofty to be realized in our later days? Not, O my brethren — not if we could receive it in all its fulness and all its simplicity. Not surely in vain did the architects of successive ages raise this glorious edifice as we now behold it, in its vast and delicate proportions, in this our day more keenly appreciated than in any other since it was first built; designed, if ever were any forms on earth, to lift the soul heavenward to things unseen. Not surely in vain has our English language grown to meet the highest ends of devotion with a force which the rude native dialect or barbaric Latin of the Confessor's age could never attain. Not surely in vain has a whole world of sacred music been created, which no ear of Norman or Plantagenet ever heard, no soul of Saxon harper or Celtic minstrel ever conceived. Not surely in vain has the knowledge of God's word and work, in the Bible, in history, and in nature, always steadily increased, century by century, to unfold to us the mind and the operations of Him with whom we have to do. Not in vain, surely, has the human heart, by God's grace, kept its freshness whilst the world has been waxing old, or the most restless and inquiring of human intellects been led by deep experience to know that the Everlasting arms are still beneath us, and the Eternal God is our refuge, or that "prayer is the potent inner supplement of noble outward life."

So surely, even now, may this Abbey be a witness to

[1] Hooker, *Eccl. Pol.* v. 23.

that one Sovereign Good, of that One Supreme Truth; a shadow of a great rock in a weary land, a haven of rest for human hearts and souls in this tumultuous world, a breakwater against the waves upon waves which beat unceasingly against its island shores.

IV. This leads us to one concluding thought. For those human hearts and souls outside, that perhaps never are brought within these walls at all — for them also this day and its consequences have a true significance. Around the church and the grave of the Confessor has sprung up, by a natural effect, the stir of life and activity which now encircles it. If he was the founder of the Abbey, he was hardly less the founder of the City, of Westminster. And assuredly those souls of the poor, the friendless, the sick,[1] the suffering, are precisely those for whom the good King most cared, and who cherished the deepest and longest affection for him. If S. Peter, the Prince of the Apostles, was the saint before whom the Confessor trembled with a dark, mysterious awe, S. John,[2] the Apostle of Love, was the saint whom he venerated with a child-like, familiar tenderness. By that loving spirit he was endeared to the Saxon race, as the pattern of a better age. Through this, the sense of an oppressive or unjust tax was to him like a cruel wound. Through this, the name of Edward was multiplied far and wide over English families, as the pledge of kindly, honorable, Christian regard to the wants and the rights of others.

Much, thank God, has been done in former days, by . those who have served the Abbey of Westminster, for the multitudes collected round it. Many a labyrinth of

[1] The alms collected on this occasion were devoted to the Westminster Hospital, which stands on the site of the Confessor's Sanctuary, within the original precincts of the Abbey.

[2] See the comparison of the Confessor's devotion to S. Peter and S. John in Ailred of Rievaulx.

poverty and infamy, as intricate and as formidable as those tangled thickets which Sebert or Edward cleared away, has been levelled by the active beneficence of modern times; many a hand has been stretched out to offer spiritual aid to those most in need. But the need still continues, still grows, out of the necessities engendered by the ancient selection of this spot as the centre of the English Empire.

And from this centre of the English Empire whenever the need arises, we may surely appeal to the heart of the English people, as now, in the name of this great Dedication, at this midwinter of our year, in the name of all the recollections which have made us what we are, in the name of the eight long centuries of God's continued goodness to us, that whatsoever each one finds to do, he will do it with all his might, to cause, as best he can, and in all manifold senses, this place, and all around it, to be indeed the House of God and the Gate of Heaven.

And now, for these our mercies, and for these our needs, let us join our thanksgivings and our prayers to Thee, the Giver of all good, and the Source of all strength.

O Almighty God, who hast knit together Thine elect in one communion and fellowship, and built Thy Church on the foundation of the Apostles and Prophets, Jesus Christ Himself being the chief cornerstone, who out of the mouths of babes and sucklings hast ordained strength; we thank Thee for the work of our Royal Founder, who out of weakness was made strong to dedicate this Church to Thy honor; and we pray Thee that there may never be wanting a succession of Thy faithful servants to carry on what he began.

O Almighty Father, of whom all the families in earth are named, and who makest men to be of one mind in a house, we thank Thee that Thou hast caused this sanctuary to be the home of the English people, and the seat of the Imperial throne; and hast in it ever turned the hearts of the fathers to the children, and the hearts of the children to their fathers. Grant that "the free and princely spirit of wisdom and of government, of knowledge and of true godliness, of counsel and of strength," here invoked on the crowned head of our Sovereign Lady the Queen, may evermore descend on her and her children's children, " to lead this people in the way wherein they should go," [1] and from us "we beseech Thee to take away all hatred and prejudice and whatsoever else may hinder us from godly union and concord: that as there is but one Body and one Spirit, and one Hope of our calling, one Lord, one Faith, one Baptism, one God and Father of us all, so we may now and henceforth be all of one heart and one soul, united in one holy bond of Truth and Peace, of Faith and Charity." [2]

O Almighty Lord, whose never-failing Providence ordereth all things both in heaven and earth, we thank Thee that, through the changes and chances of eight hundred years, Thou hast so guided this nation that in its passage through things temporal it has not lost the things eternal; we thank Thee that in this sacred edifice, preserved by Thy goodness from fire and flood, from lightning and tempest, from war and tumult, Thou hast permitted us from generation to generation to offer to Thee the sacrifice of prayer, and to gather together the dust and the memorials of those whom Thou hast raised up with special gifts to adorn this Church and Commonwealth to Thy glory and the welfare of mankind. May this great people serve Thee

---

[1] Prayer from the Coronation Service.
[2] Prayer from the Service for the Accession.

more and more with a wise and understanding heart, in righteousness and true holiness! May this ancient sanctuary ever be devoted to the offering of Thy true and spiritual worship, to the manifesting of Thy blessed presence, and to the communicating of Thy heavenly grace! Let Thine ear ever be attentive to the prayers of Thy people, which within these walls they shall make to Thee. Let Thy peace visit the troubled spirit and heal the wounded conscience of him that cometh hither in penitence and faith. Let Thy consolations wait upon the afflicted and the mourner. Let Thy Spirit of Truth be here with those who teach, and with those who learn, to guide them into all truth. And we beseech Thee that we who serve in this holy place may "have the fulness of Thy grace, that those things which our duty requires [1] we may faithfully perform to the praise and glory of Thy name, and the enlargement of Thy Church," and that we may all with thankful hearts show forth Thy strength to this generation, and Thy power to all those that are yet for to come, through Him who is the same yesterday, to-day, and forever.

Praise ye the Lord! Hallelujah! Amen.

[1] Prayer at the Installation of the Deans and Canons of Westminster.

THE CORONATION OF WILLIAM THE CONQUEROR, AND ITS CONSEQUENCES.

Christmas Day, 1866.

Every battle of the warrior is with confused noise, and garments rolled in blood; but this shall be with burning and fuel of fire. For unto us a Child is born, unto us a Son is given. — ISAIAH ix. 5, 6.

THE Prophet in these words goes back to the famous events of his country's history, to the day of Midian,[1] when Gideon routed the mighty host, amidst the terrors of a midnight panic, and amidst the carnage of the Raven's Rock and the Wolf's Winepress. It was indeed "a battle of the warrior with confused noise, and with garments rolled in blood." But he then foretells a time when out of these wars and tumults there should come a period of deep peace, when these warlike implements should be burnt to ashes, according to the practice of ancient times which heaped sword and spear and armor as on a huge funeral pile, when the victory was won, to proclaim that the strife was over, that the chariots were burnt with fire, and the spears broken asunder.[2] And he saw that this peace would come, because within his own time or hereafter — he knew not clearly which — a Son, a King, should be born, who would be the Prince of Peace, the founder of a new and eternal kingdom, clothed with a majesty which should put to silence the contentions of men, and with a power which should

---

[1] Isa. ix. 4; Judg. vii. 22-25.   [2] Comp. Ps. xlvi. 9.

compress and unite the most divergent elements. May
I on this Christmas Day take up the Prophet's thought,
first recalling to you an event from our own history,
of which this day is the anniversary, this house of God
the scene, and then drawing from it lessons congenial
to the Prophet's teaching and to the glad tidings of this
season?

You may remember that last year we celebrated on
the Feast of Innocents' Day the eight hundredth anniversary of the foundation of this Abbey by the last hereditary Saxon king. We have now advanced another
year, and this day on which I now address you is the
eight hundredth anniversary of the first authentic coronation celebrated in this place, the coronation of William
the Conqueror. That coronation is remarkable, not only
as being the first in the long series which has since been
one of the chief glories of the Abbey, but from its own
intrinsic interest, and from the marvellous lessons which
it conveys to us. I shall not scruple to describe it to
you at length. The great battle which had decided the
fate of England had been fought in October. William
entered London as a stranger and a conqueror. But he
was determined to mount the throne according to all
the forms which ancient usage had prescribed. Here,
therefore, by the grave of the last Saxon king, whose
heir he claimed to be, on this Christmas Day, the usual
coronation day of the Anglo-Saxon sovereigns, in the
heart of what was to be henceforth, as never before,
the capital of England, he appeared with his courtiers
and his army. Here, in the newly finished Abbey, he
took his stand before the altar, beside King Edward's
tomb, the huge, unwieldy, indomitable conqueror,
strange contrast to the feeble, gentle. fantastic prince
of whom we spoke last year. Outside the church, to
guard him from the attacks of his new subjects, were sta-

tioned troops of Norman cavalry; inside were crowded together Norman nobles and Saxon people. The two nations, distinct from each other as Frenchmen and Englishmen, took an equal interest in the event of that day. To each the question was addressed, to the Normans in French, by a French prelate, the Bishop of Coutance, to the English in English, by an English prelate, the Archbishop of York, whether they would have this king to reign over them. Each returned a shout of welcome. But the shout was so loud and fierce, the discord of the two rival languages and nations so harsh, that the Norman soldiers without, hearing but not understanding the uproar, burst in upon the church. A wild panic, a confused flight, and a bloody massacre followed. The Abbey was left almost empty. The King, with the assistant clergy, stood alone by the altar. He, for the first time in his life, was so terrified by the scene, that he remained trembling from head to foot in the extremity of fear. They, hurrying as best they could through the sacred forms, poured the oil over his face and planted the crown on his head; and thus was inaugurated the English Monarchy, thus was begun the series of those august ceremonials which have since never ceased to be celebrated within these walls.

It was indeed "a battle of the warrior with confused noise, and with garments rolled in blood." Who could have thought on that day that those discordant nations could have ever been knit together; that those languages, so unintelligible each to each, should have ever been blended into one; that the dynasty, so darkly enthroned on that seat of blood, could have ever been firmly fixed in the affections of the people? Yet so it has been, and it is for this reason that it is no unworthy subject of contemplation even on this sacred day. Those ancient implements of warfare have indeed been

" burned with fuel of fire ; " their ashes are scattered to
the winds.   The proud Norman and the humble Saxon
are united indissolubly in one nation, the great English
people ; the French tongue and the English tongue are
welded together into one speech, the great English language ; a Sovereign, the descendant at once of William
the Conqueror, and of his rival Edgar Atheling, has
been seated on the throne of Edward the Confessor,
the centre of the English Constitution, the head of the
British Empire.

This of itself is an example, always encouraging, of the
way in which good springs out of evil, and troubles sub-
side, and peace returns, when its return would have
been thought impossible.   But in this case there is
something yet more consoling.   That peace, that glory,
that good, which grew out of this Norman coronation,
is the natural result of the original discordance. " Two
nations," we have seen, were in the womb of the Abbey,
in the womb of the Church and State of England on
that day ; but out of those two nations came the gifts
which each most wanted to make up a perfect whole.
Without the Norman conqueror we should have had no
progress — without the Saxon subject we should have
had no solidity.   Both qualities have marked our history
ever since.   We have been a two-sided, doubly-gifted
nation ; antiquity and novelty, liberty and authority,
aristocracy and democracy, have been interwoven with
our Constitution and with our character, as you will
find them nowhere else interwoven in any part of Europe.   By this means the internal harmony of our kingly
Commonwealth has been preserved, by this means peace
and good-will have been maintained amongst us on occasions when they have perished everywhere else.   Christmas Day to us is not as on that first Christmas Day in
the Abbey, a stormy signal for bloodshed, massacre, and

misunderstanding; but it comes home to every part of the nation equally, as binding man to man, and both to God, equally with the bonds of Christian and of English sympathy. "Unto us," even in this lower sense, "a Child is born, and He shall be called the Prince of Peace."

I might apply this even to private quarrels. I might say to two neighbors who are at variance, to two friends who have quarrelled, and who think that they can never be reconciled, Do not despair; you are not more at enmity than were the Normans and Saxons on the Christmas Day of 1066. Whatever may be the differences which divide you each from each, they may in like manner change and fade away. The old pagan philosopher used to say, "Look upon your friends with the thought that they may one day prove your enemies." The Christian philosopher says (and it is certainly one lesson from the Norman Conquest), "Look upon your enemies with the thought that they may one day prove your friends." Look upon them with the experience which this day furnishes. Think that the Norman may be one day blended with the Saxon. Think that the Saxon will one day bless the Norman.

But may I go a step farther, and point out how this double element, which has pervaded, without destroying, the English Nation, has also pervaded, without destroying, the English Church? Two nations, two parties, two tendencies, have from the first been in her womb also. They have been in the Church of England, for the very reason that it is the Church "of England." The Church of England is a mixed and double Church, because England is a mixed and double nation. If it were not so, it would not be the national Church. At this moment of conflict between two great sections in the Church, it is but the same which has been again and again in the State, in the language, in the Constitution of our country. Look at the words of the first Exhortation in the Liturgy. It is half Norman, half English. It is composed of the same two elements of speech that resounded in such fearful discord through the Abbey on the day of the first coronation: "acknowledge," is Saxon; "confess," is French; "meet together," is Saxon; "assemble," is French; "humble," is French; "lowly," is Saxon; "goodness," is Saxon; "mercy," is French. Even by these trivial signs let us be reminded that the battle of the warrior and the garments rolled in blood have been forever burnt with fire, and melted down into one harmonious language.

But no less, as we go through the Prayer-book, and find expressions which sometimes suit one frame of feeling, and sometimes another, let us not be offended by them; let us not distort them; let us acknowledge that each gives our opponents (if so we choose to call them) an advantage; but let us see in them also a blessed continuation of the same unity which has elsewhere with us overcome the difference of race and language.

Some of us may lament that one set of expressions should have been left, which savors of the old superstitions of the Church before the Reformation. Others may lament that expressions have been admitted quite contrary to these, breathing only the rational or the spiritual atmosphere of modern times. But nevertheless these expressions have existed together, and the two parties may exist together; and the only real breach of Christian faith and Christian charity is when each insists on having the Church and nation to itself, when each endeavors to cast out the other.

Take even that question which has so much agitated many minds at this time — the divergence of opinion respecting the blessed Communion of the Lord's Supper,

in which we are this day to partake. Ever since the
Reformation, there have been two opposite tendencies,
two opposite frames of thought on the subject. Some,
with the Church of Rome and the German Reformer,
Luther, have found pleasure in figuring to themselves
" a real presence," a special nearness to Christ in the
outward tokens of bread and wine, even identifying
these tokens with Himself, even feeling as though they
handled Him with their hands, and saw Him with their
eyes. On the other side, there have been those who,
with the Swiss Reformer Zuinglius and the great mass
of the Reformed Churches, have found pleasure rather
in believing that their Saviour's Presence was in the
heart and in the spirit, within and not without, spiritual
like Himself, brought near to us by remembrance, by
love, by reason, by faith, not by the mere outward act,
or the mere outward ceremony. These two tendencies
have prevailed in this or that mind, according to the
natural turn which disposition or circumstance has
given ; and have prevailed, with all the innumerable
shades of intervening opinion and feeling, from the very
outset of the Reformation down to the present day.
They have left the traces of their conflict in the very
words with which the sacred elements are administered.
At the first beginning of the English Liturgy, just
emerging from the old Church and its peculiar forms,
the words were with us, as in the Churches of Rome
and of Luther, " The Body of our Lord Jesus Christ
preserve thy body and soul unto everlasting life." [1]
When the Reformation had advanced farther, and the
Church of England had become entirely a Reformed
Church, these words were omitted, and in their place
were substituted, " Take and eat this in remembrance
that Christ died for thee, and feed on Him in thy heart

[1] In the First Prayer-book of Edward VI., 1549.

by faith, with thanksgiving." [1]   When, after the accession of Elizabeth, it was desired by her and her wise
counsellors to make the Church as comprehensive and
as national as possible, the two forms were united together.[2]   And so they have continued till our own day,
a pledge and token to us, that the true policy of the
Church of England, may we not say of the Church of
Christ, is not to exclude entirely either of these feelings,
but to blend them together, and in that most solemn
act of Christian fellowship to feel ourselves not two,
but one people.   Many a time, on this and on a thousand other questions, has each party striven to drive the
other out.   Each for the moment has partially succeeded; each has succeeded to its own great loss; each
has done that which would have been done, had the
Normans at the first coronation succeeded in stamping
out the Saxons forever, or the Saxons forever repelled
all contact with the growth and progress of the Normans.   But the spirit of the English nation, the spirit
of the English Church — may we humbly say, the Spirit
of Christ our Lord in the better spirits of both Church
and nation? was too strong for the violence of any
single party.   Oh may it be so still!   May we still, both
as a nation and a Church, deserve the glorious reproach
of keeping together those who elsewhere have been
divided asunder!   May we cherish the blessed privilege
of holding social intercourse, maintaining Christian
communion, between those who in other days, perhaps even in our own, would deny and excommunicate
each other!   Prove and show as much as we will, and
as much as we can, the folly, the exaggeration, the dis-
proportion, the futility of the views which we think
wrong.   But still remember that there is a worse evil

---

[1] In the Second Prayer-book of Edward VI., 1552.
[2] In the Prayer-book of Elizabeth, 1559.

than error, and that is, injustice towards those in whom the error exists. Remember that, if our adversaries have labored with untiring zeal to drive us out, the true Christian retaliation is for us to labor with untiring forbearance to keep them in. The true weapons by which to put down error are argument, reason, knowledge ; the true armor by which error can best be repelled is love of truth, candor, charity.

To other times and to other countries belong "the battle of the warrior, with confused noise, and garments rolled in blood," the sword and stake, the rage for verbal distinctions, the ceaseless desire to find causes of division, partiality, and strife. To ours belongs, or ought to belong, the ceaseless desire to burn up these causes with fuel of heavenly fire. To us belongs, or ought to belong, the determination to "have the faith of our Lord Jesus Christ without respect of persons," to bear with the practices in which we cannot participate, even whilst most strongly condemning them ; providing only that they are not forced on those who wish not for them, that they have liberty of conscience for themselves, not dominion over the faith of others. To us belongs the heaven-born trust, that with the fire of zeal about the greater matters of the law, justice, mercy, and truth, those lesser things of hay, straw, stubble, will be burnt up and destroyed. To us belongs the hope of a true Christian peace, founded not on artificial fusions of outward form, or ill-assorted unions of ecclesiastical organization, but on the greatness of God's love, and on the greatness of man's duty. "For unto us a Child is born, unto us a Son is given," who will unite us together, if we cleave to Him with heart and soul, for this very reason, that He is greater than any of the sects or Churches which call themselves by His name. "He came" — I quote words, far better than

my own, of an English historian educated in this place
— " He came, bringing with Him the knowledge that
God is a Being of infinite goodness ; that the service
required of mankind is not a service of form or ceremony, but a service of obedience and love, obedience
to the laws of morality, and love and charity towards
man.   The God made known in Christ demanded of
His children no other sacrifice than the sacrifice of
their own wills, and for each act of love and self-forgetfulness bestowed on them the peace of mind which
passed understanding.

" Such a Gospel, had it remained as it came from its
Founder," — nay, if even now we can return to it, —
" would have changed," may yet change " the aspect of
the earth.   It would have knit together," it may yet
knit together " in one common purpose, all the good,
all the generous, all the noble-minded, whose precepts,
whose example would serve as a guide to their weaker
brethren.   It would not have quarrelled over words
and forms.   It would have accepted the righteous act,
whether the doer of it preferred Paul or Cephas.   In
that religion, if ever it is fully believed, hatred would
have no place, for love, which is hate's opposite, is its
principle.   The essence of it is something which is held
alike by Catholic and by Protestant, by Lutheran and
Calvinist." [1]

It is for this reason that Christmas with its high
glory to God is also the time of peace and good-will to
earth.   The greatness of God is the true rebuke to the
littleness of men.   The greatness of Christ is the true
rebuke to the littleness of Christians.   The war of
words and names and forms sinks into nothing in
His presence, because in Him there is neither Jew
nor Greek, Norman nor Saxon, circumcision nor un-

---

[1] Froude's *History of England*, vol. ix. p. 300.

circumcision, ritualism nor anti-ritualism, rationalism nor anti-rationalism; because He is not Paul, nor Apollos, nor Cephas, but infinite Grace, and Purity, and Truth; because He is, above and through all these things, "the mighty God, the everlasting Father, the Prince of Peace."

THE ALTAR OF WESTMINSTER ABBEY.[1]

Easter Day, 1867 and 1873.

On the first day of the week, very early in the morning, they came unto the sepulchre, bringing the spices which they had prepared; and they found the stone rolled away from the sepulchre. —LUKE xxiv. 1, 2.

ON this Easter Day, when we once more open to view the accustomed place of our Holy Communion, on which so much care and labor have been spent, these words seem not unsuited to express our thoughts. They came, that faithful band, to pay their tribute of affection and respect to the place where the Lord was laid; they came, as one of their number had come before, with an alabas-

---

[1] The Communion Table or Altar of Westminster Abbey has had a long and varied history. In the first Abbey, as built by Edward the Confessor, it stood at the eastern extremity of the church. In the Abbey, as rebuilt by Henry III., it stood where it has remained ever since, in front of the Confessor's shrine. Of this Altar the only remnant now existing is the richly-painted frontal, discovered by accident some years ago, and now in the south aisle of the church. In the fifteenth century the screen was erected behind the Altar, shutting off the shrine of Edward the Confessor from it, as was common at that epoch. Of this screen or reredos the eastward or hinder face still remains, with the legendary life of the Confessor carved on its frieze. The westward front has long ago perished, and has been since replaced, first, by the marble altarpiece of the time of Queen Anne; next, when this was removed in 1824, by a plaster screen, intended in some degree to imitate the ancient forms; and this was finally replaced within the last ten years by the present reredos, which was erected under the direction of Sir Gilbert Scott. The Communion Table, which now stands in the position which it has occupied since the Restoration, is of cedar wood, carved by Messrs. Farmer and Brindley. The frieze of the reredos consists of sculptures of the history of our Lord, corresponding to that of the life of Edward the Confessor on the other side. The space beneath

50

ter box of ointment of spikenard very precious, as she beforehand to anoint His body for the tomb, so they to anoint and guard it afterwards. They knew well the sacred spot; they knew the little garden, outside the city walls; they knew the rocky hill, out of whose ancient face was hewn the sepulchre wherein never man before was laid; they knew its deep recesses; they had seen the clean linen cloth infolding the frame, and the napkin wrapped about the head; they had watched the huge stone door drawn across the mouth of the cavern; and now, as the first light of the sun broke over the dark summit of the Mount of Olives, they approached the tomb once more with their charge of aromatic stores, to honor the memory of Him whom they had lost.

It was the natural reverence of the human heart for great recollections and sacred places, it was the natural reverence of the Christian heart for all that belongs even to the outward service of our Divine Redeemer. This reverence is not itself religion; far from it. Even the

is filled by a large mosaic, from a design of Messrs. Clayton and Bell, representing the Last Supper. On each side of this are four statues — which, as well as the frieze, were executed by Mr. Armstead. In the centre are St. Peter and St. Paul, the two Apostles to whom the Abbey is dedicated, representing the two divergent tendencies of Christianity; on the north is Moses, as the Lawgiver, looking towards the north transept, which contains the tombs of the statesmen; and, on the south, David, as the Royal Psalmist, looking towards the south transept, as containing the tombs of the poets. Of these statues and their meaning an account is given in the sermon on "The Religious Aspects of Sculpture." The porphyry which furnished the three circular slabs in front of the Altar was brought from the East by Lord Elgin at the same time as the Elgin marbles, and was presented to the Abbey by his grandson in 1870. The last additions were the gilded canopies above the mosaic picture, and underneath it heads of the holy women of Scripture — Ruth, Anna, Elisabeth, the Virgin Mary, Mary Magdalene, Martha, and Dorcas. The whole work was completed on Easter Day, 1873; its earlier portion had been completed on Easter Day, 1867, and the substance of the present sermon was preached on both those occasions, in the presence of those who had been concerned in the sculpture, carving, and arrangement of the whole.

Holy Sepulchre, which they thus came to adorn, has been the cause of some of the most cruel wars, and the scene of some of the most senseless discords, that have ever disgraced the Christian name.   When the Angelic voice invited the women on the morning of Easter Day "to come and see the place where the Lord lay," their thoughts were immediately directed upwards.   "He is not here; He is risen."   Still, with this reservation the feeling is permitted — it is the common instinct of mankind, it is part of the natural gospel (so to speak) of Him who took our nature upon Him.

I propose therefore to set forth some of the reasons which give a special significance to the glorification or our Altar.

It has been sometimes said that the history of the sacrament of the Eucharist might be made a history of the Christian Church.   So it might be almost said that the history of the Holy Table in this Abbey might be made a history of the English Church.   The original form and position of the Table of the early Christians had long passed away before the erection of our first altar.   It stood at the extreme east end of the building, thus representing the period when the primitive idea of the early church had been effaced, but before the more complex doctrine and structure of the Middle Ages had arisen.   Then came the period from the Plantagenets to the time of the House of Lancaster, during which it was brought to the almost central position that it now occupies, recalling something of the original arrangement of the Basilica; but entangled with the various forms of strange devotion with which those ages abounded.   Then, as these fantastic forms multiplied, there sprang up the screen, which parted it from the Eastern chapels, and divided asunder the building, as with a wall of partition, unknown to ear-

lier times, forming, after the manner of that perplexed
age, church within church, division within division, in
ever narrower circles.   Then descended the tempest
of the Reformation, scattering right and left the ancient figures that stood around, and planting in the
place of the old altar the plain wooden movable table,
in imitation of the original primitive usage, sometimes
standing where it now stands, sometimes in the midst
of the church.   Next, in the reign of Anne, when the
arts took a new turn, when the classical dome of St.
Paul's Cathedral was rising from its ruins, and our own
Western Towers were added by the hand of the great
architect of that period, were raised the sculpture and
painting — highly esteemed in that age, and lasting
down to times within our own memory in the beginning of this century, when they too vanished before
the first faint revival of mediæval antiquarianism.
Each of these changes coincided with the development
of fresh thoughts and fresh feelings in the Christian
Church, each containing much that each succeeding age
lamented, whilst receiving the footprint of new ideas
through the changing periods of the history of our
Church and nation.   Each, were this the time to enlarge upon it, has some peculiar lesson of its own.   But
there is this lesson belonging to them all. — We sometimes think that it is the Transitory alone which
changes, the Eternal which stands still.   Rather it is
the reverse.   The Transitory stands still, decays, falls
to pieces.   The Eternal, though changing its outward
form again and again, endures.   It is therefore, as we
might have expected, that whilst the subordinate parts
of the church have remained comparatively unchanged,
or changed only by the mouldering lapse of time, this,
the most sacred part, has continually kept pace with
the altered feeling of each succeeding period.   Those

memorials of mortal men, as the Apostle freely spoke
of the patriarch David, are dead and buried; after
they had served their own generation they fell asleep,
and were laid with their fathers, and saw corruption
and decay. But He whom God raised again saw no
corruption. The memorial of His life and death has
been changed it may be according to the poor con-
trivances of men, but remains still alive, and kept alive
by its inherent vitality.

The everlasting mountains are everlasting, not because they are unchanged, but because they go on
changing their form, their substance, with the wear and
tear of ages. "The Everlasting Gospel" is everlasting, not because it remains stationary, but because,
being the same, it can adapt itself to the constant
changes of society, of civilization, of humanity itself.
Such a new step we have now again made, in accordance with the feelings of our own generation; and we
would take occasion of it to ask, What are the reasons why, according to the principles of our Church,
and according to the natural instincts of Christendom,
this Holy Table should be the chief point of attraction
and interest in this our ancient and splendid sanctuary?

I. It is the LORD's Table.

Whatever else is the purpose of that sacrament which
we here celebrate, its main object is to bring before us
Christ our Saviour. Other consecrated spots there may
have been in this church, other objects of reverence,
which, from time to time, have attracted deeper attention. There have been times when the main interest
of the congregation was centred on the tomb or shrine,
now of this king, now of that — now of this illustrious
hero, now of that; or, again, when the preacher was
more regarded than any other part of the service, and
every eye and ear hung on the pulpit; or, again, when

the throne of our sovereigns has been the centre of all the thoughts and feelings of the vast assemblage gathered in these walls. But in our ordinary worship this is not so; the Holy Table must always be the chief object of our interest, for this simple reason, that it brings before us Christ the Lord, and no one else.

Take away the belief in Christ, and all meaning vanishes from this spot; take away this sacred table, and there will remain no other outward object in the church which specially reminds us of Christ — the Lord in the fulness of His Spirit — the Lord, not in any one aspect of His appearance, but in the whole of it. To grasp the entire spiritual truth of Christ's manifestation, to make it the food of our souls, and the strength of our minds, is the justification of this sacred ordinance, is the glorification of this sacred place. This is the true secret of the mysterious power of the ordinance of the Lord's Supper, that more than prayer, more than meditation, more than any other single holy act or word, it brings us into close communion with the Divine Person, whom truly to know is life eternal.

It is He who invites us to come. No Man, no Priest, no Church, steps between us and Him. It is the Lord's Table, not the table of any particular school or minister; each communicant draws near on his own responsibility, for his own good, on the dictates of his own conscience. Our Table is not fenced by any artificial discipline. It is not guarded by any fantastic scruples. Whosoever cometh to it, and to Him whose Table it is, "earnestly repenting of his sins, in love and charity with his neighbors, and intending to lead a new life " — shall in no wise be cast out by the wise and merciful Saviour whose strength he seeks to gain. And this remembrance of the pre-eminent greatness of Christ our Saviour, dear to Christians everywhere, ought to be specially precious to Christians and to Englishmen in this church. Here, where we not only live, but worship in the midst of so many recollections of a stirring past, so many thoughts of a stirring present, it is doubly needful to have constantly kept before us that there is One Name, which is above every name, One Master in whose presence no one else is master, One whose faith we hold without respect of persons, One whose Spirit, rightly understood, is the source of all the strength, and freedom, and light, which makes our country great and glorious, One whose Cross is a rebuke to all our selfishness, and ignorance, and narrowness. Look at these marbles and colors; and when, as after the Passage of the Jordan, your children shall ask their fathers, now or in time to come, " what mean those stones " of porphyry and alabaster, those golden canopies, those glittering mosaics, then shall you let your children know that they tell us of the glory of Christ our Lord, that is, of the glory of Justice and Truth, Purity and Love ; the glory of the love of God to man, the glory of the love of man to God. It reminds us that the kingdoms of the earth which have their throne and seat in this place are become the kingdoms of the Lord and of His Christ. It reminds us that communion with Him and following in His footsteps is the highest blessing that can be sought for any worshipper under this roof, from the Queen to the peasant.

II. It is the Lord's TABLE. That word recalls to our minds at once what is the special act of His life which it commemorates. It is His farewell to His disciples — it is the fact that in that last farewell, He blessed to their use, and sanctified by His blessing, common bread and common wine, our ordinary fare. It is the constant memorial that Religion and Common Life are mixed together, one and indivisible ; that our common joys

and sorrows, the joys of social intercourse, the sorrows
of parting and bereavement, are all sanctified by our
Christian hopes and fears.

The *Table;* its very name and shape and material
remind us of that simple repast in the upper chamber
at Jerusalem.   So it was always called in the early ages,
so it is still called in the Eastern Churches, so it is
always called in our own Prayer-book.   In itself we
need care little of what it is made — wood or stone, or
gold or brass; yet assuredly, if for a moment one may
dwell on such a mere outward detail, it is interesting to
remember that wood, the usual material of our ordinary
tables, was the material from the earliest times, in East
and West, of our holy Tables also; that such, too, after
a long interval, it again became at the Reformation;
and that such in the midst of all these brilliant sur-
roundings it is still in this place.   Our richly-adorned
Table is the successor of the plain board which served
for the Last Supper at Jerusalem, of the rough planks
which still at Rome represent what is believed to be the
holiest and most venerable Altar in the City of St.
Peter, of the simple oaken table which, from the
Reformation almost down to the present century, stood
in this place.   Despise not the name, or the thing, or
the form; the more we remember how homely it was in
its origin, how primitive in its outward shape and fashion, the more does it deserve to be honored as the monument of the most sacred and pathetic parts of the
Christian story.   It is the fittest memorial of Him,
whose home was the home of the humble workman, the
carpenter Joseph, of Him who was Himself a carpenter,
laboring with the toil of an Eastern workman, under
the hot sun of the East, till the day's work was over,
of Him who adorned by the first miracle that He
wrought the festive gathering at Cana, who declared

His acts of mercy chiefly by His feeding the hungry
multitudes, who was known to His disciples chiefly by
the breaking of bread, by the sacred meal in which
He parted from them, by the sacred meal in which He
met them again in the joy of His Resurrection. They
who kneel before it, who receive from it the strength
which its sacred ordinance gives, will remember that its
holy and elevating power depends on its homely significance — the Table of all our common tables, as the Bible
is the Book of books.

III. Another name by which we call the Lord's Table
in common speech is the COMMUNION Table. This
name, though not expressly sanctioned by the law of
the Church, indicates a peculiar truth of which we
sometimes lose sight. "The bread which we break,"
says the Apostle, "is it not a communion" — that is, a
joint partaking — "of the body of Christ? The cup
of blessing which we drink, is it not a communion"
— a *joint partaking* — "of the blood of Christ?" The
whole force of the word and of the Apostle's argument,
is that it is a communion with each other, through our
joint, common, mutual partaking of the same bread and
the same cup. Round that Table, we become one with
each other, because we become one in Christ. And
here, again, the original position of the Table in all the
older churches of Christendom was a testimony to this
solemn truth. In all the churches, where the ancient
arrangements have been preserved, the Table stands not
at the Eastern extremity of the church, but in the centre; the clergy on one side, and the congregation on
the other; literally in the midst of the whole congregation. So also it was placed in all common English
churches for the first century after the Reformation.
So also during some portions at least of that period it
was in this Abbey. But even before that time, in fact,

since the thirteenth century, it has, owing to the peculiar conformation of the building, been far more nearly
in the midst of the church, than in most cathedrals;
and, though this arose from other causes, yet when we
look at it in its present position, with the long vista
extending behind it eastward, and before it westward,
we may remark that this central situation represents to
us the original idea of the primitive Eucharist, the centre of the whole Christian worship;.the meeting-point,
as of old, between the clergy and the laity, so here,
between the past and the present, between the dead and
the living; the dark shades which lie in solitary chapels
and mouldering tombs, behind it; — the living stir of
human souls, spreading to the right and left, before it.
In this sense may the blessed Sacrament, which is here
administered, be forever a bond of union between all
the different classes of our countrymen — between the
thoughts which belong to ages past and gone, and the
thoughts which belong to ages present and to come!
It is the pledge and sign of the duty of carrying on, as
best we can, this great Christian Society which we have
inherited; every grade of social life, every mode of
thought, every temper and disposition continuing to
help forward every other in the cause of good.

IV. We are thus brought to one other word which
we apply in common language to the Holy Table — the
ALTAR. This is a title which, unlike the others of
which I have been speaking, has no direct warrant from
Scripture, from the primitive Church, or from the
Prayer-book. The name "Altar" is not applied to the
Holy Table in any part of the New Testament, or in
any author of the first three centuries (with perhaps
two doubtful exceptions), or in any part of the Prayer-
book. But it is so commonly employed, that we may
well ask whether there is not a sense in which it may,

after all, be lawfully used. If the name may be anywhere lawfully used, it is here. In the Coronation
Service which has the authority of the Privy Council
of the Sovereign, and which is used within these walls
and nowhere else, our Table is called " an Altar." This
one exception, therefore, will justify us in considering
in what sense the word " Altar," according to common
usage, may be employed for our Sacred Table, what
additional reason is hereby given for its embellishment
and glorification.

"An Altar" means a place where Sacrifice is offered.
Is there any sense in which the Bible and the Prayer-
book acknowledge the offering of Sacrifice at our Holy
Table?   There is one passage, most impressive and
most important in our Communion Service, and one
alone, in which the word " Sacrifice " is so used. It is
that prayer in which, after the Communion, we offer to
God " the reasonable, holy, and living sacrifice of ourselves, our souls and bodies," to be accepted, notwithstanding our manifold unworthiness, "as our bounden
duty and service."

This is the true Christian Sacrifice, which may well
entitle any place where we offer it to be called an Altar.
This Sacrifice, not made by the Priest or Minister, but
by the People, this offering not of dead or dumb materials, but of living, spiritual beings, this pledging of
ourselves to our Master's service, is that which specially
belongs to the Holy Sacrament of the Lord's Supper,
and which may make the spot at which we offer it to
be, in an especial sense, the true Altar of the Christian's worship.

And well may it thus be called in the one service of
our Church, where, as I have said, it is so called — in
that great solemnity in which the Sovereign is pledged
to maintain the welfare of the people and the faith of

Christ in this sacred ordinance. That is indeed the Sacrifice of the prayers and praises of a whole nation, the Sacrifice of the highest life in this Church and realm to the good of man and to the glory of God.

And how much is the solemnity of this Sacrifice of ourselves enhanced, when we make it on the same spot and in the same ordinance, as brings before us the great Sacrifice of Christ our Saviour! That Sacrifice is finished; it is full, perfect, and sufficient in itself; it belongs to the past; it lives only in our grateful memory, or in its lasting consequences. But, in the sense in which I have been speaking, it can, and ought, in its measure, to be repeated, by ourselves, that is, by the Christian congregation, every time that we approach the Sacred Table. The Holy Sacrament is the holy "oath" or pledge of Christian soldiers to their heavenly Captain. Each one as he kneels there, with all the past mercies of God full in his remembrance, and all his present and future duties full in view, declares himself ready to follow in the steps of the great Self-sacrificer. "Each [1] one, when he hears the words, This is My body which is given for you, do this in remembrance of me, declares himself as answering, Yea, Lord, I am ready in remembrance of Thee to give also myself for the advance of Thy kingdom. Each one as he hears the words, This is My blood which is shed for you and for many for the remission of sins, ought to make the answer in his heart, Yea, Lord, I am ready to shed my blood also, if thereby the sins of many may be blotted out."

So viewed, the Holy Table does indeed become an Altar in the grandest and highest sense, for it combines within itself the memory of the historical Sacrifice of

---

[1] These words are taken from a highly instructive passage in Wilson's *Bampton Lectures on the Communion of Saints*.

Christ long ago, and the perpetuation of the moral and spiritual Sacrifice of Christians now. "Hereby perceive we the love of God because He laid down His life for us, and we ought to lay down our lives for the brethren."

And there is yet one other Sacrifice, mentioned in the same prayer in the Communion Service, which I reserve for the last, because with this I will conclude — our Sacrifice of praise and thanksgiving. This is the true *Eucharistic* Sacrifice. "Eucharist" is thanksgiving. "It is meet and right, and our bounden duty, to give thanks to God at all times and in all places, but chiefly" in this sacred ordinance, when we commemorate the innumerable benefits of Christ's death and passion; chiefly on this day, when we have brought to its desired completion the work which has been wrought out with such loving care by those who planned and by those who executed it. They who, month by month, and week by week, have watched its rise, and raised it like a tender plant, whose hands have made and fashioned its delicate work and traced its gracious forms, they who in their different stations, and with their different crafts, have labored with exceeding toil to bring it to its final completion — they may well offer to God their grateful thanks for having been permitted to bring to a successful issue the work which they may well call their own. In it their name and fame, their labor and their skill are enshrined as a gift to God. "We, God's humble servants, entirely desire His fatherly goodness to accept these" as our oblation, our Easter offering. "The earth is the Lord's and the fulness thereof;" every thing that there is of beauty in sculpture, poetry, painting, or architecture, every thing that there is of skill in mechanical contrivance, has its religious side, has the link, if it can be found, which binds it round the throne of God and the gates of heaven. The alabaster from our Midland quarries, the marble from our Cornish rocks, the mosaic colors from the isles of Venice, the porphyry from the shores of the Nile or of the Bosphorus, the jewels from the far-off coasts of Asia and America, combine as truly now in the service of Him, who has "given us the heathen for our possession, the uttermost parts of the earth for our inheritance," as did the gold of Ophir and the sandalwood of India for the temple of Solomon. It has been our endeavor not to destroy the old, but to retain from every age that which can still be used for good, and to add only that which was required by our increased insight into Divine Truth, our increased growth of human knowledge. Our forefathers did what they could in former times, according to their light; we have done what we could in our day according to our light. It is the privilege of our time that we can admire the shell, without believing it to be the kernel; and that we can, whilst we cherish the form, retain the spirit. The truest worshipper is he who, whilst he does not despise the accompaniments of earthly beauty, remembers that appreciation of the past may be combined with hope for the future; that art may be made to minister, not only to the lower objects of religious reverence, but to the worship of the One Supreme Good and the One Supreme Truth; that the spiritual and inward is a thousand times more precious than the material and the outward, and that the simplicity and sincerity of our service is a thousand times more beautiful than any decoration however gorgeous, or any form however graceful.

It is the last change which this our sanctuary has witnessed, the last probably that this generation will witness. Let us hope that every sacrament celebrated under its newly-raised tabernacle may become more and more what every spiritual communion, and every spiritual sacrifice, ought to be — a sacrament, or ordinance, in which the outer form is less and less thought of, and the inner spirit more and more. Let us hope and pray that the centre of this Abbey, thus adorned and thus beautified, thus bringing before us in all its grace and simplicity that which is the centre of all Christian doctrine — the life and death of Christ — may become the focus and spring of Christian light and life to the ever-multiplying population around us. Let us hope and pray that every marriage of which that Altar witnesses the celebration, may grow more and more into the fulness of an English and a Christian home. Let us hope and pray that when in far distant years, in each succeeding reign, the Crown of England is taken from that Table to be placed on the Sovereign's head, every time that the throne is placed before it to receive the new occupant, every time that the blessing of Christ in His holy ordinance is thus invoked on this our kingly Commonwealth — let us hope that the happiness and peace of our Church and kingdom may spread wider and deeper, as from a more glorious centre, as from a purer spring, as from a higher source. "Lift up your heads, O ye gates of future times, and be ye lift up, ye everlasting doors of the greatness of England, of the opportunities of Christendom, and the King of Glory shall come in." Who is the King of Glory? It is the Lord strong and mighty, the Lord mighty in battles, the Lord who has been victorious in a thousand battles over sin and evil in all their forms; who in the great battle-fields of the world has put down our ancient foes of slavery and superstition, and cruel tortures, and oppressive tyranny, and who will put down no less our present and future foes

— indifference, intolerance, drunkenness, anarchy, respect of persons, party spirit, and luxurious selfishness.

It is the Lord of hosts, the Lord of all the armies and all the soldiers who ever have fought, and ever will fight for the cause of God; the Lord of the beneficent ruler and of the enlightened statesman, of the heaven-inspired poet and of the skilful artist; the Lord no less of the humble and faithful servant, of the artisan honest in his calling, of the father, husband, son, and brother, struggling each in his own vocation, to build up a pure and happy home — the Lord of those Warriors and Priests of the ancient faith, who served the old Altar which has passed away, no less than of those Pastors and Teachers who shall have ministered at the new Table which has risen in its place. The Lord of hosts, He is the King of Glory, of a glory which belongs to every deed and thought of secret goodness, to every humble striving after truth — the glory which we, whether "beholding" or reflecting "as in a glass, are changed to the same image from glory into glory by the Spirit of the Lord."

THE RELIGIOUS ASPECT OF SCULPTURE.

Easter Day, 1871, on the occasion of the erection of four statues in
the reredos of Westminster Abbey.

*In the midst of the throne, and round about the throne, were four
"living creatures," . . . and they rest not day and night, saying, Holy,
holy, holy, Lord God Almighty, which was, and is, and is to come; and
they give glory and honor and thanks to Him that sitteth on the throne,
who liveth for ever and ever. —* REV. iv. 6–8.

THIS is part of the vision of the Apocalypse, which is
intended to express, in imagery taken from the outer
and lower world, the worship which all creation offers
up to its heavenly Lord. The four figures which thus
appear around the throne are described as having the
strength of the ox, the majesty of the lion, the swiftness
of the eagle, and the intelligence of the man. The
word which is translated "beast" in the Authorized
Version is properly rendered "living creature," as the
corresponding Hebrew word is in the Prophet Ezekiel
(reserving the word "beast" for a totally different
phrase which occurs in the later chapters to designate
the monsters of the deep). The expression "living
creatures" is well chosen to indicate that all created
life is intended to be included in the act of adoration.
The vividness of these words well suits the expression
of thankfulness for God's mercies which the festival of
Easter calls forth. May I be allowed also to take them
as bearing on the illustration of this same truth, by
the erection of the Four Statues which have just been
placed in the vacant niches of this sanctuary?

66

I. In the first place, this vision of the Apocalypse is a sanction of the faculty which we call, from this power of creating images, by the name of "imagination."

(1.) These figures described in the Apocalypse have (as we know well) no actual existence in the courts of heaven. But they none the less bear witness to the truth that such forms are warranted under the Gospel. The letter of the second commandment, prohibiting the making of any graven image, had already been abandoned, when in Solomon's temple the art of the sculptor had graven the figures which adorned its cedar walls and supported its brazen laver.[1] But the abundant use of like images, both in the older prophets and in the Apocalypse, not indeed by the hand of the inspired artist, but by the words of the inspired poet, has carried on the principle into detail. The stern simplicity of the old Mosaic law belongs to the time when " the hardness of the heart" of the ancient people could not in any other way be kept from idolatry. But this stern necessity gave way, as in other matters, so in this, before what St. Paul calls " the riches," the wealth, the abundance of new thoughts and new resources in the human mind opened by Christianity. From this time poetry, painting, music, and sculpture have poured in a flood of sacred imagery on the world. Sometimes, no doubt, this has been abused; sometimes it has been perverted to false science, false taste, and false religion. But in proportion to its perfection it has ministered to the beauty and sublimity of Christian sentiment; and a wise man has well remarked that it is not the perfection, but the rudeness of the art which leads to superstition.[2] The veneration of outward objects is often

---

[1] Josephus, *Ant.*, viii. 7, § 5. See *Lectures on the Jewish Church*, vol. ii. pp. 220, 222.

[2] See Milman's *History of Latin Christianity*, ii. 152, 153.

more debasing in the East, where all sculpture is forbidden, than in the West, where it has been encouraged. There is often a superstition quite as gross in iconoclasm as there is in idolatry ; and it is by an intelligent, Protestant, Christian use of all the arts, whether of the musician, the painter, or the sculptor, that this abuse is best prevented.   Therefore it is that, whilst there is hardly a corner in this Abbey where the ancient Israelite or the modern Mussulman would not be shocked at the representation of living creatures, as if in violation of the commandment that forbade the erection of graven images, it is also true that every one of those countless statues, whether of statesman or poet, whether of allegorical figure or actual human being, is a witness to the true liberty of the Gospel which has broken loose from the bondage of the law, and uses freely every faculty wherewith God has endowed the human soul ; and every such figure that lives again beneath the sculptor's hand joins, as it were, in the never-ending, never-ceasing cry of all creation — " Holy, holy, holy, Lord God Almighty, that is, and was, and is to come." They proclaim, or ought to proclaim, the nobleness and the purity of " the human face divine," which bears on its front the image and superscription of the Almighty, the marvellous workmanship of that human frame which is " fearfully and wonderfully made ; " they record for after ages the head that planned, and the eye that saw, and the hand that wrote, and the mouth that spake, all those burning words and melting thoughts by which this State and Church have been kept revolving round the Eternal throne.

(2.) May we not also say that this same glorious art is an illustration, almost an example, of that great truth of Life and Immortality which the festival of Easter commemorates ?   Those who have seen the workshop of a statuary will enter into the famous saying of one of the greatest of-modern sculptors (Canova), that " a statue is *born* when it is produced in clay, that it *dies* when it is reproduced in plaster, that it *rises again* when it is finally reproduced in marble." That is exactly what ought to make every such labor of the sculptor, both to him who works and to him who sees it, a type and likeness of the transforming changes wrought in our outward frame and inward character by the Great Artificer whose workmanship we are.

There is the clay, the soft ductile clay, as in the hands of the potter, as in the time when " day by day our members were fashioned when as yet there were none of them," when our characters were not yet formed, but were being moulded by the force of circumstance or companionship, or human genius, or divine grace, just as the clay of the statue by the finger of the artist — here an addition, there a subtraction — is renewed daily, we might almost say born again, under the pressure of his watchful care.

There too is the cold dull outline, when life has vanished, when the shroud is around us, when there remains nothing but the fragile, featureless form, as in the dead lifeless plaster.

And, lastly, there is the Resurrection. Out of the block of marble, as if they had been buried within it, come forth at the successive strokes of the chisel, the bright, ideal face, and outstretched hand, and firm foot, by efforts which are indeed likenesses of that transformation described to us by St. Paul, when he tells us how the " corruptible shall put on incorruption, and the mortal shall put on immortality." And the marble figure which so emerges is a pledge — faint and remote, perhaps, yet still not to be despised — of the undying force of the human spirit, which thus outlasts the violence of revolutions and the slow decay of time. If we look on the face of one whom we ourselves have known thus "immortalized," as we say, by the sculptor's art, if yet further we see the face of one that we have never seen at all, brought near to us, looking out of the years that are past and gone, if we see this, not only in the case of those who have lived within our own time and country, but in ages long buried, and in countries far removed; if we see the Cæsars on their pedestals at Rome, or the yet more distant Pharaohs in the sands of Egypt, not hundreds but thousands of years ago; yet more, if we see those of whose form and figure we know nothing, but for whose disembodied spirits the skill and genius of later times have furnished forth an outward frame to enshrine the ideal of what we think they must have been — then indeed we feel that there is something in the human mind triumphant over matter, that there is even on earth a victory stolen from the grave, and a sting from death; we feel that after the natural earthly body has perished there may well be a spiritual ideal body for each human soul, "one glory for one, and another for another" — that God, out of His infinite treasure-house, may well give to each a new form and existence, "as it shall please Him."

(3.) We learn thus to appreciate the bright future, the lofty ideal of human nature and of human destiny. It is of little matter to us whence we have descended, out of what materials our first ancestors were created, even though it be, as the Bible tells us, from "the very dust of the ground." But it is of infinite moment to us to feel, to know what we actually are, what the high capacities we possess, what the great responsibilities which rest upon us, what the eternal destiny which may be in store for us. It is for this that every noble exercise of the faculties which God has given us, every con-

scientious work, in which we labor to produce something which shall outlast ourselves or our generation,
is a gift as from immortal spirits to an Immortal Spirit.
"God is not a God of the dead, but of the living."
Those bright ideas, those finer qualities of the human
soul which art labors to perpetuate, and which science
delights to explore, are the pledges that God will not
despise the works of His hands, that we shall live on,
in spite of death and time.

II. Such is the general lesson of the contemplation
of the creation of man, and of the efforts of Christian
art to perpetuate its glories.

And now let us briefly describe the special ideas intended to be conveyed by the Four Living Creatures—
the four gifted human beings — whose images have just
been erected around the Holy Table.

They represent four characteristics of the human
race in its highest perfection, which seemed the fittest
homage to be paid in this place to our Creator and
Redeemer.[1]

The two figures which stand in the centre are the
two chief Apostles, always united in primitive art, as
they are in the Bible itself.

The one on the right of the Table is St. Peter, to
whom, from the special predilection of our Founder,
this Church was dedicated. He represents the solid
rock, the outward framework, on which and in which
the Church was built — its ancient, universal, catholic
aspect. He stands erect like a pillar of the fabric;
the keys of government are in his hands, and on his
book are written those words of universal comprehen-

---

[1] The new statues here described, the work of Mr. Armstead, are
placed in the vacant niches above the Communion Table, on each side
of the mosaic picture of the Last Supper, and underneath the frieze
representing the events of the Gospel history.

sion by which he opened, as with a golden key, the kingdom of heaven to the whole race of man, — " *God is no respecter of persons.*"

By his side is St. Paul, who, on the other hand, represents the fervor, the life, the freedom of the Church, to which St. Peter gave the outward framework. He stands with outstretched hand, as on Mars' Hill at Athens, as on the Temple stairs at Jerusalem, or before Agrippa at Cæsarea — the great teacher, the fiery preacher; and he grasps the sword by which he suffered martyrdom, but which is also the emblem of the word that he preached, "quick, and powerful, and sharper than any two-edged sword, piercing even to the dividing asunder of soul and spirit," "rightly dividing the word of truth," in those weighty epistles on which is inscribed the corresponding name of "*the sword of the Spirit.*"

These are the two great human forces of our religion — which, in their widest form, are called Christendom and Christianity — the vast outward framework and the moving inward spirit. All that constitutes the true strength of the ancient Catholic Church in Peter, all that constitutes the true strength of the Reformed Churches in Paul, is represented in them. Lovely and pleasant were the two Apostles in their lives, and in their deaths they were not divided. Truly do they here bring before us the union of the old and the new, the depth and the breadth, which is the glory of all Christian worship and of all Christian faith.

And now let us turn to the farther right and to the farther left. On the right of Peter is the great lawgiver of the old dispensation, who by the early Christians was regarded as his forerunner — Moses, the founder of the Jewish Commonwealth, as Peter of the Christian

Church. There he stands, as he came down from Mount Sinai, bearing in his hands the tables on which are written the first words of the Ten Commandments; and in him we see the representative of the general idea of statesmanship and law. He gathers up in his person the memories of our own famous statesmen, buried in the North aisle of the Church, towards which he looks — lawgivers, rulers of the people, pillars of the State, who are in the world at large what Peter and Peter's true spiritual successors have been in the Church.

On the other side, corresponding to St. Paul, is the greatest teacher of the Jewish Church — David, the royal poet and prophet, who, by the lofty spirit, the eternal truths, of his Psalter has sanctified, for every age, the philosophy, the learning, the poetry of all mankind. As Moses looks towards our buried statesmen, so David stands beside our buried poets. As Moses combines with Peter to represent the solid forces which bind together the commonwealths and churches of the earth, so David combines with Paul to represent the ethereal grace, the prophetic zeal, the poetic fire, which still, through a thousand voices, breathe the ancient " *Hallelujah* " first adequately expressed by the strains of his harp, on which it is inscribed.

These are the Four Living Creatures which have been thought worthy to stand round the central figure of our departing Master, the four elements of life, which are the fitting emblems of the purposes of this sacred building — the all-embracing order, the all-awakening energy, which give life to the Church, the sustaining force of heaven-sent law, the informing force of inspired genius, which give life to the world. We cannot spare any of them from our earthly existence. Let us remember them in our spiritual worship. Let us, as we see them thus exalted, remember that they all, and we with them, have the same divine function of giving "glory and honor and thanks to Him that sits on the throne, who liveth for ever and ever" — to Him "who was dead and is alive for evermore."

A THREEFOLD CALL.

June 28, 1868, the anniversary of the Queen's coronation, on the occasion of the public thanksgiving for the escape of H.R.H. the Duke of Edinburgh and for the success of the Abyssinian War.

Speak, Lord; for Thy servant heareth. — 1 SAM. iii. 9.[1]

So spoke the youthful Prophet and ruler after he had thrice heard the Divine call. It was in the darkness of the early morning; the seven-branched candlestick alone lighted up the curtains of the Tabernacle. There knelt the innocent child, as we see him pictured by the greatest of English painters; his little hands clasped in prayer; his bright eyes looking upwards towards a light which none but he could see, towards a voice which none but he could hear — the likeness of that touching sight which every parent knows who sees his little ones first beginning to falter their infant prayers, and murmur their infant hymns.

But the same truth which is taught us by the sight of our children at their prayers — all attention, all reception — by the story of the young Hebrew Prophet thus receiving deep into his soul the first of that long succession of prophetic revelations, is forced upon us by the more impressive events of the lives, whether of nations or of individuals. Again and again a call is made to us, as distinct, if we would but listen to it, as that which came to Samuel. A call to duty, a call to thankfulness, a call to better and serious thoughts; and what is

---

[1] First Lesson of the Evening Service.

needed is that we should be able to say, "Speak, Lord; for Thy servant HEARETH." That is the difficulty. The whirl of business, the succession of enjoyments, the clatter of voices around us, the strife of parties, the drowsiness of indolence, the blindness of passion, the deafness of prejudice — all these distract our attention, shut our eyes, close our ears. It is this need of a pause, of a lull, which makes it good for us to have our thoughts arrested and diverted by any marked anniversary, by any solemn remembrance of public events, by any stirring incident in our own experience. A silence then falls around us; a still small voice can then make itself audible. The Lord speaks; and for the moment our ears are open to hear His call.

Such a call, in more ways than one, this day brings to us.

I. It is now just thirty years since this Abbey was the scene of the most splendid and moving spectacle that our generation has witnessed. It was on the 28th of June, 1838, that the nobles, commons, and clergy of England were gathered within these walls to welcome to the throne a Sovereign, whose youthful promise and queenly grace awakened again a flame of loyal devotion, a spring of serious hope, such as was thought to have well-nigh died out from amongst us. To her, on that bright summer day, came the awful, yet inspiring summons to preside wisely and justly over the great people here represented around her. And to the nation at large, not only in this Abbey, or in this metropolis, but in many a rustic church, and in many a retired village, throughout the Empire, was brought home the feeling that we were one people and one family, with one heart and one soul, bound together to promote each other's welfare, and to lift our thoughts upwards to whatsoever things were true and honest, just and pure, lovely and of good report. It was this common feeling of national unity and national duty — this electric sentiment with which the whole air was charged, that gave a deeper meaning to every word of that solemn ceremony, a fresh significance to every splendor of that grand pageant. The Queen was in the midst of her people; each on that day was given to each; a new era seemed to open for each; an era of new happiness and usefulness for the one, of new glory and greatness for the other — of Christian progress towards perfection for both.

Thirty years have passed away, thirty years of how much loss and of how much gain to all of us! How many have been snatched away from the home, or Church, or State, or Throne of which they were the stay and support. How many have been the noble opportunities passed by, how many the good deeds not attempted until it was, or seemed to be, too late! And yet how much also has been added to us; how happily round that royal seat have risen up the children, and the children's children of the future dynasty; how much of pure renown has been added to the English name in peace and war; how many a noble Christian deed has lighted up far and wide the dark corners of our land! In the mere thought of these vicissitudes — in the grateful remembrance of what has been done for us, of evils extinguished which, we trust, shall never reappear, of good accomplished which, we trust, shall never be reversed — in the bitter grief for good which might have been done and has been left undone — in the enkindling hope of all the splendid and useful and holy works that still remain to be done — in all these thoughts the call is repeated this day; and may each of us, from the highest to the lowest, renew that covenant which then was made, and say, "Speak, Lord; for Thy servant heareth." The nation has advanced fast and far on its way; the nineteenth century itself is moving towards its close. It is for each one of us to keep pace with it, to feel that on each and all of us depends the right direction of that onward journey. "Speak, Lord;" let us hear and understand Thy will; we are indeed all ears to hear, and all eyes to see, if Thou wilt but guide us rightly.

II. And now there come to us two special calls again, from most different quarters, awakening most different feelings, yet still pointing to the same end; calls from the uttermost extremities of the earth, which reached our shores within the same twenty-four hours, and which by this very coincidence made us feel the vastness and variety of the sphere, the loftiness and breadth of the task, which Englishmen have before them.

Let us ask what is the call conveyed to us in each of the two events, for which we are invited to express our thankfulness to Almighty God, and which are thus happily combined on this auspicious day. In each there is a lesson beyond the event itself. Let us open our ears to hear it.

Look first at the victory with which our arms have been crowned in Abyssinia. Rarely indeed in the annals of warfare, has a great purpose been carried out so exactly within the limits of time and space, foreseen and prescribed, as that which the endurance of our soldiers and the skill of their chiefs have accomplished in that distant land. For this blessed close of deep anxiety, for these marvellous gifts of God's Spirit to our race and country, we offer our unfeigned thanks. But even more than these is the mercy vouchsafed to us of the power of showing in the light of these achievements, the bright example of a war unstained by the slightest tinge of ambition, by the slightest taint of gain — a war, reluctantly undertaken, laboriously car-

ried out, magnificently successful, not for the sake of
territory or wealth, but for the sake of redeeming from
captivity a handful of Englishmen, with their wives
and children. The European world looked at our
armament with wonder; they treated with incredulous
scorn our protestations that so vast an enterprise was
undertaken for so small an object; they could not think
it possible that a great nation would enter on so great a
war for so simple and so barren a purpose. Thank
God, we have shown that it was possible; and therefore
when we read of that long march for many a weary
league, over Alpine heights, and under burning suns,
of that fierce fight on Good Friday morning, of the
entrance into that mountain fastness on Easter Monday, it is not so much over the fall of Magdala, or the
death of its chief, that we triumph gloriously, as over
the false and wicked doctrine that nations can only
fight for unworthy objects, and soldiers be courageous
only when their recompense is plunder. It is not so
much for the valor of the enterprise or the splendor of
the achievement that we thank Almighty God, as because He has, by that valor and that splendor, enabled
us to set "on a hill which cannot be hid" the great
Christian principle of uniting might with right, power
with forbearance. "Better is he that ruleth his own
spirit than he that taketh a city." As a just cause
is a sufficient ground for a mighty war, so also a just
cause is its own sufficient and exceeding great reward.
"Speak, Lord," to England and to Europe — "speak,
Lord," and let Thy servants hear. Let us hear in those
trumpet-calls of Abyssinian victory, the call to justice
and mercy, wherever God shall lead us. Let us, as our
hearts throb in receiving back our soldiers from that
strange mysterious country, welcome in them the true
successors and sons of the knights of old, who fought

for truth and right, not for gold or land; let us feel that in their deeds humanity itself has made a step onwards, and that the kingdom of God which is not of this world has acquired a new possession in the heart and mind of Christendom. Let us be taught to value the Divine gifts of courage and skill; but let us be taught to value still more deeply the Divine duties of justice, generosity, and self-control.

III. There is another call of God from a yet more distant shore, which comes still nearer home. It is that which reaches all our hearts through the merciful Providence which has sheltered from death a Prince of our Royal House.[1]

The horror of a reckless crime, the thankfulness for a life full of youthful hope rescued from an untimely end, the sympathy with those who have thus regained, as on this day, a son, a brother, from the grave — these are the natural Christian feelings which rise unbidden to every heart, and which are but weakened by the reflections of preacher or teacher. As in the most pathetic of all the Gospel miracles, the great Healer of sorrows has raised from the bier "the son of his mother." "Young man, I say unto thee, arise. And He delivered him to his mother; and she was a widow." In the words also of the most pathetic of all the Gospel parables, " It is meet that we should make merry and be glad; for this thy brother was dead and is alive again, was lost and is found."

" It is indeed very meet, right, and our bounden duty, that we should at all times and in all places give thanks to Thee, O Lord, Holy Father, Almighty Everlasting God," whenever the springs of pure domestic love are stirred within us, whenever a sudden shock awakens us

---

[1] Referring to the attempt to assassinate the Duke of Edinburgh at Sydney, March 12, 1868.

to the sense of the nearness and dearness of family ties, and home-affections. Never may we cease to feel the force of that sacred passion. Never may we cease to rise above ourselves into the fellow-feeling of delight with which the brother welcomes home the brother, and the mother the son. "Speak, Lord," on this, and like occasions, to all our hearts. We are silent; our common, vulgar, baser, selfish murmurings and babblings are hushed. Speak to us, for Thy servants hear; speak to us of tender kindly emotions; speak to us of the blessedness of peacemakers; speak to us of the purity and loveliness of domestic affections; speak to us of the infinite preciousness of a life, of a living soul, rescued from sudden destruction, preserved for all those noble and beneficent purposes which God places before each human spirit, specially before those whom He has set in the high places of the earth, and endowed with the capacities of greatness.

And here again, as in that other call of which I spoke, there comes a voice of yet deeper import, a strain of a yet higher mood, than at first catches our ears. That life which has been rescued is not a mere private life. It is one of a house which belongs not only to the nation but to the Empire. In those far-off regions where it occurred, the bright side of this dark event has been, that it has awakened a sentiment of loyal, generous, unselfish, enthusiastic affection for the country and for the throne of England, such as even here we rarely see, such as there we hardly knew to exist. Old men, they say, wept for grief to think that such an inhospitable deed should have darkened their shores; the whole community went beyond and beside themselves in tokens of sympathy with the youthful sufferer, of thankfulness for his deliverance. By that one act the whole vast continent of Australia — the whole range of English settlements along the coasts of all the Australasian

Islands was moved in oneness of heart and soul with this their mother-country. They and we have been alike made to feel that we were members of one race and family, children of the same sacred hearth, subjects and fellow-citizens of the same royal commonwealth, heirs of the same great name, of the same exalted duties. To awaken such a feeling as this is the true mission of an English Prince. To furnish this link between the old world and the new, between England as she is and has been, and England's sons wherever they wander over the wide world's surface, is indeed the very task to which the children of our regal house are called, and which their royal parents fondly dreamed for them. To have become the centre of such a sympathy is indeed worth living for, is indeed a recompense for hairbreadth escapes, for suffering days and nights, the true reward of all kingly and princely labors, "good measure, pressed down, and running over, given into their bosom."

"Speak, Lord; for Thy servant heareth." Not for ourselves do we act, but for others; not for our own circle only, but for the great country which is our inheritance; not for England only, but for all those multitudes of men and nations, that bear the English name and speak the English tongue, do our actions, some more, some less, extend their influence for good or for evil. In the silence of that vast expectant multitude, in the presence of those thousands and tens of thousands, seen or unseen by us, we have to perform our parts in this our generation. Speak, Lord; our souls are hushed to hear what Thou hast to say to us. Great is the stake, overwhelming may be the risks — most glorious are the opportunities. Speak, Lord, and show us what our duty is — how high, how difficult, yet how happy, how blessed — show us what our duty is, and, O great God and Father, give us strength to do it!

THE NATIONAL THANKSGIVING.

I. — DEATH AND LIFE.

December 10, 1871, during the illness of the Prince of Wales.

To live is Christ, and to die is gain. — PHIL. i. 21.

ON a day like this, when there is one topic in every household, one question on every lip, it is impossible to stand in this place and not endeavor to give some expression to that of which every heart is full. By a natural Christian instinct, the whole nation is gathered into one focus. We all press, as it were, round one darkened chamber, we all feel that with the mourning family, mother, wife, brothers, sisters, who are there assembled, we are indeed one. The thrill of their fears or hopes passes through and through the differences of rank and station; we feel that, whilst they represent the whole people, they also represent and are that which each family, and each member of each family, is separately. In the fierce battle between Life and Death, for the issues of which we are all looking with such eager expectation, we see the likeness of what will befall every individual soul amongst us; and the reflection which this struggle, with all its manifold uncertainties, suggests, concerns us all alike.

I have thought, therefore; that it is best to fix our

minds for a few moments on what that struggle involves — to ask what are the true lessons of Life and
of Death; to ask why it is that. whether as men, or
citizens, or Christians, we desire with such prolonged
earnestness that Life, and not Death, may be the issue
of this mortal agony.

In doing so, let us be guided by the words of St.
Paul. He is writing to his best-beloved converts. He
opens his heart more fully to them than to any others.
He admits them, as though they were his own brothers
and friends, to his innermost chamber. He discloses to
them his doubts, his anxieties, his weaknesses. He
describes to them the danger in which he is — danger,
we know not whether of natural sickness or of a violent
end. He looks on Death and he looks on Life, and he
knows not which to choose; he sees the good of each.
At last he decides that what might have seemed the best
for him is not really the best; that what might have
seemed the worst for him is not really the worst. He
tells us, in short, what are the reasons for desiring
Death; but he tells us still more strongly what are the
reasons for desiring Life.

It may seem almost cold thus to balance and weigh
the searchings of the heart at such moments. Yet
it was not coldness in the Apostle; it was the depth
of tenderness. It is not coldness in us; it is the only
channel into which we can profitably turn our thoughts
on such an occasion, and make it yield its proper lesson.

I have, before this, in quite another connection,
used these words of the Apostle. I know not how
to do better than to use them again to-day, sharpened
and pointed as they are by the feelings of the moment,
even to "the dividing asunder of soul and spirit, and
discerning the thoughts and intents" of our innermost
hearts.

To die is gain. Who is there that has not from time to time felt this, as he looks at the sufferings of this mortal life; as he thinks of the wearing nights and days of sickness, of the restlessness, the sinking, the pain, the despair, the distress of the watchers, the prolonged agony of the bystanders; as he looks at the miseries of this sinful world — the disappointments of brilliant hopes, the sore temptations to evil, the multiplied chances of failure? Who, as he thus thinks of himself or of others, has not been moved to say, from time to time, " Oh that I had the wings of a dove, that I might flee far away and be at rest!" It is the feeling beautifully expressed by the greatest of our poets, when he says: —

> Tired with all these, for restful death I cry, —
> As, to behold desert, a beggar born,
> And needy nothing trimm'd in jollity,
> And purest faith unhappily forsworn,
> And gilded honor shamefully misplaced,
> And right perfection wrongfully disgraced,
> And art made tongue-tied by authority,
> And folly, doctor-like, controlling skill,
> And simple truth, miscall'd simplicity,
> And captive Good attending Captain Ill :
> Tired with all these, from these would I be gone.

So wrote Shakespeare in his famous sonnet, and so felt even the great Apostle when, amidst the desertion of friends, and the hard struggle of truth against falsehood and good against evil, he desired to be at rest and be with his Master beyond the grave, which, he says, " would be far better."

So, too, we for ourselves, and for those that we love, and for those whose lives are fraught with so many chances of fatal shipwreck, may well long for that day when we and they shall have shuffled off this mortal coil ; when we shall have done with the anxious trials, the paltry quarrels, the baffled hopes, the grinding toil of the great Babylon of this harassing world ; when we shall have escaped from the burden and heat of the day, from the roar and tumult of the swollen torrent of life, to be with those beloved departed,

> Who in the mountain grots of Eden lie,
> And hear the fourfold river as it murmurs by.

In this sense death is, and must be, a gain to all. And it is by reflecting on this clear gain that the mind bows itself to the Supreme Will, and the heart nerves itself to the terrible thought of the last dread summons from all that we see and love in this earthly scene. It is for this that, in the language of our Visitation Service, we commit the soul with such assured confidence into the hands of its faithful Creator and most merciful Saviour.

But the Apostle tells us that, after all, there is something yet greater than the gain and rest of Death, and that is the struggle and victory of Life. Death was gain to him, but Life was something more. " *To live is* CHRIST." Death in one sense is the gate of Life eternal ; but Life — this mortal life — is the only true gate of a happy and peaceful death. It is in Life — in the wear and tear of Life — that those graces must be wrought and fashioned which perfect the soul, immortal over Death. " Reckon yourselves," says the Apostle, " to be *dead to sin*." But there is something much more than this, " Reckon yourselves *to be alive* to God through Christ." He preaches with all his heart and soul, not the worthlessness, but the infinite preciousness of Life.

Those lines from our great poet, which I quoted just now, describing his weariness of the world, close with the one thought which reconciled him to remaining : —

> Tired with all these, from these would I be gone,
> Save that, to die, I leave my love alone.

That, doubtless, is one chief thought that makes earthly life dear to us — the thought that it contains those whom our departure would leave desolate and alone. But in fact this sense of human love is a likeness, like all pure earthly affections, of a feeling far higher. When the heathen, when the unbeliever have often sought escape from the troubles of life by self-destruction, they have done so to escape from that which to them had no sacred value. But the Christian, the believer in God and in Christ, has, or ought to have, the abiding consciousness that in Life there are not only (it may be) the dearest objects of his earthly affection, but that there is the very work, the very presence of Christ. It is one of the points of coincidence between true Christianity and true civilization. As mankind advances in civilization, human life becomes more sacred, more precious ; as mankind advances in Christianity, the human soul, which is but another word for human life, becomes more precious, more sacred also. By leaving our work here before the time, we should leave His work undone. By turning our backs in self-will or impatience on this mortal scene, we should be turning our backs on Him who is in those very sufferings and struggles most surely to be found.

Every kindness done to others in our daily walk, every attempt to make others happy, every prejudice overcome, every truth more clearly perceived, every difficulty subdued, every sin left behind, every temptation trampled under foot, every step forward in the cause of good, is a step nearer to the life of Christ,

through which only death can be really a gain to us.
Death may be great, but Life is greater still.   Death
may be a state to be desired for ourselves, rejoiced in
for others, but Life is the state in which Christ makes
Himself known to us, and through which we must make
ourselves known to Him.   He sanctified and glorified
every stage of it.   He was a little child, and showed us
how good it was to be obedient to our parents, how dear
to a mother a child could be ; how He never forgot her,
but even on the cross thought of what would soothe and
comfort her.   He grew up to boyhood, he showed us
how to learn, both by hearing and asking questions ;
how early He could be busied in doing His Father's
work.   He showed us in full manhood how, in the midst
of the world, and of constant pressing duties, many coming and going, in feasting and in company, no less than
in serious moments, He was still the same Divine Master and Friend.   He showed us in the desolation and
solitude of Gethsemane and Calvary, when He seemed
to be left, unsupported, to Himself, that He was yet not
alone, because the Father was with Him.   This is the
way in which this poor human life may become a Divine life, may become a life of Christ.

Therefore, when we apply these words and thoughts
to ourselves, what is it but to dwell not on the misuse,
but on the use of our existence?   Think how much yet
remains to be done in the thirty, twenty — yes, even in
the ten years, or perhaps in the one year, perhaps even
in the one day, that yet may remain to us.   Despise it
not, neglect it not ; cherish, enlarge, improve this vast,
this inestimable gift, whilst it is granted to us with its
endless opportunities, with its boundless capacities, with
its glorious hopes, with its indispensable calls, with its
immense results, with its rare chances of repentance,
of improvement, even for the humblest and weakest
among us.

To rise above ourselves, to lose ourselves in the thought of the work, great or small, that God has placed before us — to live in that life which is indeed eternal, because it belongs both to this world and the next — for the sake of doing this the Apostle could consent to live, could prefer life with all its sorrows to death with all its gain. "God is not a God of the dead, but of the living." Christ is not a dead Christ, but a living Christ. "The living, the living, he shall praise Thee, he shall serve Thee." The varied duties of common life — the trivial round, the common task — are the means by which we carry on the true Apostolical succession of Christ's first servants. "There may be everywhere" — I quote the words of a devoted Christian of another country — "there may be everywhere a silent apostleship, a persuasive and incessant sermon — namely, the natural brightness of a profound and true content. Never can the immortal hopes to which our devotion renders its sacrifice be so well proclaimed by our words, as by the radiant tranquillity of that inward repose which comes up from the heart to the countenance." "I find" — so said this same saint-like person — "I find Death perfectly desirable, but I find Life perfectly beautiful."

And what is true of the life of individuals is true also of the life of great communities. There is, indeed, both of individuals and of nations, a life which is not a life, empty, dead, barren, a mere existence, vanity of vanities. But the collective life of thousands of English Christian souls — the life of the heart of a great people — life, not stagnation, life, not idleness, — is the very element, the living element in which the spirit of man lives and makes others live, of which the Spirit of Christ, which is Christ Himself, is the life and the light. This is what is meant by saying that the Church — that is the Christian society, the living company of all good men, the souls and hearts of Christian men and women — forms "the Body" of Christ. We, whether singly or collectively, are His representatives; we are (so the Bible repeatedly tells us) His very self. In all that is best and purest in us, in our duties, in our hopes, He lives. Because He lives we live. Because we live He lives. It is sometimes asked — it was asked the other day by an eloquent preacher in the great neighboring Cathedral — whether the Christ, the Historical Person who lived eighteen hundred years ago, is still alive amongst us. It is also sometimes asked, in many forms, and with many forms of reply, how and where Christ's presence is to be found and felt. But the best answer to all these questions is the answer of the Apostle, "To live is Christ." It is so, as I have said, on the smallest scale in our individual existence. It is so on the largest scale. "The Life of Christendom is the Life of Christ." That is the proof, the evidence, the direct continuation of the Life of Christ. It is through the multitudinous mass of living human hearts, of human acts and words of love and truth, that the CHRIST of the first century becomes the CHRIST of the nineteenth. Each successive age, each separate nation, does His work on a larger and still larger scale. The arts, the literature, the sciences, the charities, the liberties, the laws, the worship of the commonwealths of Christian Europe are all parts of the living body of CHRIST. Their influence on us is part of His influence. Their benefits to us are part of "the innumerable benefits of His Cross and Passion." To live under the best influences of Christendom, to live under the best influences of Christian England, this for us, and this only, is — the Apostle allows us to say so — is CHRIST Himself.

And now, O my brethren, if there be an individual

life to which much that I have already said be applicable; a life dear to hundreds of loving friends, and to a most loving family; a life which in their service and affection finds its best inspirations and its best vitality; a life which had till now (humanly speaking) long years of usefulness and happiness before it — then for the preservation of that life, for the sake of him who now lies on the dark confines of hope and fear, and for the sake of those most near and dear to him, we may, and must earnestly pray, and trust that it may by God's blessing be preserved. And when we add the further thought that this is a life which may, if so be, influence to an untold degree the national existence of which I just now spoke — a life which, if duly appreciated and fitly used, contains within it special opportunities of good such as no other existence in this great community possesses; a life which may, if worthily employed, stimulate all that is noble and beneficent, and discourage all that is low and base and frivolous; which, from its exceptional position, will have the power of moderating the extremes of party zeal, and of pursuing the common weal of all with an energy not weakened or divided by local or partial claims; a life which, if spared, may be the instrument for making us more and more to be of one mind and heart in all that is just and good, even as at this moment the fear of losing it has brought us all together with one heart and one soul — such a life is worth living, is worth praying for. And for such a life, for such a Royal life — which is so dear now to those who watch its fluctuations from hour to hour beside and around the bed of sickness, which may, with God's blessing, be so precious for our children and our children's children — we pray that it may yet be prolonged for the good of men and the glory of God, through Jesus Christ, our Lord, who is "the Resurrection and the Life, in whom whosoever **believeth,** though he were dead yet shall he live."

II. — THE TRUMPET OF PATMOS.

December 17, 1871.

*I was in the Spirit on the Lord's day, and heard behind me a **great** voice, as of a trumpet.* — REV. i. 10.

THE new Calendar of Lessons, which has been followed for some months in this church, introduces for the first time in the Services of this Sunday portions from the Book of the Revelation of St. John. The history of the reception of that book in the Church is curious and instructive. For the first three centuries it was not regularly received amongst the Canonical Books of Scripture, and even after it was received, even at the time of the Reformation, very few lessons were selected from it to be read in public. The reasons for this are obvious. The book is in fact exceedingly obscure — and it has been made even more obscure by the fancies of interpreters. It was also in ancient times looked upon askance, because it was the favorite text-book of those who were then thought heretics, and in modern times because it has been the favorite text-book of angry polemics and fanciful diviners of the future — the source whence have been drawn weapons of offence against theological adversaries, or imaginary pictures of the history of modern Europe. But in spite of these objections, it has, by the force of its sublime poetic form and its high moral tone, held its ground; and the true instinct of Christendom has been shown in the fact, that without the sanction of Councils and against the opinion of great prelates, this mysterious book has gradually forced its way into the Canon of Scripture, and now at last, after having been almost excluded from the public service of the English Church, it has been appointed to be read during the last month in the year, when its lessons naturally fall in with the season of Advent. Some chapters are still omitted, as fit rather for the solitary student than for the mixed congregation. But there is enough given to express the general tenor of the book, and it is of this general tenor that I propose to speak, and of this with its special application to ourselves.

The Prophet (for as such we must regard the author of this sacred book) was on the solitary island of Patmos, withdrawn from earthly things, like Moses on Sinai, or Elijah on Carmel. Round about him was the bright Ægean Sea, with its hundred isles and the neighboring mountains of Asia Minor, within whose circle lay the familiar Seven Churches to which his epistles and addresses were sent.[1] And it was on the Lord's Day. He was wrapt in the stillness and devotion of the day, already even in that early time set apart for the contemplation of heavenly things. Such was the external framework of the prophecy. It was in this solitude, in this solemn scene, from this lonely peak of speculation, that there was unrolled before the eye of his spirit that vision of the future which is called the "Apocalypse," that is the "Revelation," the "Unveiling" of the will and purpose of Providence.

Amidst all that is obscure and difficult, there are two main features of this Revelation which may be easily described and easily understood. The first is that, as in all the prophetic visions of the Bible, the outward

---

[1] See Appendix to *Sermons in the East*, pp. 225-31.

imagery is taken from the objects and circumstances immediately at hand and around. Not only do the bright sky, the wide sea, the lofty mountains, the grotesque rocks, the sandy beach, of Patmos and the adjacent islands enter into the picture, but the whole tissue of the visions themselves is drawn from the events with which the atmosphere of that portentous time was charged. It was the period which witnessed the fulfilment of those signs in earth and heaven which are set forth in the Gospel records brought before us at this season. The long peace which had prevailed throughout the world down to the death of the Emperor Nero had just been broken up. It was the epoch which the Roman historian describes as " teeming with disasters, terrible in war, rent with faction, savage even in peace." From the Northern Ocean to the Ægean coasts, all was in confusion and alarm; wars and rumors of wars, earthquakes, volcanoes, armies marching and countermarching, the fall of Jerusalem, the burning of Rome, the overthrow of the cities of Herculaneum and Pompeii, the barbarians hanging on the frontier, dynasty after dynasty succeeding each other on the imperial throne, " the powers of heaven shaken, men's hearts failing them for fear of those things that were coming on the earth." This was the horizon on which the Prophet looked out, and it was the thought of these calamities which presented to him the imagery of those prophecies which have themselves continued the like imagery for all such convulsions in every age. The " thunderings and lightnings and earthquakes," " the trumpets of war " and " the vials of wrath," the overthrow of the Imperial city on her seven hills, the bottomless pit, and Death on his pale horse, all these are the signs which he read in the lowering heavens and the distracted earth of his own times. And on the other hand, the martyrs

under the throne, the white-robed army of saints, the
new Jerusalem coming down as a bride adorned for her
husband, were suggested by the thought of the little
band of Christians already spreading through the Empire, already becoming the centres of light and life and
truth amidst a corrupt, decaying, and dissolving world;
struggling against their fanatical persecutors in the Jewish Church, and their heathen persecutors in the Roman
Empire, yet still holding their own, and containing
within themselves the pledge of the future of civilization and of Christianity. It is needless, it is futile to
seek in these chapters for the detailed history of our
own recent times. They have no relation to modern
events; they belong, as far as their letter is concerned,
to the States and the Churches which formed the horizon, far or near, of the Seer on the rock of Patmos, in
the first century of the Christian era — not to the States
and Churches of Italy, France, Germany, or England,
in the sixteenth, or eighteenth, or nineteenth, or twentieth centuries, as some in all succeeding generations
have vainly tried to find them.

There is much in them that we shall never understand
— they are riddles of which the key is lost; "the times
and the seasons that the Father has put in His own
power," and "which are not known to the Angels of
God, nor even to the Son of Man," are not likely to be
discovered by any process of interpretation, however
ingenious, from this sacred book, which, as regards these
outward things, was addressed to the generation not of
some future age, but of that which its author was specially sent to waken and to warn.

But, secondly, there is an eternal truth wrapt up in
these sublime visions — in their spirit, and not in their
letter; in their general principles, not in their details.
On that great Lord's day St. John was not in the flesh,

not in the time or space of any particular scene or spot on earth, but "in the Spirit." And "in the Spirit," under these outward forms, he described how through struggles, through miseries and confusions of every kind, the cause of goodness and truth, the spiritual man (so to speak) of the whole human race advances towards perfection. From that solitary rock he saw the shaking of empires, the ruin of nations, the persecution of the saints, the blood of the martyrs; yet he felt persuaded, and in his bright and beaming words of hope and triumph, he has stamped on the mind of Christendom his persuasion, that purity and truth would come out victorious at last. It is at times a hard doctrine to receive. It seems at times as if the advance of civilization, of religion, of goodness were so irregular that we almost despair of the ultimate purposes of Providence, of the final perfection of humanity. Yet the Seer of Patmos did not despair, nor was troubled beyond measure; and so, neither should our hearts fail.

In the voice of the trumpet that spoke behind him, however varied its tones, he recognized, and we should recognize, the voice of God. Even when, as then, the progress of humanity seemed to be thrown back, and ancient superstitions seemed to be regaining their hold, he clung, and we may still cling, to the hope that good will be wrought out of evil; even when we look on the grievous crimes and follies which have brought about the fall of nations, we may speak of them, as even in that hour of judgment St. John himself spoke of them, with a feeling of human sympathy for the wreck of Imperial greatness and world-wide splendor.

These, then, are the two main features of the Apocalypse. First, the interest, which the public events of our own time are intended to awaken in the hearts of Christians. Secondly, the moral and spiritual effect which such an interest is intended to produce.

Other signs, other striking events, have occurred in the earlier part of this year, on which I have before dwelt,[1] as like to those greater convulsions of which the Revelation speaks. But it seems to me that we shall be also following out the spirit of this sacred book, if we fix our attention on the one public event, close at hand, which has recently filled our minds; if we concentrate our thoughts on that one single trumpet-call, and ask what permanent good we may learn from it.

We were all of us engaged in our several pursuits; most of us as much withdrawn from any of the concerns which were going on outside of our own immediate circles as St. John was removed from all thoughts of the great Roman Empire in his seclusion in the isle of Patmos. Suddenly, like him, we every one of us were roused from these separate individual cares — every one, however high or however humble, in the midst of our several distractions and occupations, as though we heard "the voice of a trumpet talking with us." It came not from falling thrones, or blood-stained battle-fields, or burning cities, but from a single sick chamber in a secluded English county. At each successive reverberation of that thrilling voice, as it was repeated from city to city in countless messages, it hushed the strife of angry disputants, it silenced the eager gathering, it broke up the festive banquet, it rang on from shore to shore through the vast range of the whole empire; the whole nation of Englishmen became on a sudden possessed with one thought and one desire. Even the remote subjects of our dominion, of other races and other creeds, joined in one united prayer for one single youthful life, that it might be sustained in its fierce struggle with death. And now that the tones

---

[1] In sermons preached in the earlier part of 1871, during the troubles of France and the conflagration of Paris.

of that trumpet are changed from mourning into joy, from despair into hope, not the less are its vibrations felt in every household and in every heart.

My brethren, there is not yet such absolute confidence as that we can indulge in assured thanksgiving for the answer to our hopes; and it is not till that day arrives that we can look forward, as we then ought to look forward, with solemn and serious thoughts to the fresh duties which the gracious mercy of God will then, if so be, impose both on him who is spared, and on us who have so earnestly trusted that he might be spared.

But we may, even now, before the recollection of our strain of eager expectation and anxiety has faded away, ask ourselves what this voice was intended to teach us; we may seek to give the reasons to ourselves and to other nations why our hearts have thus burned within us, why, by the mortal struggle of a single existence, our souls were so deeply stirred.

There were many feelings which this unexpected trumpet-call awakened in us, that made it like a voice from a better world.

Let me speak of a few of these. I confine myself to those which apply to all of us alike.

The first lesson of such a summons is that it called us out of ourselves. Nothing is so narrowing, contracting, hardening, as always to be moving in the same groove, with no thought beyond what we immediately see and hear close around us. Any shock which breaks this even course, any thing which makes us think of other joys and sorrows besides our own, is of itself chastening, sanctifying, edifying. We are, or ought to be, the better for having had our souls filled with the thought of others, whom many of us never saw, with hopes and fears which went far beyond the small span of our own lives into the distant future.

Secondly, it touched a chord which vibrates even in the least responsive hearts. It appealed to our sense of the sanctity, the preciousness of family ties; it drew us round one family hearth. In every condition of life a natural instinct prompted an instantaneous sympathy with and for the sufferer and those who were watching around him, because in every household the same scene might at any moment be enacted. It made us feel, according to the trite saying, that royal persons are of the same flesh and blood with us; but it also made us feel — which is no less important — that we are of the same flesh and blood with them. That strain of suspense, that sorrow, that joy which we all of us have felt, was a testimony to the true nobleness and greatness of home affections. Let us, as we think over this week, thank God that He has planted these instincts within us. Let no one be ashamed to own, let every one be eager to cherish, these pure and sacred feelings, which a whole nation has been proud to exhibit, and which are in fact the foundation of all true national and all true Christian life.

Thirdly, it has brought before us how, amidst all our dissensions and party strifes, we are still Englishmen — Englishmen, first and foremost, whatever we may be besides. This is not the first time that the like penetrating sympathy with a single member of the royal house has knit together the hearts of all. So it was, as our fathers have told us, when the Princess Charlotte was snatched away in a moment of time with her infant child. So it was on that sad day which, on its tenth anniversary in this past week, filled every mind with dark forebodings, when the illustrious Prince, whose loss is still felt throughout the Empire, was called away in the midst of his beneficent career. So it has been in that alternation of grief and hope which has wavered

round the sick bed of the Heir of the remote future.
This it is which gives to the Family that represents the
whole people so rare, so singular an interest. It brings
before us in a living, present shape the fact that above
and beyond all sects and parties there is such a thing as
an inextinguishable feeling towards our common country, a sacred bond in the thought that one familiar name
calls up all our patriotic emotions, a charm which gilds
the wear and tear of politics with a personal devotion,
such as no mere abstraction could enkindle. I have
often before and elsewhere dwelt on the sacredness of a
Christian State, on the paramount supremacy of the
English Crown and the English Law. It is impossible
to imagine a more striking tribute than that which has
been just rendered to this sometimes forgotten and disparaged truth, by the spontaneous outburst of every
class and of every party. There are nations, and there
have been times, in which the devotion to the reigning
family has been a thing separate and apart from the
love of country. There have been times and places,
where the love of country has existed with no loyal
feeling to the reigning family. Let us thank God that
in England it is not so. Loyalty with us is the personal,
romantic side of Patriotism. Patriotism with us is the
Christian, philosophic side of Loyalty. Long may the
two flourish together, each supporting and sustaining
the other! .

And, finally, this universal movement has shown —
what in the last resort Englishmen have always shown
—that we are (I say it not in any spirit of boastful-
ness or ostentation) a Godfearing and religious people.
What was the natural expression of our hopes and fears,
our sympathy and our anxious expectation? It was the
united sacred language of prayer to the Supreme Ruler
and Father of the Universe. Not only in the churches

in which, as here, day after day, the names of the Sovereign and her children are habitually mentioned, and where, in silent meditation, each of those names has through the whole of this long suspense been commended to God, not only in the solemn prayer which on last Sunday was offered up with one consent in every proud cathedral and humble village church which owns the Queen's authority, but in every church and chapel of every sect, however far removed from our mode of worship or doctrine; in temples of other faiths in regions far away; in journals at home, however cynical and worldly; in assemblies however secular, the same awful Name was invoked, the same devout wish was expressed, the same sacred petition breathed, differing in words, but in substance the same. This is indeed a true Christian communion; this is to keep the unity of the Spirit in the bond of Peace. We need not penetrate into the inscrutable secrets of Providence, we need not perplex ourselves with precise questions on the mode in which Prayer is answered. It is enough for us to know and feel that it is the most natural, the most powerful, the most elevated expression of our thoughts and wishes in all great emergencies. It is enough to know that, in the most severe of all trials, the most sustaining and comforting thought is the fixed belief that we are in the hands of an All-wise, All-merciful Father. To Him we turned in anxious suspense, to Him we turn again with grateful thanks. Into His Hands we commended the spirit of the sufferer, hovering between life and death, to be strengthened, purified, and, if it might so be, restored to us. Into those same Hands of infinite compassion we commend once more that same youthful spirit, returning, as we trust, from the gates of the grave to a higher, better, grander life than ever before.

May we be strengthened by the voice of the heavenly Trumpet to fulfil more faithfully, more loyally, more courageously our duty towards him; may he be strengthened by that same voice, as from another world, to fulfil more actively, more steadfastly, more zealously his duty towards us! "Unto God's gracious mercy and protection we commit him. The Lord bless him and keep him! The Lord make His face to shine upon him, and be gracious unto him!"

III. — THE DAY OF THANKSGIVING.

March 3, 1872.

I was glad when they said unto me, We will go into the house of the Lord. — PSALM cxxii. 1 (Prayer-book version).

THESE words, taken from the Psalms of the 27th day of the month, which I have caused to be again repeated here to-day, met the eyes of thousands in the course of the past week, inscribed over the western portico of St. Paul's Cathedral. They fitly expressed the feeling which swayed the heart of the whole metropolis. We were glad, we rejoiced, because our Sovereign and her people had said, "We will go into the house of the Lord." It was a gladness which made itself felt even to the distant extremities of our mighty Empire. It was a gladness for the gracious gift, as if sent direct from heaven, of a precious life which we had earnestly sought. It was the gladness of beholding the Sovereign whom we loved once more trusting herself amongst us, and receiving with radiant smiles, with unshaken courage, the tokens of her people's loyalty. It was the thankful gladness, we may say, for the Thanksgiving itself, the grateful relief, that a day so long expected with such eagerness — we had well-nigh said with such awe — as its morning dawned with its mighty burden of innumerable human souls, had come and gone amidst such almost unclouded brightness, such almost unbroken order and pure unstained enjoyment.

But it was not mere gladness, not mere thanksgiving. When we felt that the centre of all those myriad movements was not the seat of commerce, or legislation, or pleasure, but the consecrated house of the Lord; when we looked down on the multitudes covering that vast area, or upwards to the multitudes suspended in that soaring cupola; when after the long hours of waiting, there fell over all those dense masses a stillness, as of an unseen Presence; when, as the voice of praise and prayer went up from thousands of lips and thousands of hearts, the whole atmosphere became, as it were, charged with worship — we felt assured that the ages of faith are not yet run out; that Religion, in its widest and deepest sense, still holds its sway over the hearts of Englishmen, that it shall be, as far as human foresight can reach, the crown and consummation, and best expression of our noblest and purest feelings. And when further we remarked, how, under that spacious dome were gathered (with the single exception of one exclusive body) the representatives of every Christian, nay, of every religious community in England, how all of these felt that, agreeing here or disagreeing there, they yet on the whole could join in the utterances of religious faith and hope as embodied in the venerable forms of the National Church — it was a living proof that such united worship within one common national sanctuary is not an idle dream; it was a sign that a

National Church, so bound up, heart and soul, life and limb, with the Nation and the State, could alone furnish such a common meeting-point of religion and patriotism — it was a pledge that as long as the memory of that day remains, England will not willingly consent to make over her noblest historical and sacred edifices, her purest and highest aspirations after God, to the keeping of any single sect, or to the mere rivalry and contention of private interests.

When further we thought how he who was the central object of that vast gathering, was there not merely as an ordinary worshipper, but as one who had, by a marvellous recovery returned from the very valley of the shadow of death, and that, by a singular coincidence, the Primate's words of sober and simple counsel were uttered by one who had himself been recalled by a recovery not less wonderful to health and activity amongst us — a dying man, speaking as to a dying man of the duties of the living to which both had been alike brought back; when we remembered how around that youthful form life and death had battled, for long days and nights, like mortal combatants, in a strife of which the whole English race were the awestruck spectators; when we glanced at the mother, wife, brothers, sisters, and little children, in whose anguish, and anxious expectation, and returning happiness all the nation found the impersonation of their own peculiar joys and sorrows — then, again, we felt that it was not merely a solemn service, a sacred act of adoration, but a service, a worship, of the most living reality, because it rose from and gathered round a living human being, with passions, hopes, fears, duties, such as each one of us knows in himself, needing the same strength from above, struggling with the same terrible temptations, wrought in the same English mould, inheritor of the same individual destiny for weal or woe, according to the deeds done in the body, whether they be good or whether they be evil. Other services might be more ornate, more dramatic; other appeals to the feelings more exciting; other forms of devotion more eager to pry into the secrets of the eternal world, or explain the unrevealed mysteries of Providence. We were content with the simple expression of heartfelt gratitude, as of sons to a Father, for a mercy received; and if that natural expression rose to gigantic proportions, it was only because the whole nation was resolved to bear its part therein.

But yet more; not only was this a solemn religious festival, not only did it concern the welfare of a human soul, which, whether of Prince or peasant, is equally precious in the sight of the Eternal God — but it was the response in every English heart to the sense of the union, too subtle for analysis, yet true and simple as the primitive instincts of our race, which binds the people of England to their monarchy, and the monarchy to the people. It is the feeling of which the Psalms are so noble a rendering, and which make them so fit an exponent of our national hopes and fears. — "There is the seat of judgment. There are the thrones of the house of David. For my brethren and companions' sake, I will wish thee prosperity; yea, because of the House of the Lord our God, I will seek to do thee good." So spoke the Psalmist in the inspired thanksgiving, from which the text is taken. And so in a yet more exalted strain, another Psalmist drew a picture of what such a monarchy should be — "Give thy judgments, O God, to the king, and thy righteousness to the king's son. He shall judge thy people with righteousness, and thy poor with judgment. He shall deliver the needy when he crieth, and the poor also, and him that hath no helper. In his days shall the righteous flourish, and abundance of peace, so long as the moon endureth."

Such was the ideal of a just and beneficent Monarchy more than two thousand years ago. Such, to all who can feel or think, it still is, amidst whatever mixture of personal and national infirmity, amidst whatever changes have been wrought by differences of time and race and country, in our modern existence.

Look for a moment at the serious, philosophic, Christian aspect of such a monarchy, at that which alone rendered possible the feelings of the week that is past. It is the one name and place amongst us which unites in almost unbroken succession the whole range of our island story, which is the common property of the whole British people, we might almost say of the whole Anglo-Saxon race. No other existing throne in Europe reaches back to the same antiquity, none other combines with such an undivided charm the associations of the past, the interests of the present. It is the one name and place which, being raised high above all party struggles, all local jealousies, over all causes and over all cases, ecclesiastical as well as civil, is the supreme controlling spring which binds together, in their widest sense, all the forces of the State and all the forces of the Church. It is the one name and place which, being beyond the reach of personal ambition, beyond the need of private gain, has the inestimable chance of guiding, moulding, elevating, the tastes, the customs, the morals of the whole community. It is the one institution, which, by the very nature of its existence, unites the abstract idea of country and of duty with the personal endearments of family life, of domestic love, of individual character. This is the

bright side of that ancient and august possession, which
has steadied the course of our onward progress, and
given us peace in the midst of tumults, and freedom
in the midst of disorder. It is because of the greatness
of this possession, that we so fervently pray and hope
that he who is its destined heir shall be worthy of his
noble inheritance. He knows, and we know, that on
him henceforth, as by a new consecration and confirmation, devolves the glorious task of devoting to his
country's service that life which is in a special sense
no longer his but ours, for which his country's prayers,
his country's thanksgivings have been so earnestly
offered. He knows, as few in like positions have
known, the mighty power for good which has, within
our own memory, been exercised in that lofty sphere
by one who, from early manhood to his sudden and untimely end, wore "the white flower of a blameless life,"
unscathed and unspotted even in that "fierce light which
beats upon a throne." He has learned by the experience of these eventful weeks, he has had borne in upon
him by thousands and tens of thousands of voices, that
"of him to whom much has been given, of him shall
much be required." Hardly ever, in the long course
of our history, has so heart-stirring a prospect been
opened, of beginning life afresh, of taking the lead in
all that is true and holy, just and good, of finding in
the hundred calls of duty a hundred openings for the
best and purest enjoyment, of strengthening the relaxed
fibre, if so be, of English morals, of raising and purifying the homes of the poor and the tone of every grade
of English society, of becoming by the sheer force of a
stainless and guileless life a terror, not to good works,
but to the evil.

Over the tomb of a famous Prince, who lies buried
in this Abbey, and whose first entrance on a new career

of goodness and usefulness began from the moment
when he stood by his father's deathbed within these
precincts, there is carved the flaming beacon or cresset
light, which, says the ancient chronicler, " he took for
his badge, showing thereby that as his virtues and good
parts had been formerly obscured, and lay as a dead
coal waiting light to kindle it, . . . notwithstanding
he being now come to his perfecter years and riper
understanding, . . . his virtues should now shine forth
as the light of a cresset, which is no ordinary light."
Such a kindling of such a beacon light, which shall
reach as far as the fame of this Thanksgiving has penetrated — such may God grant to him whom the nation
hopes by its prayers to have won back to itself forever.
" Give, Oh give thy servant wisdom and knowledge,
that he may go out and come in before this people . . .
that is so great."   " The Lord preserve his going out
and his coming in, from this time forth for evermore."

But if this be what we expect from the Throne, let
us ask ourselves what the Monarchy, what the Empire,
what the world expects from us.   It is the glory of
England that if the welfare of the Prince is the welfare
of the people, not less is the well-being of the people
the only safeguard of the well-being of the Prince.   It
is not with us, as in some Eastern or despotic States,
where the Royal House dwells apart, withdrawn from
all the surrounding influences of the country or the age
in which their lot is cast.   The breath of public opinion, of good or evil example, in our mixed and varied
society, rises upwards as much as it descends downwards.

It is in our power, in the power of the people of England, to drag down the Throne, even in spite of itself,
to the level, if so be, of our own meanness, triviality,
or self-indulgence, as it is, thank God, also in our power,

by the purity of our homes, by the sincerity and the
loftiness of our purposes, to create the atmosphere in
which the Throne must become pure and lofty, because
it cannot help receiving the influences which ascend to
it from below and from around.   We, by raising up a
constant succession of just, upright, loyal, single-minded
citizens, of enlightened and energetic teachers, of far-
seeing and unselfish statesmen, form a body-guard
around the Royal House of England, even as the
statues and monuments of famous Englishmen in this
Abbey stand like a guard of honor round the shrines
which contain the dust of our Princes and our Kings.
Any breach in that sacred line of honest English hearts,
any failure of duty, of vigilance, or of faithfulness on
our part lays open the way for the destroyer to come
in and lay waste the innermost sanctuary of the State
itself.   Our prayers, our thanksgivings, if they are to
last beyond the passing moment, must take the shape,
not of idle flattery or fond endearments, but of stern
requirements of duty both from others and from ourselves.

We look down with mingled indignation and contempt on the miserable outrages attempted in former
years against the Gracious Majesty of these realms.
We are accustomed to regard with scorn the handful
of misguided men, who seek to win popular favor by
appeals to the prejudices, the passions, and the ignorance of the people.   But let us remember that these
are not the only or the chief dangers against which the
Nation is bound to protect the Throne.   If there be,
as there have been in other times and in other countries, those who, hovering round the footsteps of the
great, either for their own selfish ends, or from mere
weakness and complaisance, or from mere vanity of
vanities, strive to serve them by smoothing the path to

sin, by making a mock at goodness, by hiding the unwelcome truth, or repeating the welcome falsehood;
if there be any who, under the guise of friends, play
the part of tempter and evil counsellor, who lie in wait
for every occasion to flatter, to indulge, and to corrupt
— if there be any such anywhere, these, far more than
wild fanatics or the feeble parasites of the multitude,
these are the real traitors, the real enemies of Sovereign, Prince, and people all alike.

It is for the growth of such as these that we, the
nation of England, are, in great measure, responsible
before God and man. They are bone of our bone and
flesh of our flesh. It is by our levity, if so be, that characters such as these are encouraged in their wretched
folly, as it is by our firmness that they are discouraged
and cowed. They come out when the moral atmosphere
has been made dark around them, "wherein all the
beasts of the forest creep forth for their prey." But
"when the sun ariseth," when the bright burning light
of a sound public opinion is brought to bear upon them,
"they get themselves together and lay them down again
in their dens."

On these then, and such as these, whosoever they be,
men or women, high or low, the Day of Thanksgiving
is or ought to be a Day of Doom. Against these, and
such as these, the nation is called upon to echo the
voice of most just judgment that goes up from every
honest heart. On these, if on any human being whatever, Christian society, English society, ought to place
its deliberate ban, its unmistakable mark of righteous
indignation. Whatever may have been before, yet now,
if after the experience of these never-to-be-forgotten
weeks and days — if, after this solemn recognition of
the value of our great institutions, of the incalculable
importance of the character of our rulers — if, after

this, the nation relaxes its hold on the high vocation, which has thus been marked out, our last state shall indeed be worse than our first. If, after this, any such as I have described, shall be found, betraying, misleading, ensnaring those whom by every call, human and divine, they are bound to lead into all good and keep from all evil, such, if there be any such, deserve the contempt of man and the vengeance of GOD, as amongst the meanest, or the weakest, or the most detestable of mankind.

There is yet one more topic on which I would dwell. In those ancient days of the Jewish monarchy and Jewish people to which the text belongs, it was customary, on solemn occasions when, as we read, " the King and the people made a covenant with each other and with God," to erect some monument, some towering pillar, some massive altar, as a permanent witness to themselves and to the world, in order that they and all might forever be reminded of what they had pledged themselves to do. It was a just and natural safeguard. Human emotions are so transitory that they need some such external monument or form in which they may be consolidated and fixed. Such a monument we are asked now to erect — most suitable to the occasion, most lasting in duration, most significant to the eye and the mind of England for all future time.

It is the restoration, the completion of the great metropolitan Cathedral of St. Paul, that witnessed the solemn service which we here this day, in the sister Abbey of St. Peter, have also met, in our humbler measure, to commemorate. It is in accordance with the varying characteristics of these two venerable and majestic Churches, that, whilst the Abbey of Westminster is interwoven by a gradual, silent, continuous chain, as by the links of " natural piety," with the even tenor, the stately pageants, the silent departures of our country's rulers and heroes, St. Paul's Cathedral derives its historical interest from single stirring incidents, from the sudden and terrible vicissitudes of its own rise and fall, from the thunders of the Reformation at its pulpit cross.   It has received the burst of national exultation at the destruction of the Armada, the victories of Blenheim and of Trafalgar.   It has mourned with a mourning people over the graves of Nelson and Wellington —

> Who is he that cometh, like an honor'd guest,
> With a nation weeping, and breaking on my rest?
> Mighty seaman, this is he
> Was great by land as thou by sea.

It has rejoiced with the universal rejoicing at the unexpected recovery of an aged Sovereign at the close of the century that is past.   It has now rejoiced, yet again, with the still wider joy, over the yet more wonderful restoration of the youthful Prince.   In the circles of that same dome, round those same wide-embracing walls, that witnessed the covenant, as it may well be called, between the Heir of the Throne and his future people, shall now be carried on that glorious work which the mighty architect of the Cathedral was compelled to leave unfinished, which its most venerable historian and illustrious divine labored in vain to accomplish, but which, when completed, shall make the great Protestant Cathedral of England worthy to look in the face the great Roman Basilica, of which it is even now a noble rival, — worthy also of the magnificent future which more and more seems opening before it, as the centre of instruction and edification to the thousands of worshippers, week by week, assembled within its almost illimitable space.

For such a completion as this the greatness of the

Imperial Thanksgiving demands the united help of the British Empire. For such a completion as this, let every Englishman give, far and near, according to his means. Let none think they can give too much, let none think their contributions too insignificant, to commemorate a day in which they have all taken part — towards a great work, a world-renowned edifice, which ought to have been finished long ago, which, so long as a National Church exists amongst us, every Englishman may call his own, from the Queen in her palace down to the humblest peasant or the most remote Nonconformist, throughout the length and breadth of the land.

And when, in after days, Prince and people alike shall gaze with admiration on its vast interior, bright with all the splendors which art and wealth can bestow, as even now they look from far on those sublime proportions which rise above all the smoke and stir of this bewildering multitudinous city — may he and we be ever reminded of the solemn thoughts which have now filled our hearts, may he and we be always able to look back upon this week with thankfulness and not with shame, may he and we then behold in that august edifice a standing memorial of good resolutions, not broken but accomplished; of noble hopes, not disappointed but fulfilled; of splendid opportunities, not lost but cherished to the utmost; of generous devotion, on our part, to our Queen and country, not wasted in party strife but spent in the common good; of love for God's holy Name, not shown in futile and fierce disputes about trifles but in the great causes of justice, charity, and truth! May we all be able to say ten, twenty years hence, with as much sincerity as now, "I was glad when they said unto me, Let us go into the house of the Lord!"

ENGLAND AND INDIA.

October 11, 1875, being the day preceding the departure of H.R.H. the Prince of Wales for India.

Now it came to pass in the days of Ahasuerus, (this is Ahasuerus which reigned, from India even unto Ethiopia, over an hundred and seven and twenty provinces).

There is a certain people scattered abroad and dispersed among the people in all the provinces of thy kingdom.

How can I endure to see the evil that shall come unto my people? or how can I endure to see the destruction of my kindred? — ESTHER i. 1; iii. 8; viii. 6.

WE have reached that point in the Lessons in our Church Services where the history of the people of Israel blends with the history of the other nations of the earth — Babylon, Persia, Greece, and Rome. I propose to take, as the subject of my sermon, a book which is more exclusively devoted to this outside world than any other book in the Bible, and which, perhaps on this account, is never read in our Sunday services. It is the Book of Esther.

The scene of the Book of Esther is not Palestine, but Persia; not Jerusalem, but Shushan or Susa. The king Ahasuerus is that famous prince whom we know in Grecian story under the name of Xerxes. The events took place in the palace of Susa, in the great hall of which we know the exact form and figure from that of which the ruins still remain at Persepolis — the most magnificent hall, it is believed, that ever was raised for regal splendor. There sate "the great king," as he

114

was called, surrounded by the seven princes of the realm. Round his throne we trace the peculiar customs of the Persian Court, which, with but little change, have continued down to the present day.

What is it which, with all these foreign associations, gives to such a book its place in the records of the chosen people? It is because it is the description of the most signal deliverance of the vast body of Jews, who were settled throughout the different countries comprised in the vast territory of the Persian Empire. "There is a certain people scattered abroad and dispersed among all the people in all the provinces of thy kingdom, and their laws are diverse from all people." Such was the account given of them to Ahasuerus, and we know from other sources how true it was. Along the banks of the river Euphrates numbers had remained, with schools and universities and sacred places; so that it was a proverb, "Whoever dwells in Babylon is as though he dwelt in the land of Israel." High up in the mountains of Kurdistan the descendants of those who were transplanted thither are said to be found even to the present time. In the green fields of Egypt there was a powerful colony established, which afterwards formed the materials of the great Jewish community in Alexandria.

These settlements were suddenly doomed to destruction by one of those violent acts which characterize the policy of Eastern sovereigns. The anger of Haman, the king's chief minister, was roused against one of this body because he refused to do reverence before a mortal man; and in his anger he included the whole race. Posts, after the manner of the Persian Empire, were sent into all the provinces "to destroy, to kill, and to cause to perish, all Jews, both young and old, little children and women, in one day, even upon the thirteenth day of the twelfth month, which is the month Adar."

This is the subject of the book, and its main interest hinges on the mode of the deliverance. They were delivered by what we might call three remarkable coincidences, any one of which would have failed of itself, but all together combined to produce the result as surely as if the Divine Presence had been manifested in flames of fire, or with twelve legions of angels. There was the singular chance, as we should say, that, owing to a quarrel in the Court of Susa, a Jewish captive was at that critical period the favorite queen of the Persian king, and that she had the spirit and courage, at the risk of her own life, to reveal her origin, and to plead for the lives of her countrymen. There was next the accident, that the king, on a sleepless night, was suddenly reminded of a service that years before he had received from the hands of Mordecai. There was, lastly, the good fortune that when Haman cast the lot at the beginning of the year, to find an auspicious moment for the execution of his designs, it ·postponed the time from day to day, and from month to month, till it was deferred to the thirteenth day of the very last month of the year. According to the custom of the Medes and Persians, which forbade any royal decree to be altered, it was impossible for the king, even on the entreaty of Esther and Mordecai, to withdraw his rash and cruel order; yet, owing to this long interval, there was still time left to issue a counter decree, permitting the Jews in every city to gather together and defend themselves to the death. It was still early in the year — still the third month — when this second decree was issued; and in the interval which thus elapsed, before the dreaded thirteenth day of the twelfth month arrived, they had time fully to organize their defence; and when at last the attack was made, the spirit of their enemies was broken down, " the fear of them fell on all people;" the rulers of the provinces helped them; they stood at bay against the hunters of their lives, "and no man could withstand them."

I. Such briefly are the main points of the story of Esther. Let us now ask what lessons are taught by it.

(1.) First, then, let us turn to the structure of the story itself. In one respect the Book of Esther stands absolutely alone amongst all the books both of the Old and the New Testament. From one 'end of it to the other the name of God, so common everywhere else, is entirely absent. So startling has this peculiarity seemed that in the early times of the Christian Church there were those who wished to exclude the book from the Scriptures altogether, while others, as we may see from the additions which we find in the Apocrypha, endeavored to introduce and invent the religious phrases which the original narrative did not contain.

But it is this very peculiarity of the Book of Esther which is so instructive. It is necessary for us that in the rest of the sacred volume the name of God should constantly be brought before us, to show that He is all in all to us and to the world. But it is expedient for us no less that there should be one book which omits it altogether, to prevent us from attaching to the mere name a reverence which belongs only to the reality. We cannot doubt that Esther and Mordecai were really animated by the faith and love of God. We cannot doubt that the quarrel of Ahasuerus, the sleepless night, the delay of the lot, although all these occurrences were what we should call accidents, yet worked out the will of God as completely as the parting of the Red Sea or the thunders of Sinai. Let the Book of Esther be a token to us that in the daily events, the unforeseen chances, of life, God is surely present; that in little unremembered acts, in the fall of a sparrow, in the earth bringing forth fruit of herself, springing and growing up into a bountiful harvest, we know not how, His will is accomplished as truly as by fire and earthquake. The name of God is *not* there, but the work of God *is*.

Let us learn from the admission of such a book into the Bible not to make a man an offender for a word or for the omission of a word. There may be many who, without any outward confession of faith, are as faithful servants of God as those who are full of religious expressions; many who, from reverence or reserve, or want of fluent discourse, abstain altogether in public from using the names of God and of Christ, and yet are true servants of God, true missionaries of Christ, by deed or look, though not by word. "There is neither speech nor language, but their voices are heard among them. Their sound is gone out into all lands, and their words unto the ends of the world."

By acts of silent goodness, by a humble faith, that does not express itself in speech, the presence of God is often as surely indicated as in the actual calling on His name in prayer and praise, in teaching and preaching.

When Esther nerved herself to enter, at the risk of her life, the presence of Ahasuerus — "I will go in unto the king, and if I perish, I perish " — when her patriotic feeling vented itself in that noble cry, "How can I endure to see the evil that shall come unto my people? or how can I endure to see the destruction of my kindred?" — she expressed, although she never named the name of God, a religious devotion as acceptable to Him as that of Moses and David, who no less sincerely had the sacred name always on their lips.

It is the same truth as is conveyed by our great dramatist, when he describes how, amongst the three

daughters of the British king, the true affection was to
be found, not in the two that made the loudest professions, but in the one who, from fear of overstepping in
the least degree the bounds of truth, answered nothing,
and kept all the proof of her love for the tender care
which she showed when all others turned against him: —

> Thy youngest daughter does not love thee least;
> Nor are those empty-hearted whose low sound
> Reverbs no hollowness.

(2.) Secondly, our attention is called to the great
significance, not merely of the Jewish community which
was fixed in the Holy Land and in the Holy City, but
of that vast body of Jews scattered over the world, and
known by the name of the Dispersion. What, we may
ask, was the importance of their preservation? We
have only to look at the Acts of the Apostles to see,
far more surely than Esther or Mordecai saw, the infinite
consequences of their exertions, of God's intervention
at that moment. It was those very congregations of
dispersed Israelites that furnished the link between
Jews and Gentiles through which the Gospel spread
from one to the other. What the Jews in Palestine
and Jerusalem were for the first foundation of Christianity, that the Jews in Babylonia, in Egypt, in Asia
Minor, in Greece, in Italy, were for its subsequent propagation. From their ranks came Stephen and Apollos,
Barnabas and Paul; out of them were formed in every
instance the nucleus, the basis, round which the Gentile
Churches gathered. From the earnest prayer of Esther
to Ahasuerus, from the various chances which aided that
prayer, was drawn, by a long succession of consequences,
the golden chain which has brought the isles of the
Gentiles into the Church of God.

These are the chief religious lessons of the Book of

Esther. The details of the Imperial splendor and the strange intrigues of the Court of Xerxes, however interesting in an historical point of view, have no special edification for us. The bitterness of Esther against Haman's innocent family belongs to the hardness of that old dispensation which is condemned by Christ our Lord, and which the Jewish race themselves, at least in this country, have long since laid aside. The fierce anathemas that once were uttered in their synagogues whenever the feast of Purim was celebrated — stamping with their feet and shaking their fists whenever the name of Haman was mentioned — have dropped out of their worship, as the like expressions are gradually disappearing from Christian worship also.

It was for these harsher and more worldly characteristics of the Book of Esther that Luther hesitated to receive it into the Bible. "It is too full," he said, "of heathenish naughtiness, and it Judaizes too much." Yet, amidst that "heathenish naughtiness" and that narrow Judaic spirit, it carries with it lessons of enduring value for all time. It is a book which, in spite of all its defects, ranked amongst the Jews as the very most precious portion of the whole Bible after the Law — more precious than even the Prophets, or Psalms, or Proverbs. We need not rank it so high as this. We perhaps may regard it as the least important of all the sacred books. But even this humblest part of the Bible is not without its use if it can teach us those inestimable lessons of silent courageous patriotism which are as much needed in England as in Persia, and those duties of energy and self-denial which are as essential for Christians as for Jews.

II. Let us apply the story more especially to ourselves.

Is there any race of men, now, as were then the dispersed Jews, with like high issues dependent on their good or evil fortune?

"There is," now, as there was then, "a people scattered abroad and dispersed through all the provinces," not of one kingdom only, but of an almost boundless empire — raised up, and preserved, through a long succession of ages, by a protection not indeed miraculous, but as truly providential as that by which the Jews were saved in the time of Esther — a people the fear of whom is on all the nations in a wider and better sense than was that of the Jews on the heathens with whom they dwelt — a nation with power and knowledge such as make it in a still higher degree than those ancient Jewish colonies, "a light to lighten the Gentiles, and to be the glory of God's people Israel."

We all know without another word what that nation is. It is ourselves — we say it in no boastful spirit — our own widely dispersed English, British, Anglo-Saxon race.

And to speak only of one portion of that great dispersion of Englishmen, there is that vast Eastern Empire of which the name is for the first time mentioned in the Bible in the first words of the Book of Esther: — "This is Ahasuerus, which reigned from *India* even unto Ethiopia." In India, so marvellously acquired, sometimes by force and fraud, sometimes by just and beneficent rule; in India, whose trophies fill many a niche in this church; in India, so mercifully saved to us through dangers and escapes as remarkable as any that are recorded by history; in India, whose ancient religion, philosophy, and language have in our generation been for the first time brought to light by the labors of German and English scholars; in India, glorified with a dubious splendor by the names of Clive and Hastings, and sanctified, with a purer and milder lustre, by statesmen like Bentinck, soldiers like Havelock, missionaries like Henry Martyn, pastors like Heber and Cotton — in that vast province of the British Empire, surely, if nowhere else, we as Englishmen have to express our thankfulness, as truly as ever did the Jews of old, for our signal deliverances, for that eminent greatness to which God has raised us in former times, and from which in these latter days He has not allowed us to be cast down.

And what are the corresponding duties? Can it be doubted that, as in those ancient Jewish settlements of the Dispersion, so, and much more, in all those various portions of the world whither our commerce, and our arms, and our enterprise, have carried us, but especially in India, the sons and daughters of the English race are the true missionaries for good or for evil to the rest of mankind?

Is there any one in this congregation who has travelled or has intended to travel, for pleasure or for business, to those distant regions? Is there any one who mourns for the dead received back from those dangerous climes only just in time to breathe at home their parting breath, or who looks back on bright courses of usefulness, prematurely closed, of the servants of their country and their God, sleeping far away beneath the shadow of the Himalayan heights, or in the bed of the rolling Ganges, or by the surf-beaten shore of Madras? Is there any one who has friends, brothers, sons, in that Eastern Empire occupying the positions almost of kings, with an influence extending over vast populations such as will never again fall to their lot, such as rarely falls to the lot of any human being? If there be any such (and it is the peculiarity of every English congregation that there may be such in every church throughout the land), let them remember the heavy responsibility, the glorious privilege, which rests upon them and theirs.

The Book of Esther teaches us — what our own experience and common sense teach no less — that it is by the lives as well as by the lips, by deeds as well as by words, nay, by deed even more than by word, of our countrymen in foreign parts, that the truth and beauty of Christian life and Christian doctrine are to be made known, if ever Christianity is to spread beyond its present limits. The name of God may perchance be withheld; but the presence of God may be made as clear as light. According as an English traveller, an English soldier or sailor, an English magistrate or merchant, an English governor, presents an image of justice or injustice, of purity or impurity, of reverence or of profaneness, of kindly appreciation or of dull indifference, will be the likeness which the Mahometan and the Hindoo will form in their own minds, and retain perhaps to their dying day, of our country and our religion. According as the life and conduct of an Englishman, in camp or in field, in business or in pleasure, attracts or repels, conciliates or offends, elevates or corrupts, those with whom he comes into contact, will be the rapid advance or the indefinite delay of the kingdom of God in the sphere in which he moves.

It is recorded that some Brahmins, conversing with the Danish missionary Schwartz, replied to his arguments in behalf of Christianity. "We do not see your Christian people live according to that Holy Word. They curse, they swear, they get drunk; they steal, they cheat, they deal fraudulently with one another; they blaspheme and rail upon matters of religion, or often make a mock of those who profess to be religious; they behave themselves as badly, if not worse, than we heathen. Of what advantage is all your profession of Christ's religion, if it does not influence the lives of your own countrymen? Should you not first endeavor to convert your own countrymen before you attempt to proselytize Pagans?" But turning to him they said, "Of a truth you are a holy man, and if all Christians thought and spoke and lived as you do, we would without delay undergo the change and become Christians also."

And if such is the duty of those who are thus called to foreign parts, what is that of those who remain at home? We have heard it a thousand times. It is by all the means in our power to build up and strengthen all the elements of Christian life in our countrymen who depart from us to fields so full of interest. It is for us to make them feel the manifold instruction which they may receive, as in a second education, by moving amongst scenes and races so unlike to those with which they have hitherto been familiar.

It is our duty to foster here, in the focus of English civilization, the public opinion, the private influence, which shall keep alive in our countrymen abroad the conviction that of those " to whom much has been given shall much be required." It is according as we treat their conduct with levity or with seriousness, with indifferent apathy or with generous sympathy, that they will go out to their callings there in a low or in a lofty spirit. If they take in hand so great an enterprise unadvisedly, lightly, and wantonly, it will be in large measure because we have not done our best to raise them to the consciousness of their high vocation. If we insist on their entering upon it advisedly, reverently, and in the fear of God, we shall have delivered our own souls, and they, it may be, will rise to the level to which we insist that they shall reach. The ancient founders, the ancient princes, of the Grecian colonies took out with them to their distant settlements a spark of the sacred fire which was always kept burning on the hearth of the parent country. It is for us to see that the sacred fire on our hearth is always kept bright and pure. If its ashes grow cold with us, the spark which is taken from it will dwindle and sink far away. If it blazes warmly here, its heat will be felt to the extremities of the Empire. And when we think how, amongst those dispersed countrymen, our own friends and brothers and children may hereafter, if not now, be found; when we think how honorable may be their success, how miserable their failure, in proportion as their opportunities are used wisely or foolishly, well or ill — is it possible to help joining in the spirit of Esther's petition, "How can I endure to see the evil that shall come unto my people; or how can I endure to see the destruction of my kindred?"

We were roused to fury in the days of the Indian Mutiny. We could not endure to see, we could not endure to hear, of the evil that came to our people during that dark time. We could not endure to see or to hear of the destruction of our kindred by murder, or pestilence, or famine. But surely any man who has in him (I will not say the heart of a Christian, but) the spirit of an Englishman, ought to feel no less keenly, How can we endure to see the evil that will come to our people far away by our careless living, by our folly or recklessness, by our insolence or intemperance or indolence? How can we endure to see the moral destruction of our kindred, the imperilling of our Empire, the discrediting of our name, our race, and our religion, by the unworthiness of us who are its representatives and its witnesses?

For the blessings or the curses which accompany, for

the good or evil influences which inspire. those who go forth to our vast dependencies, or who rule them, or who dwell in them, we who form the public opinion of England must be more or less responsible. It is the necessary consequence of the principle. which is as true in the State as in the Church. that, "if one member suffer, all the members suffer with it ; or if one member be honored, all the members rejoice with it."

Many of you will have perceived why this subject has been chosen for our thoughts at this time. when for the next five months our attention will be specially turned to India. To-morrow the first Heir of the English throne who has ever visited the Indian Empire starts on his journey to those distant regions, which the greatest of his ancestors. Alfred the Great. a thousand years ago. longed to explore. and which now forms the most splendid jewel in the British crown.

On this eve of that departure. solemn to him and solemn to us, we pray that the Eldest Son of our Royal House. in whose sickness and recovery. four years since, the whole nation took so deep an interest, shall now once more be delivered from perils by land and perils by sea, from "the terror by night and from the pestilence that destroyeth in the noonday ;" we pray that he may be restored safe and sound to the Mother, the Wife, and the little children. who wait with anxious expectation his happy and prosperous return.

But we pray, or we ought to pray. yet more earnestly, that his journey may be blessed to himself. and to those whom he visits, in all things high and holy. just and pure, lovely and of good report. We pray that he and they who attend him may feel how sacred a trust is committed to them ; we pray that we who remain behind may never ourselves forget, or suffer others to for-

get, how arduous and (if ~so be) how noble a duty
they have undertaken. We pray that we, by our sympathy in all that is good, by our detestation of all that
is base, may, like those of old time, hold up the sinking
arms and strengthen the wavering hands of those who
are charged with the responsibility of this mission of
good-will, of duty, and of hope. We pray that they
may be so filled with the spirit of power, of love, and of
a sound mind, with the spirit of justice and wisdom,
with the spirit of courtesy and purity, that, wheresoever
they go, the name of England and of English Christendom shall be not dishonored, but honored ; that the
fibre of Indian society, whether amongst our countrymen or amongst natives, shall not be relaxed, but
strengthened ; that the standard of our national morality shall not be lowered, but raised ; that the bonds
of affection between the ruling and the subject races
shall be not loosened, but confirmed. We pray that
this visit, long desired and at last undertaken, to those
marvellous lands, may, by God's mercy, leave behind,
on the one side (if so be) the remembrance of graceful
acts, kind words, English nobleness, Christian principle,
— on the other side, awaken or renew, in all concerned,
the sense of graver duties, wider sympathies, loftier
purposes.

Thus, and thus only, shall that journey on which the
Church and nation now pronounce a parting benediction, be worthy of a Christian Empire and worthy of
an English Prince. For the building up, in truth and
righteousness, of that Imperial inheritance, for the moral
and eternal welfare of his own immortal soul, may the
LORD preserve his going out and his coming in, from
this time forth for evermore !

THE RETURN OF THE TRAVELLER.

May 14, 1876, being the Sunday after the return of the Prince of Wales from India. Preached in the presence of their Royal Highnesses the Prince of Wales, the Princess of Wales, the Duke of Edinburgh, and the Duke of Connaught.

I was glad when they said unto me, Let us go into the house of the Lord. — PSALM cxxii. 1.

THIS Psalm is one of a series from the 120th to the 134th, which are called in our version " The Songs of Degrees," but more properly " The Songs of the Return " — the songs in which the Israelites, after their exile in Babylon, expressed their joy at finding themselves once more in sight or in prospect of home. The Psalms and Prophecies of the time describe the delight with which the travellers started on their westward journey; how they mounted ridge after ridge, and caught the first view of their own [1] country; how the beacon-fires [2] flashing from their native hills welcomed them onwards; how at last their feet [3] stood " fast within thy gates, O Jerusalem." This is one part of the feeling of the Return of the Exiles, and it became the root of that patriotic sentiment which flourished henceforth in the Jewish nation with a vigor never known before.

There is another feeling in the background which gives additional force to this passionate homesickness and patriotic fervor. They had not merely been absent from home. They had been sojourning in a mighty

---

[1] Ps. cxxi. 1, cxxvi. 1, lxxxiv. 7.   [2] Jer. vi. 1.   [3] Ps. cxxii. 2.

128

empire wholly unlike their own. They had seen the splendors of Babylon; they had mixed with the princes and potentates of Chaldea, Persia, and Media; they had drunk in all the influences of those far-off seats of Oriental wisdom. Their ideas of religion, of history, and of science had become enlarged. If in some respects they were a lesser nation than they were before the Exile, in some respects they were much greater. For they had received a new and serious impulse, which ended in nothing less than the greatest event of the world's history — the advent of Christianity.

These, then, are the two feelings of the human heart which are consecrated by the Psalms and Prophets of the Return — The value of Home; the value of new and wide experience.

(1.) There is not one single human being in this congregation to whom this is not one of the nearest and dearest thoughts. There is not one of us who does not in some measure respond to the appeal in which the poet asks, in words almost too familiar to be quoted:

> Breathes there the man with soul so dead
> Who never to himself hath said,
> 'This is my own, my native land!'
> Whose heart hath ne'er within him burn'd,
> As home his footsteps he hath turn'd
> From wandering on a foreign strand?

There has not been a generation of men for the last three thousand years, there will not be a generation of men to the end of time, in which some will not read with sympathy that story on which the greatest master of ancient poetry has spent all his art — which tells of the return of Ulysses after his long absence; the wife counting the weary days in the hills of Ithaca; the dog leaping up in his master's face and dying of joy; the aged servants recognizing their long-lost chief as he treads once more his father's threshold. To any man worthy of the name, the thoughts of mother, and wife, and children, and brothers, and sisters, are amongst the most inspiring, the most purifying, the most elevating of all the motives which God has given us to steady our steps, and guide our consciences, and nerve us for duty, through all the changes and chances of this mortal life. Happy, thrice happy, is he or she who keeps this sanctuary pure and undefiled. False to his country, and false to the true interests and the holy progress of mortals, is he or she who undermines or betrays it. Not charity only, but all the virtues of which charity is the bond, begin and end at Home.

(2.) And yet in this wide world Home is not, nor can be, all. Even by the changing scenes of this life we learn that "here we have no abiding city," but are "strangers and pilgrims upon earth;" and that at times it is good for us to be so. That famous story of the return of the Grecian chief which I just now quoted derives half its significance from the tale of the many cities and many men that he had beheld; of the perilous adventures by land and sea that he had encountered; of the strange forms and faces that had passed before him since he quitted the shores of his native island. There are doubtless many to whom this knowledge is denied, to whom the same circle of duties and of pleasures suffices, and must suffice, from year to year. For such "untravelled travellers" "the trivial round, the common task," the world-exploring book, or the unfathomable depths of the solitary soul in joy or in sorrow, may take the place of the largest survey or the most extraordinary surprises of distant scenes. But for those who have been allowed to wander and to return, who have annexed to the realm of their own hearts and minds the sights and sounds of all that is

greatest and strangest on earth — there is or ought to
be given a new sense of the greatness of God and of man,
a new lever whereby to move the sluggish world within
and around us, a new zest to the duties of our own special sphere, a new glory to the destinies of our race.

My brethren, You will have perceived what has led
me to speak to you on this double subject. There has
been a return from distant wanderings, in which the
whole country has taken a heartfelt interest, an interest
which ought to make every one of us ask more seriously
what is the blessing of Home, and what is the blessing
of those larger experiences which lie without.

The blessing of Home. — Is there a mother, wife,
child, who cannot understand the joy which welcomes
back a dear son, a beloved husband, an affectionate
father? who does not feel the heart warmed at the
thought that the forebodings and pangs of the parting
seven months ago are now past and gone; and that the
delight which almost all of us have known under like
circumstances is shared by the most familiar, because
the most exalted, household in the land? Is there any
Englishman or any Englishwoman so dead to the greatness of our country, so dead to the instincts of humanity, as not earnestly to desire that the household thus
blessed by Providence in these outward deliverances
from sickness, and sorrow, and danger, shall be blessed
also in all those things which alone can make a home
truly happy and a family truly noble and truly royal?
Can we any of us fail to recognize at such a moment
that a fresh responsibility is laid upon all those who,
whether near or far, have any concern in the interests
of the State or the grandeur of the Throne? Ought
we not all to feel impelled afresh to watch with double
vigilance over their welfare, to foster with every encouragement their efforts for good? Can we any of us

fail to be assured that a double measure of infamy and shame will be the deserved judgment on those, if any there be, who by word or by act, by speech or by silence, make temptation more easy, or goodness more difficult, or duty more irksome, or sin more pleasant, in the way of those by whose virtue we are all raised, in whose shortcomings we all suffer? At this moment, in the touch of nature which makes the whole country kin, we are all one family. Oh, may God grant that to every member of that great family of the English race the grace may be given to seek not our own, but others' good; not the passing amusement or success which is for the moment, but the eternal happiness which outlasts the grave, and defies the world, and is the bulwark alike of households, and of States, and of Churches!

And let us also remember on this day wherein consists that other blessing — the blessing of enlarged experience. Home itself becomes doubly dear after long absence. Our power of serving our country is multiplied by the knowledge gained of every other country. That was a fine saying of the old Cavalier: —

> I could not love thee, dear, so much,
> Lov'd I not honor more.

That is a true sentiment also which makes us feel that we do not love our country less, but more, because we have laid up in our minds the knowledge of other lands, and other institutions, and other races, and have had enkindled afresh within us the instinct of a common humanity, and of the universal beneficence of the Creator.

And if this be so in regard to ordinary experience of foreign parts, how much is the duty increased when the foreign parts are our own dependencies, and when the contrast exhibited is the greatest contrast which this earth affords — the contrast between East and West, between Heathenism and Christianity, between the civilization of the ancient world of bygone ages and the civilization of modern Europe! If, as we know from the long growth of history, the English rule includes not merely a Kingdom shut up between the four seas, but an Empire on which the sun never sets — if "the Imperial Parliament" rejoices in that time-honored name which it bears by virtue of its far-reaching sway — if there be any truth in the saying of an illustrious foreign statesman, "that the conquest and government of India are the achievements which give England its place in the opinion of the world" — then any event which brings these distant regions before us ought to remind us that the morality, the justice, the humanity of our country affect the welfare, not only of the inhabitants of these little islands, but of those vast dominions where active Parsee, and subtle Hindoo, and haughty Mussulman, as well as the settlers of the English race, or the savage on many a lonely shore or immeasurable continent, look up to us for guidance, direction, and example. Do not think that this breadth of view and depth of experience diminish for one instant the importance of our insular and domestic sphere. In a famous discourse which was intended to show how true religion is best carried out in the business of common life, the preacher — himself one of the greatest orators of our age — illustrated the possibility of combining the grandest thoughts with the homeliest duties from the fact of the latent but powerful influence exercised over a public speaker by the consciousness of the presence of his auditory. "No exertion requires a greater concentration of thought or attention than this of speech. And yet amidst the subtle processes of intellect — the selection and right

ordering and enunciation of words — there never quits
the speaker's mind for one moment the idea of the
presence of the listening throng. Like a secret atmosphere, it surrounds and bathes his spirit as he goes on
with the external work."

This illustration in that discourse was carried on to
the thought of "the One Auditor, the Awful Listener,
ever present, ever watchful, as the discourse of life
proceeds." But what is there said of the effect of a
listening audience on one who speaks is still more true
of the effect of vast multitudes of distant spectators
on one who acts. It is not for nothing that to many
of us there have been of late called up the visions of
the "numbers numberless" of the swarming populations of our Indian cities; or that we have tracked in
presence or in thought the scenes of the splendid, if at
times harsh and violent, deeds by which India was
won, or of the heroic courage and endurance by which
in the time of the Mutiny it was preserved to us. It is
not for nothing that we have seen or heard of the mon-
strosities of idolatrous worship, or the debasement of
unchecked superstition; or, on the other hand, of the
marvels of the sacred river, or the snow-clad tops
of the highest of earthly heights, or the luxuriance of
the loveliest of tropical forests, or the grandeur of monuments which Christendom has never surpassed and
rarely equalled. All these things have been unrolled
before us for our own good and for the good of others.
Those countless multitudes, those fairy cities, all henceforth become the close spectators of our actions, the
near recipients of our beneficence. Every crying need
for spiritual help, every just complaint, every high
aspiration, from those distant shores ought henceforth
to find a more ready access to our hearts. Every act
of grace or courtesy which we have shown or can show

towards those subject-races — every firmer grasp on the eternal principles of justice and purity that we can exhibit in our relations with them, will henceforth strike with double force on those who have been drawn towards us by the bonds of personal regard and personal knowledge. Every deed of good or ill that we perform is henceforth enacted, not only in "the fierce light that beats upon a throne," but in the presence of the gazing eyes and listening ears of peoples, and kindreds, and nations. "Wherefore, seeing we also are compassed about with so great a cloud of witnesses, let us lay aside every weight, and the sin which doth so easily beset us, and let us run with patience the race that is set before us."

"I was glad when they said unto me, We will go into the house of the Lord." Once before I have preached within these walls on this text. It was when the whole of this vast city and nation was stirred as one man to go up to the great Metropolitan Cathedral to return thanks for the recovery of their beloved Prince from the terrible struggle of life and death which for weeks the people had followed with thrilling eagerness and anxiety.

That was five years ago. In those five years much has passed — opportunities, mercies, visitations.

And now has come another moment, less exciting, less tragical, than that solemn festival. Yet it reminds us of that other time. Here, also, is an escape from perils, if unseen, yet hardly less imminent. Here, also, there is a thanksgiving in which, from the Queen downwards, we all share. Here, again, we are assembled in a venerable church, if less august than the great Cathedral of St. Paul's, yet to many of us even more closely endeared. On that occasion I asked you to commemorate the general Thanksgiving by contributing to the restoration of that metropolitan edifice. On this occasion it happens that the time falls in with the contributions to the yet more constant and pressing need of strengthening the hands of the chief pastor of this metropolis in his efforts for the good of its poor and neglected masses, and no thank-offering can be conceived more fitting, as far as material aid and support can express the inward feelings of the heart. But, on a day like this, those inward feelings rise higher still and reach yet deeper down. The gladness of home regained, the vicissitudes of joy and sorrow that have crossed the path of many in the interval since the Royal traveller left our shores, the sense of the moral debt which England owes to India, and which India owes to England, the prospect of duties, and difficulties, and anxieties, ever multiplying and ever needing all the vigilance of man, and all the grace of God to direct aright, the voices of the living and the voices of the dead — all combine to make us feel that, for mercies such as these, genuine thankfulness in a Christian man or a Christian nation has but one adequate expression, and that is a desire for increase of goodness, increase of wisdom, increase of firmness, increased contempt of what is vile, and selfish, and base, increased determination to fight manfully in the faith of Christ crucified, and under His victorious banner, against sin, the world, and the devil.

Let us join once more, and for the last time, in the words of that Prayer which for five long months was offered every Sunday in this place — that the journey of the Heir of these realms now, by the good Providence of God, safely accomplished, may tend to his own best happiness and the happiness of those nearest and dearest to him, to the welfare, physical, moral, and spiritual, of the Indian Empire and of this our own Regal Commonwealth, to the glory of Almighty God, the Holy, the Just, the Merciful, and the Pure.

May the Eternal, who has thus blessed his going out, bless yet more abundantly his coming in, from this time forth for evermore!

LORD PALMERSTON.

October 29, 1865, being the Sunday after Lord Palmerston's burial in the Abbey.

See that ye walk circumspectly . . . redeeming the time . . . understanding what the will of the Lord is. — EPHESIANS v. 15, 16, 17.

So spoke the Apostle in the epistle of this day. He tells his readers to "walk circumspectly"—that is, with a keen, critical observance of all they see; to "redeem the time"—that is, to make the most of every opportunity that is thrown in their way, not to let any part of it escape them; to make every effort of mind and heart to "understand what the will of the Lord is" — that is, to understand what is the special intention of God, wrapped up in the different dispensations of joy and sorrow which come across them. It is this very thing which we are called upon to do this day — to look hard into the essential lessons of the great solemnity at which, on Friday last, so many of us assisted; to redeem, and make the most of, for our instruction, the opportunity of serious thought, thus afforded to us; to understand, so far as we can, what is the will of the Lord concerning us, in the national homage then paid to the illustrious dead.

It is one of the most instructive parts of solemnities of this kind, that each has its own peculiar lesson to convey. Of all the great men who are laid within these walls, every single one, probably, is laid there for a separate and distinct reason, which could not apply to any

138

one else. That grand truth which was read in our ears in the funeral lesson, from the apostolic epistle, has its special force on every such occasion here — "There is one glory of the sun, and another glory of the moon, and another glory of the stars; for one star differeth from another star in glory."

In the chambers of the dead, in the temple of fame, no less than in the house of our heavenly Father, there are indeed "many mansions," many stages, many degrees. Each human soul that is gifted above its fellows, leaves, as it passes out of the world, a light of its own, that no other soul, whether more or less greatly gifted, could give equally. As each lofty peak in some mountain country is illuminated with a different hue of its own, by the setting sun, so, also, each of the higher summits of human society is lit up by the sunset of life with a different color, derived, it may be, from the materials of which it is composed, or from the relative position which it occupies, but each, to those who can discern it rightly, conveying a new and separate lesson of truth, of duty, of wisdom, and of hope.

What, then, are the special lessons which we may learn from the character of the remarkable man who has been taken away, and from the tribute paid to his memory? I leave altogether the questions of political and religious parties, which have no place here, and confine myself entirely to those direct, practical lessons which may be applied to all, of whatever opinions, equally. I leave, also, altogether, those questions of the unseen world which are known to God only. I leave them, as our Church leaves them, to that holy and merciful Saviour, whose mighty working is able to subdue all things to Himself, who sees as man sees not, but who, we cannot doubt, commends to our admi-

ration whatsoever there is good and true in every one
of His servants, that from each we may understand the
more fully what the will of the Lord is, what the whole
counsel of God is towards us.

First, then, there was this singular peculiarity, That
the gifts by which the eminence of the departed statesman was achieved were such as are far more within
the reach of all of us than is usually the case with those
who occupy a position like his. It has been said of
Judas Maccabæus, that of all military chiefs, he was
the one who accomplished the greatest victories with
the smallest amount of external resources. It may be
said of our late chief, that of all political leaders, he
accomplished the greatest success by the most homely
and the most ordinary means. It is this which makes
his life, in many respects, an example and an encouragement to all. The persevering devotion of his days
and nights to the public service, the toil and endurance
of more than half a century in the various high stations
in which he was employed, — these are qualities which
might be imitated by every single person, from the
highest to the lowest amongst you. You, whoever you
may be, who are disposed, as so many young men are,
to give yourselves up to ease and self-indulgence, who
think every thing that costs you any trouble a reason
for putting work aside, remember that not by such
faint-hearted, idle carelessness can God or man be
served, or the end of any human soul be attained, in
this life or the next. You, whoever you be, who are
working on zealously, humbly, honestly, in your different stations, work on the more zealously and the more
faithfully, from this day forward, with the feeling
that, in the honors paid to one who was, in these
respects, but a fellow-laborer with you, the nation, as
in the sight of God, has set its seal on the value of

work, on the nobleness of toil, on the grandeur of long, laborious days, on the splendor of plodding, persevering diligence.

Again, he won his way, as we have been told a hundred times, not so much by eloquence, or genius, or far-sighted wisdom, as by the lesser graces of cheerfulness, good humor, gayety and kindness of heart, tact, and readiness — lesser graces, doubtless, graces of which some of the highest characters have been almost destitute, yet graces which are assuredly not less the gifts of God — graces which, even in the House of God, we do well to reverence and admire.   Those who may think it a matter of little moment to take offence at the slightest affront; those who by their presence throw a dark chill over whatever society they take part in; those who make the lives of those around them miserable, by recklessly trampling on their tenderest feelings, and wounding them in their weakest points; those who poison discussion and embitter controversy by pushing particular views to their extremest consequences, by widening differences between man and man; those who think it a duty to make the worst of every one from whom they dissent, and to maintain a never-ending protest against those who have ever done them a wrong, or from whom they have ever differed, — such as these may have higher pretensions and, it may be, higher claims on our respect; yet if they would understand what the will of the Lord is, a silent rebuke will rise to them from yonder grave, such as God designs for their especial benefit.   The statesman who had always a soft word ready to turn away wrath; who, if at times he attacked or was attacked justly, yet never bore lasting malice towards his enemies; who was able to see, even in those who opposed him, the true worth and value of their essential characters, —

from him, and from the honor paid to him, many an eager partisan, many a hard polemic, many an austere moralist, may learn a lesson that nothing else could teach them. How many, by praising him, have condemned themselves! How many, by making much of him, have made much of the very graces which, in all other times and persons, they have been unwilling even to acknowledge!

Yet again, the long life which has just closed was an enduring witness to the greatness of that gift which even heathens recognized, of hope, unfailing, elastic hope. "Never despair!" so the vicissitudes of the octogenarian chief seemed to say to us. From a youth of comparative obscurity, from a middle-age of constant struggle with opposition, through a shifting career of many changes and many falls, was attained at last that serene and bright old age, that calm and honored death, which, in its measure, is within the reach of all of us, if God should so prolong our years, and if we should not despair of ourselves. Never be dispirited; never say, "It is too late;" never think that your day is past; never lose heart under opposition; hold on to the end, and you may at last be victorious and successful, even as he was — it may be in still nobler causes, and with still more lasting results. Nor let us shut out the encouragement which this is designed to give us, by saying that it was, after all, only the natural result of a buoyant and vigorous constitution. To a great degree, no doubt, it was so; yet it also rested in large measure on the deeper ground of a quiet conviction that the fitting course for a man was to do what is good for the moment, without vainly forecasting the future — to do the present duty, and to leave the results to God. "I do not understand," so he once said to one who knew him well, — "I do not understand what is meant by the anxiety of responsibility. I take every pains to do what is for the best, and having done that, I am perfectly at ease, and leave the consequences altogether alone." That strain, indeed, is of a higher mood: it is the strain of the inspired wisdom of ancient days — " Whatsoever thy hand findeth to do, do it with all thy might." It is the strain, also, may we not say, of true Christian humility and courage, which may well calm many a care, and nourish many a hope, and strengthen many a faith, beside, and beyond, and above the care, and the hope, and the faith of a mere political career.

And this leads me to another and a wider view of the subject, in which, nevertheless, all, even the humblest of us, may take an interest. If any were asked what was the thought or belief which, from first to last, most distinctly guided his policy and sustained his spirit, they would say his unfailing trust in, and concern for, the greatness of England. He was an Englishman even to excess. It was England, rather than any special party in England — it was the honor and interests of England, rather than even the Constitution, or the State, or the Church of England, that fired his imagination, and stimulated his efforts, and secured his fame. For this it was that his name was known throughout the world, in the most secluded villages of Calabria, on the wild shores of the Caspian, in the monastic solitudes of Thibet. To England, and to no lesser interest, the vast length of that laborious life, with whatsoever shortcomings, was in all simplicity and faithfulness devoted. My brethren, I know well that when I thus speak there are considerations far greater than these by which the human soul must be stayed in life and death, by which the world and Church are guided on their appointed course; but on this occasion this is the thought which presses most forcibly upon

us; this is the framework in which those higher considerations present themselves; this is the special opportunity which we are to redeem, and out of which the
will of the Lord will make itself clear.   In this great
historic building, on the disappearance from amongst
us of one of our chief historic names in the sight of all
that was highest and noblest in our national life gathered round that open vault, it is the very mission of the
preacher to ask you to reflect on what should be our
Christian duty towards that kingly commonwealth of
which we, no less than he, are members — of which we,
no less than he, are proud — for which we, no less than
he, are bound in the sight of God to lay down our lives
and to spend our latest breath.

> England, we love thee better than we know!

It was surely an allowable feeling which caused one
whose voice has often been heard from this place thus
to describe the thrill of joy and exultation with which,
in a foreign land, he —

> . . . heard again thy martial music blow,
> And saw thy gallant children to and fro
> Pace, keeping ward at one of those huge gates
> Which, like twin giants, watch the Herculean straits.[1]

Some such feeling of pride as this it was which was
roused by the awe awakened in many a distant and
many a suffering nation at the sound of the powerful
name now to be inscribed within these walls.

But it is with loftier thoughts than pride or even
thankfulness that our spirits mount upwards when we
reflect on what is really involved in that idea which
so inspired the long career which has just closed —
England, and a citizen of England.   Think of our
marvellous history, slowly evolved out of our marvel-

---

[1] *Gibraltar:* sonnet, by R. C. Trench, Archbishop of Dublin.

lous situation. Think of that fusion of hostile races and hostile institutions within the same narrow limits. Think of the long, bright, continuous line of our literature such as is unknown in any other country. Think of our refuge for freedom and for justice. Think of our temperate monarchy and constitution, so fearfully and wonderfully wrought out through the toil and conflict of so many centuries. Think of our pure domestic homes. Think of the English Prayers and the English Bible woven into our inmost and earliest recollections. Think of the liberty of conscience and the liberty of speech which give to conscience and to speech a double, treble·weight and value. Think of the sober religious faith which shows itself amongst us in so many diverse forms, each supplying what the other wants. These are some of the elements which go to make up the whole idea that is conjured up by the sacred name of England for which our statesman lived and died.

And then remember that what England is, or will be, depends in great measure on her own individual sons and daughters. Nations are the schools in which individual souls are trained. The virtues and the sins of a nation are the virtues and the sins of each one of its citizens, on a larger scale and written in gigantic letters. To be a citizen of England, according to our lost chief, was the greatest boast, the greatest claim on protection and influence, that a man could show in any part of the world. To be a citizen of England in the fullest sense, worthy of all that England has been and might be, worthy of our noble birthright, worthy of our boundless opportunities, this is, indeed, a thought which should rouse every one of us, not in presumptuous confidence, but in all Christian humility, to redeem the time that is still before us, and to labor to understand what the will of the Lord is for ourselves and for our children. When, two days ago, we stood amidst the deepening gloom round the grave of the aged statesman, it was impossible not to feel that we were witnessing not only the flight of an individual spirit into the unseen world, but the close of one generation, one stage of our history, and the beginning of another. We had climbed to the height of one of those ridges which part the past from the future. We were on the water-shed of the dividing streams. We saw the last thread of the waters which belonged to the earlier epoch amongst the remains of which the ashes of the dead were laid; we were on the turning-point whence, henceforward, the springs of political and national life will flow in another direction, taking their rise from another range, destined to commingle with other seas, and to fertilize other climes. Even the oldest of living statesmen, compared with him who has gone, belongs to a newer age, and has to face a newer world. On this eminence, so to speak, we stand to-day. To this new start in our pilgrimage we have each one of us to look forward. It is not in England as in other countries, where the national will is but little felt compared with the will of a single ruler. Here, for good or for evil, the mind, the wishes, the character of the people are almost every thing. That public opinion, of which we hear so much, which was believed to be the guiding star of the sagacious mind which has just gone from us — that public opinion is moulded by every one who has a will, or heart, or head, or conscience of his own, throughout this vast empire. On you, on me, on old and young, on rich and poor, it more or less depends, whether that public opinion be elevating or depressing, just or unjust, pure or impure, Christian or un-Christian. If it be true, as some think, that to follow and not to lead public opinion must henceforth be the course of our statesmen, then our

responsibility and the responsibility of the nation is
deepened further still. The very creation of the character of our public men must then devolve in a manner
upon those below them and around them. They may
inspire us, but we must also inspire them. We must
strive with all our strength to be that in our stations
which we would wish them to be in theirs. We must
act as those act in a beleaguered city, where every sentinel knows that on his single courage and fidelity may
depend the fate of all. A single resolute mind, loving
the truth, and the truth only, has ere now brought the
whole mind of a nation round to himself. A single
pure spirit has, by its own pure and holy aspirations,
breathed a new spirit into the corrupt mass of a whole
national literature. A single voice raised constantly
in behalf of honesty, and justice, and mercy, and freedom, has rendered forever impossible practices which
were once universal.

"Brethren," — so says the Apostle in the chapter
which you have just heard in this evening's service —
"Brethren, forgetting those things which are behind,
and reaching forth unto those things which are before,
I press toward the mark, for the prize of the high calling of God in Christ Jesus." So let me call upon you,
in the presence of that grave which has been so lately
closed; in the prospect of the changes and trials, whatsoever they may be, which are now before us; in the
midst of those mighty memories by which we are surrounded; in the face of that mighty future to which we
are all advancing, forget those things which are behind.
Forget in him who is gone all that was of the earth and
earthy; reach forward in his character to all that is immortal — the kindness, the perseverance, the freedom
from party spirit, the hope, the self-devotion, which can
never pass away, and which are still before each one

of us. Forget, too, in the past and the present generation all that is behind, all that is behind the best spirit of our age, all that is behind the true spirit of the Gospel, all that is behind the requirements of the most enlightened and the most Christian conscience; and reach forward, one and all, towards those great things which we may trust are still before us — the great problems which our age, if any, may solve, the great tasks which our nation alone can accomplish, the great doctrines of our common faith, which we may have the opportunity of grasping with a firmer hold than ever before, the great reconciliation of things old with things new, of things common with things sacred, of class with class, of man with man, of nation with nation, of church with church, of all with God. This is the high calling of England, this is the high calling of an English statesman, this is the high calling of every English citizen, this is the high calling of the nineteenth century, this is the will of the Lord concerning us; this, and nothing less than this, is "the prize of the high calling of God in Christ Jesus our Lord."

CHARLES DICKENS.

June 19, 1870.

He spake this Parable. . . .
There was a certain rich man, which was clothed in purple and fine
linen, and fared sumptuously every day: and there was a certain beggar
named Lazarus, which was laid at his gate, full of sores, and desiring
to be fed with the crumbs which fell from the rich man's table: moreover
the dogs came and licked his sores. — ST. LUKE xv. 3; xvi. 19–21.

THERE are some passages of Scripture which, when
they are read in the services of the Sunday, almost demand a special notice from their extraordinary force
and impressiveness. Such is the Parable of the Rich
Man and Lazarus, read as the Gospel of this day.
There are some incidents of human life which almost
demand a special notice from the depth and breadth
of the feelings which they awaken in the heart of the
congregation. Such was the ceremony which, on Tuesday last, conveyed to his grave, within these walls, a
lamented and gifted being, who had for years delighted
and instructed the generation to which he belonged.
And if the Scripture of the day and the incident of the
week direct our minds to the same thoughts, and mutu-
ally illustrate each other, the attraction is irresistible,
and the moral which each supplies is doubly enforced.

Let me then draw out these lessons in what I now
propose to say.

1. I will speak first of the *form* of instruction which
we are called upon to notice in the Gospel of this Sun-

149

day. It is not only, like most of our Lord's instructions, a Parable, but it is, as it were, a Parable of the Parables. It is the last of a group which occurs in the 15th and 16th chapters of St. Luke, where the story is taken in each case, not as in the other Gospels, from inanimate or irrational creatures, but from the doings and characters of men. First comes the story of the Good Shepherd, with all its depth of tenderness; then the story of the Indefatigable Searcher, with all its depth of earnestness; then the story of the Prodigal Son, with all its depth of pathos; then the story of the Unjust Steward, with all its depth of satire; and, last of all, comes the story of the Rich Man and the Poor Man, drawn not merely from the mountain side, or the dark chamber, or the tranquil home, or the accountant's closet, but from the varied stir of human enjoyment and human suffering in the streets and alleys of Jerusalem. It is a tale of real life — so real that we can hardly believe that it is not history. Yet it is, nevertheless, a tale of pure fiction from first to last. Dives and Lazarus are as much imaginary beings as Hamlet or as Shylock; the scene of Abraham's bosom and of the rich man in Hades is drawn not from any literal outward truth, or ancient sacred record, but from the popular Jewish conceptions current at the time. This Parable is, in short, the most direct example which the Bible contains of the use, of the value, of the sacredness, of fictitious narrative. There are doubtless many other instances in the Sacred Records. There is the exquisite Parable of the Talking Trees in the Book of Judges; there is the sublime drama of the Patriarch and his Friends in the Book of Job; there is the touching and graceful picture of Jewish family life in the Book of Tobit, from which our Church selects some of its most striking precepts, and which, in its Homilies, is treated as if inspired directly by the Holy Ghost. All these are instances where moral lessons are conveyed by the invention of characters which either never existed at all, or, if they existed, are made to converse in forms of speech entirely drawn from the inspired imagination of the sacred writer. But the highest sanction to this mode of instruction is that given us in this Parable by our Lord Himself. This, we are told, was His ordinary mode of teaching; He stamped it with His peculiar mark. "Without a parable,"[1] without a fable, without an invented story of this kind, He rarely opened His lips. He, the Example of examples, the Teacher of teachers, "taught His disciples[2] many things by parables." Through this parabolic form some of His gravest instructions have received a double life. If we were to ask for the most perfect exposition of the most perfect truth respecting God and man, which the world contains, it will be found not in a Discourse, or a Creed, or a Hymn, or even a Prayer, but in a Parable, a story — one of those which I have already cited — the Parable of the Prodigal Son.

I have dwelt on this characteristic of the Gospel teaching because it is well that we should see how the Bible itself sanctions a mode of instruction which has been, in a special sense, God's gift to our own age. Doubtless His "grace is manifold,"[3] — in the original expression, many colored. In various ages it has assumed various forms, the divine flame of poetry, the far-reaching gaze of science, the searching analysis of philosophy, the glorious page of history, the burning eloquence of speaker or preacher, the grave address of moralist or divine. These all we have had in ages past; their memorials are around us here. These all we have in their measure, some more, some less, in the age

---

[1] Matt. xiii. 34.   [2] Mark iv. 2.   [3] 1 Pet. iv. 10.

in which we live.   But it is perhaps not too much to
say, that in no age of the world, and in no country of
the world, has been developed on so large a scale, and
with such striking effects as in our own, the gift of
" speaking in parables," the gift of addressing mankind
through romance and novel and tale and fable.   First
and far above all others came that greatest of all the
masters of fiction, the glory of Scotland, whose romances
refreshed and exalted our childhood as they still refresh and exalt our advancing years — as would to
God that they still might continue to refresh and exalt
the childhood and the manhood of the coming generation.   He rests not here.   He rests beside his native
Tweed.   But long may his magic spell charm and purify the ages which yet shall be !   Long may yonder
monument of the Scottish Duke, whom he has immortalized in one of his noblest works, keep him in our
memory, as, one by one, the lesser and later lights
which have followed in that track where he led the way,
are gathered beneath its overshadowing marble !   It is
because one of those bright lights has now passed from
amongst us — one in whom this generation seemed to
see the most vivid exemplification of this heaven-sent
power of fiction, that I would thus speak of it, for a few
moments, in its most general aspect.

There was a truth — let us freely confess it — in the
old Puritan feeling against an exaggerated enjoyment
of romances, as tending to relax the fibre of the moral
character.   That was a wholesome restraint which I
remember in my childhood, which kept us from revel-
ling in tales of fancy till the day's work was over, and
thus impressed upon us that the reading of pleasant
fictions was the holiday of life, and not its serious
business.   It is this very thing which, as it constitutes
the danger of fictitious narratives, constitutes also their

power. They approach us at times when we are indis-
posed to attend to any thing else. They fill up those
odd moments of life which exercise, for good or evil,
so wide an effect over the whole tenor of our course.
Poetry may enkindle a loftier fire, the Drama may rivet
the attention more firmly, Science may open a wider
horizon, Philosophy may touch a deeper spring — but
no works are so penetrating, so pervasive, none reach
so many homes, and attract so many readers, as the
romance of modern times. Those who read nothing
else read eagerly the exciting tale. Those whom sermons never reach, whom history fails to arrest, are
reached and arrested by the fictitious characters, the
stirring plot, of the successful novelist. It is this which
makes a wicked novel more detestable than almost any
other form of wicked words or deeds. It is this which
gives even to a foolish or worthless novel a demoraliz-
ing force beyond its own contemptible demerits. It is
this which makes a good novel — pure in style, elevating in thought, true in sentiment — one of the best of
boons to the Christian home and to the Christian State.

Oh vast responsibility of those who wield this mighty
engine; mighty it may be, and has been, for corruption,
for debasement, for defilement; mighty also it may be,
mighty it certainly has been, in our English novels (to
the glory of our country be it spoken), mighty for edification and for purification, for giving wholesome thoughts,
high aspirations, soul-stirring recollections! Use these
wonderful works of genius as not abusing them; enjoy
them as God's special gifts to us; only remember that
the true Romance of Life is Life itself.

2. But this leads me to the further question of the
special form which this power assumed in him whose
loss the country now deplores with a grief so deep and
genuine as to be itself a matter for serious reflection.

What was there in him which called forth this wide-spread sympathy? What is there in this sympathy, and in that which created it, worthy of our religious thoughts on this day?

I profess not here to sit in judgment on the whole character and career of this gifted writer. That must be left for posterity to fix in its proper niche amongst the worthies of English literature.

Neither is this the place to speak at length of those lighter and more genial qualities which made his death, like that of one[1] who rests beside him, almost an "eclipse of the gayety of nations." Let others tell elsewhere of the brilliant and delicate satire, the kindly wit, the keen and ubiquitous sense of the ludicrous and grotesque. "There is a time to laugh, and there is a time to weep." Laughter is itself a good, yet there are moments when we care not to indulge in it. It may even seem here-after, as it has seemed to some of our own age, that the nerves of the rising generation were, for the time at least, unduly relaxed by that inexhaustible outburst of a humorous temper, of a never-slumbering observation, in the long unceasing flood of drollery and merriment which, it may be, brought out the comic and trivial side of human life in too strong and startling a relief.

But even thus, and even in this sacred place, it is good to remember that, in the writings of him who is gone, we have had the most convincing proof that it is possible to have moved old and young to inextinguish-able laughter without the use of a single expression which could defile the purest, or shock the most sensi-tive. Remember this, if there be any who think that you cannot be witty without being wicked — who think that in order to amuse the world and awaken the inter-est of hearers or readers, you must descend to filthy

[1] David Garrick.

jests, and unclean suggestions, and debasing scenes. So may have thought some gifted novelists of former times; but so thought not, so wrote not (to speak only of the departed) Walter Scott, or Jane Austen, or Elizabeth Gaskell, or William Thackeray: so thought not, and so wrote not, the genial and loving humorist whom we now mourn. However deep into the dregs of society his varied imagination led him in his writings to descend, it still breathed an untainted atmosphere. He was able to show us, by his own example, that even in dealing with the darkest scenes and the most degraded characters, genius could be clean, and mirth could be innocent.

3. There is another point, yet more peculiar and special, on which we may safely dwell, even in the very house of God, even beside the freshly laid grave. In that long series of stirring tales, now forever closed, there was a profoundly serious — nay, may we not say, a profoundly Christian and Evangelical truth, of which we all need to be reminded, and of which he was, in his own way, the special teacher.

It is the very same lesson which is represented to us in the Parable of this day. "There was a certain rich man, which was clothed in purple and fine linen, and fared sumptuously every day. And there was a certain beggar named Lazarus, which was laid at his gate, full of sores, and desiring to be fed with the crumbs which fell from the rich man's table. Moreover, the dogs came and licked his sores." It is a picture whose every image is expressive, and whose every image awakens thoughts that live forever. It is true that an Oriental atmosphere hangs around it — the Syrian purple, the fine linen of Egypt, the open banqueting hall, the beggar in the gateway, the dogs prowling about the city. But the spirit of the Parable belongs to the West as well as to the East. The contrast, the inequality of deserts and circumstances, on which it insists, meets us in the streets of London, no less than in the streets of Jerusalem; and the moral which the Parable intends that we should draw from that contrast is the very same which in his own peculiar way is urged upon us, with irresistible force, throughout the writings of our lost preceptor. Close beside the magnificence, the opulence, the luxury of this great metropolis, is that very neighbor, those very neighbors, whom the Parable describes. The Rich Man has no name in the Scripture; but the Poor Man has a name in the Book of God; and he has a name given him, he has many names given him, in the tales in which the departed has described the homes and manners of our poorer brethren. "Lazarus," the "help of God"—the noble name which tells us that God helps those who help themselves—is the very prototype of those outcasts, of those forlorn, struggling, human beings, whose characters are painted by him in such vivid colors that we shrink from speaking of them here, even as we should from speaking of persons yet alive— whose names are such familiar household words that, to mention them in a sacred place, seems almost like a desecration. It is of this vast outlying mass of unseen human suffering that we need constantly to be reminded. It is this contrast between things as they are in the sight of God, and things as they seem in the sight of man, that so easily escapes us all in our busy civilization. It is the difficulty of seeing this, of realizing this, which made a Parable like that of the Rich Man and Lazarus so vital a necessity for the world when it was first spoken. But He who spake as never man spake saw, with His far-seeing glance, into our complicated age as well as into His own. What was needed then is still more needed now; and it is to meet this need that our dull and sluggish hearts want all the assistance which can be given by lively imagination, by keen sympathy, by the dramatic power of making things which are not seen be even as though they were seen. Such were the gifts wielded with pre-eminent power by him who has passed away.

It was the distinguishing glory of a famous Spanish saint, that she was "the advocate of the absent." That is precisely the advocacy of the Divine Parable in the Gospels, the advocacy of these modern human Parables, which in their humble measure represent its spirit — the advocacy of the absent poor, of the neglected, of the weaker side, whom not seeing we are tempted to forget. It was a fine trait of a noble character of our own times, that, though full of interests, intellectual, domestic, social, the distress of the poor of England, he used to say, "pierced through his happiness, and haunted him day and night." It is because this susceptibility is so rare, so difficult to attain, that we ought doubly to value those who have the eye to see, and the ear to hear, and the tongue to speak, and the pen to describe, those who are not at hand to demand their own rights, to set forth their own wrongs, to portray their own sufferings. Such was he who lies yonder. By him that veil was rent asunder which parts the various classes of society. Through his genius the rich man, faring sumptuously every day, was made to see and feel the presence of the Lazarus at his gate. The unhappy inmates of the workhouse, the neglected children in the dens and caves of our great cities, the starved and ill-used boys in remote schools, far from the observation of men, felt that a new ray of sunshine was poured on their dark existence, a new interest awakened in their forlorn and desolate lot. It was because an unknown friend had pleaded their cause with a voice which rang through the palaces of the great, as well as through the cottages of the poor. It was because, as by a magician's wand, those gaunt figures and strange faces had been, it may be sometimes, in exaggerated forms, made to stand and speak before those who hardly dreamed of their existence.

Nor was it mere compassion that was thus evoked. As the same Parable which delineates the miseries of the outcast Lazarus tells us also how, under that external degradation, was nursed a spirit fit for converse with the noble-minded and the gentle-hearted in the bosom of the Father of the Faithful, so the same master hand which drew the sorrows of the English poor, drew also the picture of the unselfish kindness, the courageous patience, the tender thoughtfulness, that lie concealed behind many a coarse exterior, in many a rough heart, in many a degraded home. When the little workhouse boy wins his way, pure and undefiled, through the mass of wickedness in the midst of which he passes — when the little orphan girl brings thoughts of heaven into the hearts of all around her, and is as the very gift of God to the old man whose desolate life she cheers — when the little cripple not only blesses his father's needy home, but softens the rude stranger's hardened conscience — there is a lesson taught which touches every heart, which no human being can feel without being the better for it, which makes that grave seem to those who crowd around it as though it were the very grave of those little innocents whom he had thus created for our companionship, for our instruction, for our delight and solace. He labored to tell us all, in new, very new, words, the old, old story, that there is, even in the worst a capacity for goodness, a soul worth redeeming, worth reclaiming, worth regenerating. He labored to tell the rich, the educated, how this better side was to be found and respected even in the most neglected Lazarus. He labored to tell the poor no less to respect this better part in themselves, to remember that they also have a call to be good and just, if they will but hear it. If by any such means he has brought rich and poor together, and made Englishmen feel more nearly as one family, he will not assuredly have lived in vain, nor will his bones in vain have been laid in this home and hearth of the English nation.

4. There is one more thought that this occasion suggests. In the Parable of the Rich Man and Lazarus, besides the pungent, pathetic lessons of social life which it impresses upon us, is also conveyed, beyond any other part of the Gospels, the awful solemnity of the other world. "If they hear not Moses and the prophets, neither will they be persuaded though one rose from the dead." So also on this day there is impressed upon us a solemnity, before which the most lively sallies of wit, the most brilliant splendors of genius wax faint and pale, namely, the solemnity of each man's individual responsibility, in each man's life and death. When on Tuesday last we stood by that open grave, in the still deep silence of the summer morning, in the midst of the vast, solitary space, broken only by that small band of fourteen mourners, it was impossible not to feel that there was something more sacred, more arresting than any earthly fane however bright, or than any historic mausoleum however august — and that was the return of the individual human soul into the hands of its Maker.

As I sit not here in judgment on the exact place to be allotted in the roll of history to that departing glory, neither do I sit in judgment on that departing spirit. But there are some farewell thoughts which I would fain express.

Many, many are the feet which have trodden and will tread the consecrated ground around that narrow grave; many, many are the hearts which both in the Old and in the New World are drawn towards it, as towards the resting-place of a dear personal friend; many are the flowers that have been strewed, many the tears shed, by the grateful affection of "the poor that cried, and the fatherless, and those that had none to help them." May I speak to these a few sacred words which perhaps will come with a new meaning and a deeper force because they come from the lips of a lost friend, because they are the most solemn utterance of lips now forever closed in the grave? They are extracted from "the will of Charles Dickens, dated May 12, 1869," and they will be heard by most here present for the first time. After the emphatic injunctions respecting "the inexpensive, unostentatious, and strictly private manner" of his funeral, which were carried out to the very letter, he thus continues: "I direct that my name be inscribed in plain English letters on my tomb. . . . I conjure my friends on no account to make me the subject of any monument, memorial, or testimonial whatever. I rest my claims to the remembrance of my country upon my published works, and to the remembrance of my friends upon their experience of me in addition thereto. I commit my soul to the mercy of God through our Lord and Saviour Jesus Christ; and I exhort my dear children humbly to try to guide themselves by the teaching of the New Testament in its broad spirit, and to put no faith in any man's narrow construction of its letter here or there."

In that simple but sufficient faith he lived and died; in that faith he bids you live and die. If any of you have learnt from his works the value, the eternal value of generosity, purity, kindness, unselfishness, and have learnt to show these in your own hearts and lives, these are the best monuments, memorials, and testimonials of the friend whom you loved, and who loved, with a rare and touching love, his friends, his country, and his fellow-men : monuments which he would not refuse, and which the humblest, the poorest, the youngest have it in their power to raise to his memory.

SCIENCE AND RELIGION.

May 21, 1871, being the Sunday following the funeral of Sir John
Herschel.

*And God said, Let there be lights in the firmament of the heaven
to divide the day from the night; and let them be for signs, and for
seasons, and for days, and years: and let them be for lights in the firmament of the heaven to give light upon the earth.*—GEN. i. 14, 15.

So the sacred writer described, in the first early
dawn of Science, and in the first early dawn of Revelation, the creation and the purpose of that vast celestial mechanism which has exercised the minds of men
ever since.   It is a striking instance of the mode in
which the Bible does and does not teach Science.   Of
details it tells us nothing, or tells us only what belonged
to the rude, unformed conceptions of those ancient
times.   Neither the gifted seer, whoever it was, that
wrote that first chapter of the Book of Genesis, nor he,
the royal Psalmist, who wrote that glorious hymn which
speaks of "the heavens declaring the glory of God,"
had any even the faintest insight into the wonders
which the telescope has disclosed to the eye and the
mind of the later generations of mankind.   The "lights"
of which the sacred historians or prophets spoke were
to them (such is the meaning of the word) burning
"lamps" or "candles" suspended in the sky.   The "firmament" of heaven was to them a solid blue surface,
spread like a canopy over the habitations of men.   The
heavenly bodies were not to them enormous masses of

162

worlds, millions of miles away, millions of ages old, but bright flashing fires, kindled for the first time to illuminate the darkness of the freshly created earth. "He made the stars also" is the one brief passing record in which the author of Genesis sums up, in his account of the fourth day of Creation, the birth of those mighty systems, each almost a universe in itself.

That corner of infinite space in which men dwelt still seemed the centre of the whole. None knew as yet the vast "ordinances of heaven;"[1] none knew "the balancings of the clouds," "the wondrous works of Him that is perfect in knowledge." It was not the Divine will that the Chosen People should be premature astronomers or premature geologists. Other and nobler truths than these were committed to the race of Israel — not the wisdom concerning earth or sky, but concerning man and God, not (as Baronius quaintly but wisely says) "the revelation of how the heaven goeth, but the revelation of how we must go to heaven."

But, although this gradual and imperfect growth of knowledge is involved in the very structure of the sacred books, although it is as unjust to the Bible as it is vexatious to Science, to endeavor to reduce scientific systems into conformity with the Biblical accounts, or to require the Bible to give us scientific systems — this does not prevent, nay, rather it assists the sacred writers, in giving us the germs, the principles, the framework, of that which has, in the slow march of ages, been developed, we may almost say, into a new revelation.

Most remarkably is this the case with respect to astronomy. There are two characteristics of the Biblical accounts of the sun and moon and stars, that contain the first stimulating thoughts of all the discoveries

1 Job xxxvii. 15, 16; xxxviii. 33.

which have since been achieved. They belong to that
side of the Bible which it possesses, not so much from
its directly didactic character, but from that grandeur
and solemnity of view which is the inalienable treasure
of every book, of every mind, of every prospect of
man or nature, in proportion as it rises, whether by
grace or genius, above the commonplace level of ordinary trivial things.

The first of these characteristics is the profound
sense which the Biblical writers display of the sublimity and beauty of the divine order of heaven and earth.
They knew not, they could not know, what it meant in
all its parts. But it struck a poetic fire out of their
inmost souls, that reproduced itself in thoughts and
words, of which the childlike simplicity is only equalled
by their inborn and supreme nobility. Human language has performed many marvellous feats since the
first chapter of Genesis was written; but the saying of
the heathen Longinus sixteen hundred years ago is still
true — that nothing more sublime has ever been spoken
than ·the words, "And God said, Let there be light,
and there was light." The hues of the rising and the
setting sun have been depicted by many a poet and
many a painter, have been analyzed by many a scientific process, by many an optic tube, since the shep-
herd-king watched the rays of the early morning dart
over the level line of the hills of Moab; yet no more
life-like description has ever been given in few words
than that of the sudden emergence of the sun's bright
face like that of a joyous bridegroom on his wedding-
day from the curtain of his secret chamber — of the
startling bound with which he leaps over the dark
ridge of the eastern mountains like a giant rejoicing to
run his course. The Grecian poets have sung of the
repose of immortals and the toils of mortals, have

handled with delicate touch the lights and shades of sea and sky; but we might search in vain for any expression of intense and abounding joyousness in the beauty of creation for its own sake equal to that which the Book of Job describes when it tells us, that at the laying of the foundation-stone of the world, "the morning stars sang together, and all the sons of God shouted for joy."[1] The Mosaic cosmogonist, the Psalmist of Bethlehem, the Idumean patriarch, could supply no theory of the universe; but they felt assured that in those glorious orbs there was an indication of divine power and wisdom beyond what they saw more closely around them. They were prepared, and they prepared others, to hear more; they put themselves and the world into an admiring, reverential, listening attitude.

And this brings me to the second point which I would name. They felt that there was something in these wonders which man was intended to understand and to read. At times they are overwhelmed by the greatness of the mystery — they look up in dumb astonishment: "When I consider Thy heavens, the work of Thy fingers, the moon and the stars which Thou hast ordained, what is man, that Thou art mindful of him?"[2] "Canst thou," it is said to Job, "canst thou bind the sweet influences of the Pleiades, or loose the bands of Orion? Canst thou bring forth the constellations[3] in their season, or guide Arcturus with his sons?"[4] But these very phrases imply a search, a yearning after the hidden truth, the very opposite of dull indifference or superstitious fear. They mount at times into the full expression of what a great French scholar calls "the grand curiosity" of a scientific and inquiring age. "There is neither speech nor language"

[1] Job xxxviii. 7.   [2] Ps. viii. 3.
[3] *Mazzaroth*, probably the signs of the zodiac.   [4] Job xxxviii. 31, 32.

(so David sings) in those distant stars; "neither are their voices heard." Yet, in spite of their silence, "their sound"—a sound of their own—"is gone forth through all lands, and their words unto the ends of the earth. Day unto day uttereth speech, night unto night revealeth knowledge."[1] Those lights which were set in the firmament of heaven were already seen to be not mere purposeless ornaments, not mere twinkling fireflies; they were set there (so the primeval historian tells us) "for signs and for seasons, and for days and years."[2] They were there for man to interpret, to explain; to hear that silent sound; to read those inarticulate words; to educe out of their mystic dances and labyrinthine movements, order and law, the ideas of time and of space, the witness which they bore to the glory of the first creative Cause, the service which they rendered to the use of the last created being.

That miserable antagonism which later ages have imagined between Religion and Science, had no place in those venerable oracles of God; that unnatural civil war which in modern times has been waged under the opposing flags of Faith and Reason, would have awakened not the slightest echo, because it would not have had the slightest meaning, in the minds of those primitive theologians, of those sacred philosophers.

If that question to Job has in our days been all but answered; if there have arisen those who have analyzed "the sweet influences of the Pleiades, and brought forth the constellations in their seasons;" if the simple reckonings "of days and years and signs and seasons" have grown up into the vast systems of astronomy and chronology, of Kepler and of Newton; if the silent language of the stars has been read and expounded in all lands from the Arctic Pole to the Antarctic Ocean

[1] Ps. xix. 2-4.   [2] Gen. i. 14.

— it is because He who set those lights in the firmament of the heavens willed that there should be corresponding lights in the human soul on earth; it is because He planted an instinct in the spirit of man, which, in the presence of these wonders of creation, longed to see them face to face, eye to eye; it is because in these early records of the Book of books there was implied and expressed that craving for an interpreter, for a translator, for an explainer of those mysteries; because, whilst clothing their bright ideas of the universe in such shreds of knowledge as they could put together, they were filled with a fearless desire for light, an eager restless movement after truth, such as best befits the truly religious mind, such as fills the human soul with the only true reverence, because it is the reverence of knowledge and not of ignorance.

This is the beginning of the world's astronomy. This is the true relation of the Bible to Science. Not a system true or false, but an opening and encouragement for all systems; not a fixed letter to control and check, but a living spirit of freedom to encourage, and stimulate, all inquiry.

I. Most instructive would be the task to trace the gradual progress of that inquiry, the full completion of that revelation. But on this day I would confine myself to such thoughts as are more immediately suggested by the passing away from us of one who was amongst the foremost interpreters of nature in these our latter days.

Such a light set in the firmament of earth to meet the light in the firmament of heaven has been bestowed on us in that gifted spirit, whose mortal remains were on Friday last laid beside his yet mightier master, amidst the mourning of all that England could show of scientific genius and research.

Of him, if of any, it might be said that he lived amongst those celestial luminaries. "Born under the giant shadow of his illustrious father's telescope," inheriting from him his aspiring tastes, and his unconquerable genius, the stars from his earliest years were his constant companions. "Light," he used to say, "was his first love." For him was reserved that task which the Book of Job describes as of superhuman magnitude — the exploration for the first time of the "wonders without number," not only in the familiar regions of the north, but in "the secret chambers of the south"[1] that Southern Hemisphere, whose marvels he has himself so eloquently described, "where a new heaven as well as a new earth is laid open to the gaze of the astronomer, a celestial surface equal to a fourth part of the heavens, the vivid beauty of the Southern Cross sung by poets, and celebrated by the pen of the most accomplished of civilized travellers" — the constellations which neither Moses, nor David, nor Galileo, nor Newton ever saw, but which shall look down on the future destinies of the teeming nations of the youngest born of the families of earth.

What the Psalmist regarded as the incommunicable attribute of divinity, was almost if not altogether achieved by those twelve years' unceasing labors and unwearied calculations of a single man — "He telleth the number of the stars, and calleth them all by their names."[2] The glorious sun, whose daily rising was in the eyes of the earlier Psalmist at once so beautiful and so mysterious, became to this latest of astronomers the absorbing subject at once of his ardent imaginings and his profoundest speculations. "Where are thy

[1] "Which maketh Arcturus, Orion, and Pleiades, and the chambers" (Hebrew, "the secret chambers") "of the south" (Job ix. 9).
[2] Ps. cxlvii. 4.

beams, O sun, and whence thine everlasting light?" seemed to those who knew him best the motto engraved as it were over his study door.

II. But this is not the place, nor is it for him who now speaks, to dwell on results which those only who fully understand them can worthily report. Here let us for a few moments speak of the moral lessons to be learnt from the conclusions which those labors suggest, and from the spirit in which they were approached by him who is gone.

It was his peculiar privilege to combine with those more special studies such a width of view, and such a power of expression, as to make him an interpreter, a poet of science, even beyond his immediate sphere. It is this which justifies and demands the development of a somewhat larger range of instruction from his career than it else would have allowed.

1. First, let us speak of that which at once appeals to the ordinary life of all — the effects of Science on our common interests. Filled as he was with a passionate love of abstract truth, yet .from that very love of those high subjects he longed to diffuse the knowledge of them as far and as wide as he could find eyes to see or ears to hear them. He was animated to a fresh enthusiasm by the conviction which he labored to impart to others, of the vast practical importance of scientific knowledge, in "showing us" (if I may venture to use his own simple but most exhaustive language) " in showing us how to avoid impossibilities; in securing us from important mistakes when attempting what is in itself possible by means either inadequate or actually opposed to the end in view; in enabling us to accomplish our ends in the easiest, shortest, most economical and most effectual manner; in inducing us to attempt and enabling us to accomplish objects

which but for such knowledge we should never have thought of undertaking." [1] These are homely rules, but they are rules which can be translated into the highest experiments and enterprises alike of scientific study, of statesmanlike policy, and of Christian benevolence.

2. He felt, too, with a strength rendered doubly strong by the profound interest which he took in the more spiritual subjects of thought, the immense advantage of Science to Theology and Philosophy, in teaching the necessity of accurate definition, and of testing theory by fact. He felt and he taught with all the persuasiveness of example no less than precept, the danger of meeting scientific questions with any other than scientific weapons, "the danger of mistrusting even for a moment the grand and only character of Truth — its capability of coming unchanged out of every possible form of fair discussion." "Ye shall know the truth, and the truth shall make you free." [2] How many a cobweb of fine-spun folly, how many an imaginary distinction of metaphysics, how many a scholastic entanglement, how many a baneful superstition — has vanished away before the touch of this Ithuriel's spear of scientific research! how firm a grasp of reality, how strong and fresh a belief in the [3] possibility of knowledge and certainty, how just a sense of the difference between false, artificial authority and true natural authority — can be given to the least scientific of us by such an interpretation of science as that which has in these latter days been afforded to us! This is no subtraction from any theology which de-

[1] Herschel's *Discourse on Natural Philosophy*, p. 94.

[2] John viii. 32.

[3] See the Duke of Argyll's *Essay* in *Contemporary Review*, May, 1871, p. 157.

serves the name. It is giving new meaning to its words, new bounds to its domain, new life to its skeleton.

3. Again, he, if any of his generation, taught us with unabated confidence the hope which Science teaches, no less than Religion, but which, whether in Science or Religion, the natural man so shrinks from receiving — the endless prospect of improvement set before mankind in its onward progress. It is the scientific version of the Apostolic text, " Forgetting those things which are behind, and reaching forth towards those things which are before." [1] Great as is the duty of humility to the student of Science and to the student of Theology, equally needed and often equally missed in both, yet not less needed for both, is the duty of hope, of boundless trust in the inexhaustible resources which the Giver of all good things has stored up in man and in nature. " The character of the true philosopher is to hope all things not impossible, and to believe all things not unreasonable." [2] We are often asked, with a mixture of incredulity and despair, when any new inquiry is set on foot, " How far will this take us ? Where will you stop ? " The true answer is that which he gave with the emphasis of calm persuasion, namely, that this is the very glory of science — " When once embarked in any physical research, it is impossible for any one to predict where it will ultimately lead him." We often hear it said — we often in our indolence think — that all truth is old, and that there is nothing new under the sun. The true answer of Science is that which again is at once the parallel and the illustration of the language of the Apostle. " The mysteries of knowledge, which in other ages were not made known unto the sons of men, are now revealed, and will be still

more revealed, to those whom God has chosen." [1]   All
these thousands of years the many uses of the sun and
moon [2] and stars "were hidden, which are now made
manifest" to all the world, even to those who least
understand whence their knowledge came, or what it
means.   It was his proud, yet reverential boast, that
the students of Science were "as messengers from
heaven to earth to make such stupendous announcements that they may claim to be listened to, when they
repeat in every variety of urgent instance, that these
are not the last announcements which they shall have
to communicate; that there are yet behind, to search
out and to declare, not only secrets of nature which
shall increase the wealth or power of men, but Truths
which shall ennoble the age and the country in which
they are divulged, and by dilating the intellect react
on the moral character of mankind." [3]

4. We often hear, from timid or anxious lips, that
the tendencies of Science lead towards a materialistic
fatalism.   It is at once a consolation and a rebuke to
be told by one who knew these tendencies well, that,
on the contrary, it is or ought to be the result of Science
that, "instead of being supinely and carelessly carried
down the stream of events, we now, by the great resources put into our hands, find ourselves, as never
before, capable of buffetting with its waves, and perhaps of riding triumphantly over them; for why should
we despair that the Science which has enabled us to
subdue all nature to our purposes, should (if permitted
and assisted by the providence of God) achieve the far
more difficult conquest of enabling the collective wisdom of mankind to bear down the obstacles which
individual short-sightedness, selfishness, and passion
oppose to all improvements?" [4]

[1] Eph. iii. 5.   Col. i. 26.   [2] Discourse, p. 308.
[3] Herschel's Essays, p. 550.   [4] Discourse, p. 74.

This is the scientific form, in which we read as in a parable the counterpart, and therefore the support, of that which Hegel truly called the most conspicuous mark of the Divinity of the Son of Man — His freedom from, His triumph over, the destiny of time and circumstance: "In the world ye shall have tribulation: but be of good cheer, I have overcome the world."[1]

5. Again, not with high-vaunting words, but with the simplest and most serious assurance, he saw in the Unity of Science the reflection, the inevitable reflection, of the Unity of one Supreme Life and Will. We are told that every theory and research of Science is converging towards absolute simplification, towards resolving form after form, and species after species, into some one common element, or some one common origin, instead of the endless multiplicity of distinctions which the more barbarous ages of the world assumed. There may be much in this which is exaggerated, much which we cannot understand, much which may startle, shock, confound us. Yet there is a reassuring side of this great argument. This truth of the unity of all things, which he in common with others of his mighty fellow-laborers has put before us, is but the statement by scientific process and in scientific language of the same doctrine which in one short, sublime sentence, was proclaimed from Mount Sinai, "The Lord thy God is one Lord," or which stands at the opening of the first page of the first sacred book, "In the beginning God created the heaven and the earth." "Chaos," as our departed teacher well put the case, "is the natural counterpart of Polytheism;" "Kosmos,"[2] the adornment, the ideal beauty, harmony, and grace, the unvarying law of the universe, is the natural counterpart of the belief in the one Supreme Mind of the one Creator and Lawgiver of

[1] John xvi. 33.   [2] *Essays*, p. 28; *Discourse*, p. 266.

all. " It is in this conservation of order in the midst
of perplexity, in this ultimate compensation brought
about by the continual action of causes which appear
at first sight pregnant with subversion and decay —
that we trace the Master wisdom with whom the darkness is even as the light." [1]   This is the Religion of
Nature ; but it is also only another formula for that
which, in the Religion of the Bible, is called the doctrine of Redemption and of Grace.

6. And yet once more, in that vast expansion of the
systems of the universe which Galileo first revealed to
us, which Newton explained, which the two Herschels
classified and analyzed, if our first feeling be one of depression and bewilderment, surely the final conclusion
of Science is also the final conclusion of the Apostle, in
the favorite text of Bacon, Oh the depth of the riches
both of the wisdom and knowledge of God!" [2]   It is
the great doctrine, faintly, dimly, imperfectly believed
by our forefathers indicated, in passing, by one obscure
word in one of the least edifying of our Creeds, but by
these wonderful disclosures, confirmed, vivified, illustrated, reverberated from pole to pole, from system to
system — the doctrine of the Divine Infinitude, the
Divine Immensity.   It is the intellectual, the scientific
side of the same attribute which in the moral nature of
God we call His all-embracing compassion, His boundless toleration, His all-penetrating justice, His inexhaustible forbearance.   " There are bodies celestial and
bodies terrestrial — one star differing from another star
in glory." [3]   This was the very image by which, even
with the imperfect knowledge of that age, the Apostle
represented the divine truth which his Master had proclaimed in the simpler form, so grand, so comprehensive, yet so tender, " In my Father's house are many
mansions." [4]

[1] *Essays*, pp. 257, 258.   [2] Rom. xi. 33.   [3] 1 Cor. xv. 40, 41.   [4] John xiv. 2.

Such are some of the relations of Science to Religion, of the relations of the heavens that are without us, to the yet greater heavens that are within us, which the world and the Church may learn from all the true students of nature, and in a special degree from him who is laid amongst us here.

III. And now let us draw aside the curtain a little further, and pass to the yet more practical lesson from the spirit in which he labored. Surely it is profitable to every one of us, to contemplate that long life wholly given to those lofty, unselfish aims — working, as he himself expressed, "like a working bee at home," working to the very end, reserving almost his only indignation for that spirit of idleness and luxury which spends life without using it, which dissipates life without civilizing it. There is no child here present who may not take heart from the thought that these memorable labors took their rise in the filial pride and affection which enkindled in him the noble ambition to complete what his famous father had begun. There is no young man here amongst my hearers who may not be stimulated in a steadfast, onward course, when he is told of those early college days, when the young Herschel with two or three of his friends vowed (like a similar band almost at the same time [1] in a great neighboring nation) that "they would put their shoulders to the wheel, and leave the world better than they found it." There is not a student or a politician, there is not an artisan or an artist, of whatever kind, who may not be moved by the burning words in which the English philosopher six-and-twenty years ago urged on his laggard countrymen to follow the example, even then bright with transcendent brightness, of the science and industry of Germany; when he implored them to bear in mind that amidst the

[1] See *Life of Baron Bunsen.*

vast overwhelming accumulation of facts forced in upon us from every quarter,[1] "what we want is Thought, steadily directed to single objects, with a determination to eschew the besetting evil of our age, the temptation to squander and dilute it on a thousand different lines of inquiry. The philosopher must be wedded to his subject if he would see the children and the children's children of his intellect flourishing in honor around him." There is not a soul engaged in the turmoils of private or of public life, of science, or theology, or statesmanship, who may not be raised beyond their petty trivialities by thinking of that venerable sage who lived through his long years above the stir of controversies, which he shunned, not from indifference, but from principle; without the slightest spark of unworthy rivalry either towards men or towards nations, fired only by that noble glow which results from companionship in honorable effort.[2] "True Science, like true Religion, is wide-embracing in its aims and objects. Let interests divide the worldly, and jealousies torment the envious. The true votaries of science breathe, or long to breathe, a purer air. The common pursuit of truth," whether sacred or scientific, "is itself a brotherhood."[3] There is no one, old or young, who may not be soothed and elevated by the remembrance of the calm, cheerful, simple, sanguine faith with which he rose towards truth and light of whatever kind, like his own favorite bird, ever soaring towards the dazzling, sunbright sky — lark-like, "true to the kindred points of heaven and home."[4] "To spring even a little way aloft, to carol for a while in bright and sunny regions, — to open out around us, at all events, views commensurate with our extent of vision, — to rise to the level

---

[1] *Essays*, p. 651. See also p. 17. [2] *Ibid.*, pp. 30, 634.
[3] *Ibid.*, p. 680. [4] Wordsworth.

of our strength, and if we must sink again, to sink not exhausted but exercised, not dulled in spirit but cheered in heart — such may be the contented and happy lot of him who can repose with equal confidence on the bosom of earth, or rise above the mists of earth into the empyrean day." [1] Such, assuredly, was his lot of whom we speak — "always eager to cast down 'the High Places and Groves of Ignorance,' and to open the doors of the human mind to let in light and knowledge; yet, always sure that right would come right at last, always content to urge the right rather than fight the wrong."

One remark in conclusion, which I will preface by a fine passage from one of his own popular addresses, in which he urges on his hearers the inestimable advantages of a taste for reading good authors. "Give a man," he said, "this taste, and you place him in contact with the best society in every period of history, with the wisest, the wittiest, with the tenderest, the bravest, and the purest of characters, who have adorned humanity; you make him a denizen of all nations, a contemporary of all ages. The world has been created for him. It is hardly possible but the character should take a higher and better tone from the constant habit of associating with thinkers above the average of humanity. It is morally impossible but that the manners should take a tinge of good breeding and civilization, from having before one's eyes the way in which the best bred and the best informed men have talked and acted." [2] It was in a yet higher mood of the same vein of thought that, many years ago, in the hearing of one who well remembers it, there fell from his lips a like saying, in a burst of fine moral enthusiasm: — "Surely if the worst of men were transported to Paradise for only half an hour, amongst the company of the great and good, he would come back converted."

[1] *Essays*, pp. 259, 737.   [2] *Essays*, p. 12.

Such, in its measure, is the privilege which we have had and may have in dwelling even for a short time on the words and thoughts of a soul so pure and noble as that which has gone from us. Such, still more, is the privilege of those who were his companions and friends; who traced him from his blameless youth to his honored grave; who were drawn round him in his quiet and simple home by the charm of his genius, by the yet more inexpressible tenderness of his affections; who now gaze up into heaven after him — the outward heaven, where his name is written in the stars, the spiritual heaven, where his name is written in the Book of Life.

For us, let us trust that he has "left the world better than he found it." For himself, let us use those humble and holy words of his own —

Enough, if cleansed at last from earthly stain,
My homeward step be firm, and pure my evening sky.[1]

[1] *Essays*, p. 741.

THE RELIGIOUS ASPECT OF HISTORY.

June 25, 1871, being the Sunday after the funeral of George Grote the Historian.

The " just " shall be had in everlasting remembrance.
PSALM cxii. 6.

IT is now more than six hundred years ago since one of the earliest fathers of English history, an inmate of the venerable Abbey of St. Alban's, which nurtured the first school of English historical learning, recounted, at the commencement of his work, how he was vexed by questions, some put by envious detractors, some arising from serious perplexity, whether the record of times that were dead and gone was worthy of the labor and study of Christian men. He replied, with a lofty consciousness of the greatness of his task, first by an appeal to the highest instincts of man; and then added, as a further and complete sanction of those instincts, the words of the Psalmist, " The just shall be had in everlasting remembrance." " *In memoriâ æternâ erit justus.*"

These are simple and familiar words; but the Chronicler of St. Alban's was right in saying that they contain the principle which vindicates and sanctifies all historical research.

" If thou," he said to his readers, " if thou forgettest and despisest the departed of past generations, who will remember thee ? " " It was to keep alive," so he added, " the memory of the good, and teach us to abhor the bad, that all the sacred historians have striven, from

Moses down to 'the deep-souled'[1] chroniclers of the years in which we ourselves are living."

The religious sense of History which Matthew Paris thus endeavored to convey has never since altogether died out from amongst us, and it may be well to express it once more on this occasion, when it has been brought to our minds by the solemn ceremony which yesterday consigned to the grave the remains of a great scholar, whose life was spent in historical study.

As on a like occasion not long ago I dwelt on the religious aspect of Science, so now I propose to dwell on the religious aspect of History. As then we were invited to express our gratitude to the Giver of all good, for the genius of one who "told the number of the stars, and called them all by their names," so now we are invited to give thanks for the gift which God has bestowed on the Church and realm of England, in the genius of one who could call up the spirits of the mighty dead, and "seek out the secrets of grave sentences, and try the good and the evil among men."[2]

Let us take the words of the text as the groundwork of our thoughts.

I. "Everlasting remembrance," "eternal memory" —"a memorial that shall endure from generation to generation." This is what History aims to accomplish for the ages of the past.

As we are reminded both by Scripture and by experience of the noble, the inextinguishable desire implanted within us, to understand and to bring near to us the wonders of the firmanent, so in like manner we may be assured that there lies deep in the human heart a desire not less noble, not less insatiable, to understand and to bring near to us the wonders of the ages that are

[1] "Pectoris Profundi," Matthew Paris, *Hist. Major*, pp. 1, 2.
[2] Ecclus. xxxix. 3, 4.

dead and buried. "I have considered the days of old, and the years that are past; I will remember the years of the right hand of the most Highest; I will call to mind His wonders of old time;"[1] "I will declare hard sentences of old, which our fathers have told us, that we should not hide them from the children of the generations to come."[2] It is this continuity of purpose, this progression of ages, this connection of the deeds and thoughts of those that are gone with the deeds and thoughts of men now upon earth, that as truly disclose the mind of God in the world of man, as the order, and harmony, and progression of the celestial bodies disclose it in the world of nature. The Astronomer is the historian of the heavens; the Historian is the star-gazer into the dark night of the past. As the philosophic discoverer enables us to distinguish the several distances of the fixed stars from each other, which to common eyes are lost in the sense of their distance from us, so the philosophic historian distinguishes, for those who cannot see as far as he, the several distances of the stars in the moral world, "one star differing from another star in glory," according to their opportunities, their age, their characters. As the telescope enables the man of science to resolve the nebulous clusters of the milky way into the distinct worlds of which each cluster is composed, so the microscope of scholarship enables the man of letters to resolve the nebulous mist of primeval tradition into the distinct elements out of which it has been gradually formed. As the celestial spheres are mapped out by the natural student to guide the mariner, and "for times, and for seasons, and for days, and for years," so the spheres of earthly events are mapped out by the historical student, and the monuments of glory and the beacons of danger are set along the shores of

---

[1] Ps. lxxvii. 5, 10, 11.   [2] Ps. lxxviii. 2–4.

the past, to direct us through the trackless ocean of the future. Happy, thrice happy he who has the ears to hear those voices of the dead which others cannot hear; who has the eyes to see those visions of the ancient times which to others are dim and dark. History may be fallible and uncertain, but it is our only guide to the great things that God has wrought for the race of man in former ages; it is the only means through which " we can hear, and " through which " our fathers can declare to us the noble works which He has done in their days, and in the old time before them."

II. And not only the religion of the natural man, but the whole structure of the Bible is a testimony to the sacredness and the value of historical learning. Unlike all other sacred books, the sacred books both of the Old and New Testament are, at least half in each, not poetical, or dogmatical, but historical. Even the poetic and dogmatic parts are for the most part materials for history. The Prophets of the Old Testament are also historians. The visions of Daniel are, as has been often observed, the first signal example of the Philosophy of History. Nor is it merely in form, but in spirit, that this truth is set forth before us in the Bible. The Religion of Christendom has, besides its other transcendent marks of superiority, this broad distinction from all other religions, that it is essentially historical. Of the three great manifestations of God to man, in nature, in conscience, in the course of human events, — "God in History" will to a large part of mankind be the most persuasive. On the great scale of the world's movements we see impressed the "unceasing purpose" of the Creator; on the smaller scale of the lives of heroes, saints, and sages, we see the highest efforts of the Creature.

Doctrine, precept, warning, exhortation, all are invested with double charms when clothed in the flesh and blood of historical facts. If there has been an " everlasting remembrance " of One supremely Just, in whom the Divine Mind was made known to man in a special and transcendent degree, it is because that Just One, the Holy and the True, " became flesh and dwelt amongst us," and became (so let us speak with all reverence and all truth) the subject of historical description, of historical research, of historical analysis, of historical comparison. The sacred historians of the Jewish Commonwealth, still more the simple, homely, but profound historians of the New Testament whom we call the Evangelists, are the most impressive of all preachers. They are subject doubtless to the same laws, to the same difficulties as other histories, and it is from the illustration of other histories that they can alone be fully understood and appreciated. But in themselves they are the enduring witness in the Book of books to the immortal power of history in the education of mankind.

III. And this power is not confined to the history of the Jewish people, or of the Christian Church. It extends to the history of " the nations " — of " the Gentiles," as they are called in the Bible.

Those of us who were present at the splendid discourse [1] which on Sunday last thrilled the vast congregation within these walls, and who heard the preacher's indignant repudiation of the common mode of dividing secular from sacred history, will not need to be persuaded of the great Catholic and Evangelical doctrine that whatever was or is good and true in any race of men, is equally precious in the sight of God; that Greece and Rome as well as Judæa had their own dis-

---

[1] Sermon preached by the Bishop of Peterborough in Westminster Abbey on the evening of June 18, 1871.

tinct parts allotted to them in the guidance and progress of the world.

Over and over again is this truth expressed in the Bible, "The just," without reserve, in whatever nation, and of whatever creed, "is to be had in everlasting remembrance." "*Whatsoever* things are true, *whatsoever* things are honest, *whatsoever* things are just, *whatsoever* things are pure, *whatsoever* things are lovely, *whatsoever* things are of good report, if there be *any* virtue, if there be *any* praise," [1] in *whatsoever* race, or under *whatsoever* form, — these things are the legitimate, the sacred, subjects which the Father of all good gifts has charged the historians of the world to read and to record wheresoever they can be discerned.

The Apostle St. Peter received the heathen soldier of the Italian band with the undoubting assurance that "in every nation he that feareth God and worketh righteousness is accepted with Him." [2] The Apostle St. Paul, in contemplating the whole Gentile world, [3] declared that "not the hearers of the law are just before God, but the doers of the law are justified; for when the Gentiles, which have not the law, do by nature the things contained in the law, these, having not the law, are a law unto themselves." The Apostle St. John declared that "he who doeth righteousness is righteous." [4] And the Master and Lord of Peter, Paul, and John, welcomed with His own special favor the Roman centurion, [5] whose faith exceeded all that He had found in Israel; and hailed the coming of the Greek inquirers [6] who sought to see Him on the eve of His departure; and declared in language not to be mistaken, that when "all the nations" should be assembled before the Son of man at the last day, His gracious

---

[1] Phil. iv. 8.   [2] Acts x. 35.   [3] Rom. ii. 13, 14.
[4] 1 John iii. 7.   [5] Matt. viii. 10, 11. [6] John xii. 20-26.

benediction would be pronounced on all those that had done good to their fellow-men, even though they had never heard His voice, nor named His name;[1] even though they had never said Lord, Lord, yet, if they had done His Father's will, if they had ministered to His brethren on earth — this, and this alone, was sufficient to win His supreme approval.

IV. And if we look yet closer into the story of that marvellous Grecian race, which we are especially called this day to consider, let us never forget that Christianity itself, if from one point of view it is as a Hebrew of the Hebrews, from another and not less important view, it has become even as a Greek to the Greeks. The language of its sacred books is not the tongue of Sinai or Jerusalem, but of Athens and Alexandria. Without Plato, without Aristotle, without Alexander, the whole preparation for Christianity, the whole development of Christianity, would have been wholly different from that which, in the fulness of time and with these riches of the Gentile world poured into it, it has actually become. There is in its very conception, if one may so say, a welcome, a stretching out of the hands to the sons of Javan and to the coasts of Chittim. There is interwoven with the very texture of the New Testament a tenderness, a humanity, a universality, a search after truth, a variety, a freedom of development, a popularity of constitution, that, humanly speaking, are not Hebraic, but Hellenic; they belong to that side of the Divine Image which looks not towards the mountains and deserts of the East, but towards the isles of the Gentiles and the uttermost parts of the western sea. Even in that Supreme Exemplar, in whom there is in one sense neither Jew nor Greek, yet in whom in another sense Greek and Jew each find

[1] Matt. xxv. 31-40; vii. 21.

their corresponding elements, there is an aspect to which, amidst a thousand differences and at an incommensurable interval, there has yet no closer parallel been suggested in the history of mankind than the highest climax of the development of Greece in the immortal story of the consecrated life and solemn end of the Athenian philosopher.

Yet perhaps it is even more from the contribution of new elements of life to the spiritual growth of man, that the Hellenic race claims "the everlasting remembrance" of those who value the inward Holy Spirit of our Christian faith yet more deeply than they value even the most sacred and imperishable of its outward forms. "To have known the history of a people by whom the first spark was set to the dormant intellectual capacities of our[1] nature"—to draw forth from the various forms of fable or legend, of strange antique observance and rare preternatural beauty, "cunningly graven in gold or silver or stone by art and man's device," the devotion of that ancient people to their thousand "unknown gods," which caused them to be considered by the Apostle as in all things "very[2] religious" beyond all their fellows—to delineate the growth of that singular freedom of discussion, and singular fidelity to law, which have since combined to make Christendom a living reality, and Western Civilization a possibility — to appreciate the various motives and forces, which,

> Through many a dreary age,
> Upbore whate'er of good and wise
> Still lived in bard or sage,

and stimulated those lofty spirits who have moulded the policy, the art, and the philosophy of all educated men in after times — to thrill the spirit of generations yet to

---

[1] Grote's *Greece*, vol. i., Preface, p. viii.   [2] Acts xvii. 22, 23.

come by recording once more in all their fulness those
heart-stirring victories of the few against the many,
of light against darkness, which will be the watchwords
of patriotism and of liberty as long as the fabric of the
civilized world endures — to inquire in what intricate
depths of those early times " could wisdom be found," [1]
and where was the primeval " place of understanding "
— to trace the rise of that heaven-sent genius which
was forever preaching on the oracle, *Know thyself*, as
the holiest of texts, which " permanently enlarged the
horizon, improved the method, and multiplied the as-
cendant minds of the whole speculative world " forever
— to have painted the gloomy side of that luminous
history, and seen our own sins anticipated or exaggerated in that highly wrought society, the sins of party
spirit and of popular superstition, the action and re-
action of democratic and despotic violence, the growth
of dark vices and of hideous crimes, even under the
surface of the most refined civilization and by the side
of the loftiest aspirations — to have gathered together
that vast " cloud of witnesses," who, though they " received not our promises, God having provided some
better things for us, that they without us should not be
made perfect," [2] yet have their memories enshrined on
the heights of fame, as trophies which will not suffer us
to sleep in the race that is set before us in the onward
progress of humanity towards the City of the Living
God ; — To have learned or to have taught any of these
lessons from the annals of that dear immortal land,

> Where each old poetic mountain
> Inspiration breathes around —

this is to have done something towards the " everlasting remembrance " of the Just, the Free, the Beautiful,

[1] Job xxviii. 12.   [2] Heb. xi. 39, 40; xii. 1, 22.

and the True — this is to have contributed something towards the glorification of Him whose name is Justice, and Loveliness, and Liberty, and Truth.

V. Such an effort, sustained through almost forty years of unremitting toil, marked the course of the aged scholar who now rests from his lifelong labors. For this end, alike in early manhood and in maturer years, he steadily forsook and set aside (so far as he could) all worldly cares and honors. For this and for the advancement of kindred pursuits, he, in a distracted and luxurious age, lived the simple and single-minded life of an ancient or academic sage.

And if, as has been the lot of other eminent historians, he was himself an example of that which he described, and grew like to that which he admired, if we feel as though we were reading of himself, when he portrays the Athenian statesman,[1] who " by his straight and single-handed course, with no solicitude for party ties, and with little care to conciliate friends or offend enemies, and by manifesting through a long public life an uprightness without flaw, had beyond all suspicion earned for himself the lofty surname of the Just," or that Spartan chief,[2] who rose above his countrymen by his " entire straightforwardness of dealing and his Pan-hellenic patriotism, alike comprehensive, exalted, and merciful;" if we almost fancy that we see living again in him the genius of historical impartiality, which once seems to have been realized amongst men in the Grecian Thucydides — then of him also, as of those whom he delineated, may those sacred words be repeated: " The just shall be had in everlasting remembrance."

To be just was the inspiring motive and the controlling check of his whole intellectual life. For the sake of preserving the exact balance of truth, he resisted

---

[1] Aristides (Grote's *Greece*, iv. 459).   [2] Callicratidas (*Ibid.* viii. 219).

what, to minds like his, in an age like ours, is an inducement stronger than love, or honor, or wealth; he restrained a fervid imagination, he sacrificed the graces of style, and the desire of effect; he never gave way to "the constantly recurring temptation to break loose from the unseen spell by which a conscientious criticism bound him down." [1]

And this passion for justice, which was the soul of his work, was also the soul of his character.

They who knew him best will tell us that of all the public men whom they had ever known he was the most unswervingly just. Those who knew him not, may be assured that whatever honor or respect he won, beyond the region of his intellectual eminence, was the tribute which mankind feel to be due to any manifestation of that most Godlike and Christlike grace, the virtue of justice. Let those whose hasty, dogmatic, exaggerated statements fall from their lips in unceasing flow, without thought for themselves, or care for others, remember (if they ever heard it) the slow, deliberate enunciation with which, even on seemingly trivial matters, he would drop out, syllable by syllable, his exact, unimpassioned judgments, as though he feared lest a single phrase should escape him that was not absolutely true — as though he had forever sounding in the innermost chamber of his conscience the sacred maxim, "By thy words thou shalt be justified, and by thy words thou shalt be condemned." Let those who think it consistent with their station, or their rank, or their religion, to treat with rudeness, or with scorn, those from whom they differ, those to whom they are superior, those to whom they are inferior, remember, if they ever saw it, the gracious urbanity, the antique courtesy, the tender consideration, with which he met the jarring circum-

1 *Ibid.* Preface, p. x.

stances and characters of life, as though he had ever
before him the Divine ideal of Him who, in the quaint
but reverent language of an early English poet,[1] has
been called —

> The First True Gentleman that ever breathed.

Let those who think that enlarged philosophy, or
daring speculation, or eager research, carries with it, as
by a fatal necessity, a fierce and scoffing spirit, a forward speech, an intolerant, insolent temper — let them
remember, if they ever witnessed it, the reverential
abstinence, the modest forbearance of that firm but
gentle nature which, alike in act and word, was the
living representation of the apostolic maxims — "In
honor preferring others; condescending to men of low
estate;" "rendering" with scrupulous exactness "to
all their due, custom to whom custom, honor to whom
honor."[2]

Such an one, whether he be of us or not, shall surely
be honored amongst "the spirits of just men made perfect" hereafter. In parting with such an one, whether
we look backwards to the dark shadows of this mortal
life, or forwards to "the Light which no man can approach unto," we may repeat for him, and urge on
others, those sacred words of which the scope is limited
to no age or country, and of which the meaning is inexhaustible: "The path of the just is as the shining light,
that shineth more and more unto the perfect day."[3]
"Blessed are they which do hunger and thirst after
righteousness, for they shall be filled."[4] "*In memoriâ
æternâ erit justus.*"[5]

---

[1] Dekker.   [2] Rom. xii. 10, 16; xiii. 7.   [3] Prov. iv. 18.
[4] Matt. v. 6.   [5] Ps. cxi. 7 (cxii. 6).

FREDERICK DENISON MAURICE.

From a Sermon on Sunday Evening, April 7, 1872.

Peace be unto you. — LUKE xxiv. 36.

THERE is a name which was given in the old Pagan religion of ancient Rome to its chief ministers — the name of *Pontiff;* and from them the name has descended to the chief ministers of the Christian religion in modern Rome. The name, as it was first applied, meant *the maker of bridges.* Why it was so used, in the first instance, we now hardly know. They were, perhaps, specially employed in constructing those mighty instruments of earthly peace and civilization — the great roads and bridges by which those old Romans tamed and subdued the world. But in a moral and spiritual sense we ought all to be *makers of bridges* still — Pontiff or no Pontiff, minister or no minister, every Christian who walks in his Master's steps, but especially those who are Pontiffs, those who do hold a high place in the Christian hierarchy, and most of all those who by their noble spiritual gifts have the power to reconcile and bring together their fellow-men.

Churches need not be united in order to be at peace. Men need not be alike in order to be at peace. Not as the world giveth, not as outward appearance giveth, is the peace which Christ gives to us. It was the saying of a great monarch of France, looking out on the neighboring country of Spain, "There are no more Pyrenees."

The power of the human will, the vaulting ambition of one man, was — so he thought — sufficient to remove even this greatest of natural boundaries. But so, even literally, it may be said that Faith and Charity have power to remove mountains. Mountains of difficulty, mountains of misunderstanding, may vanish before the power of knowledge, before the depth of philosophical analysis, before the courage which despises difficulties, before the insight which sees into a heart of stone. In those same Pyrenean mountains there is a huge cleft called the Breach of Roland, because it was believed to be hewn out by the magic sword of that renowned paladin on his passage to the field of Roncesvalles. Such a Breach of Roland, such a cleft through the hardest granite barriers that have ever parted the families of mankind asunder, has been ere now cut through by the magic sword of the paladins of true philosophy, of true theology, of the true Christian discernment of the spirits of men.

Such an example of the gift of peace in all its senses has been shown forth in a revered and saintly teacher, who on the early dawn of Easter Monday was removed from this world of strife to the peace which shall never be broken. Many in this church may have seen — many others, high and low, may have heard of — the lifelong labors in behalf of Christian truth and Christian love, which have endeared to thousands of his countrymen the name of Frederick Maurice. In one sense it was a life not of peace, but of constant warfare, of war against all that was mean and base and false; whenever and wherever he saw, or thought he saw, any one wronged or oppressed, always in the foremost rank; the champion of the fallen cause, of the forgotten truth, of the things which being eternal are not seen, because they are hid behind the things which being seen are temporal. It was a life, too, not of peaceful ease, but of incessant, unwearied toil, a bush ever burning; and, as it burned, consumed with its own inextinguishable zeal for God's house and God's honor, devouring as a burning flame the mind and the body that enclosed it; bearing every one's burden and relieving every one's grief; suffering with the sufferings of the poor and afflicted; struggling with the struggles of the inquiring soul. Who was weak and he was not weak? Who was offended and he burned not? It was a life, too, not withdrawn from earthly concerns, not wrapt up in abstruse contemplation. He lived in the very thick of the stirring influences of our time. He, if any one, was an English citizen, even more than he was an English Churchman. He, whilst clinging passionately, devotedly, to the ages of the past, yet was, if any one, full of all the thoughts and events of our own momentous century. Not a wave of speculation in Europe, not a public event of joy or sorrow in England, but called forth a sympathetic or indignant cry from that travailing soul. None of our time have in this respect so visibly been as the ancient prophets, reflecting all the movements of the age, yet themselves not led captive by them.

For this was the contrast which makes his life so deeply instructive. In the midst of all this, he was in all those senses in which we have spoken of peace, the most peaceful, the most pacific, the most peace-making of men.

Peace in himself; for, amidst the strife of tongues and the war of parties, he remained self-poised, independent, in a world above this world, in a land that was very far away, with utterances sometimes obscure, sometimes flashing with lightning splendor, yet always speaking from his own heart and conscience that which there he had truly found.

Peace for others; for he was ever striving to make himself heard and felt across the boundaries which part us asunder; a fountain of fire which irradiated even where it did not penetrate, a trumpet that awaked even where it did not convince, a music that soothed even where it was not understood. In any sacred word, whether of the Bible or of the Church, in all the great words of human speech, he labored, perhaps too eagerly, to discern — not its commonplace, earthly, party meaning, but its heavenly, ideal, catholic significance. He has been, in the high sense in which I used the word, a true Pontiff of the English Church, a true paladin in the English State. He has built bridges that will not easily be broken across the widest chasms that separate class from class, and mind from mind. He has, with a more piercing sword than Roland's Durandel, made a breach in the mountain-wall of prejudice and ignorance that will never be entirely closed.

Peace in God. In that voice trembling with emotion each time he said the Lord's Prayer or the Apostles' Creed, as though he was reading them always for the first time, as though they came to him fresh with their original freshness, yet laden with all the meaning of ages; in those eyes bright with faith in the eternal goodness and justice of God; in that mighty mouth, fixed in defiance against all falsehood, in which the heart seemed to speak, as with lips of its own, the very message which he was sent into the world to deliver — the veriest stranger could see the " Peace not as the world giveth," but as He giveth who is the giver of all that is good in every prayer, in every creed, in every truth, human or divine. By that prophetic countenance, by that inspiring voice, by that ennobling presence, the youthful listener felt that a mind higher than his own was feeling for him; the old man perceived

. that from the generations that were to come there was as much to be learnt as from the generations that were passed and gone; the student saw the unity of theology and of philosophy, of time and of eternity; the poor man felt that there was one who was filled even to overflowing with the sense of the brotherhood, the community of all men. The secret of all this (if we may venture to divine) was that of a trust absolute, unbroken, yet with a perfect understanding of what he believed, in the greatness and goodness of God and of God's dealings with the whole race of mankind. The religions of the world were all to him manifestations, more or less imperfect, of the religion of Jesus Christ. The various developments of the Christian Church were all to him various provinces of the Kingdom of Christ. The threefold name of the Father, the Son, and the Holy Ghost, was not to him a dark insoluble mystery, but a glorious revelation of the depths of the moral being of God. Believing in the truth of this revelation as positively as the strictest Pharisee or fanatic of any Jewish or Christian sect, he could afford to be as reverent as he was free, as fearlessly bold as he was perfectly humble; he was not, he could not be, afraid of any evil tidings, of any inquiry, of any research, for his heart stood fast, and believed in the eternal God.

Such was the vision of Peace which he presented to the world whilst he lived; and his reward even on earth has been that when his end came, the strife that had been provoked by the long warfare of life, the earthly passions which had cast out his name whilst he was amongst us, were hushed into respectful silence when he was taken from us. And amongst those who gathered round his grave, or who honored his memory, were many who met but there, and who there met in the Peace of God. For he, in whom the ancient faith in Jesus Christ and His Gospel could enkindle such a bright and shining light, had given the best proof that the truth of that Gospel can make us free, that where the Spirit of Christ is, there is liberty.

And from himself there came in those last hours the most touching, the most impressive, because the most characteristic, of all the utterances that could have fallen from his lips. On that early Easter morning, when the end drew near, out of the extremity of bodily weakness, out of the darkness of death, he gathered himself up and pronounced calmly, distinctly, and with the slight variation which was necessary to include himself as well as others within its range, the solemn benediction with which the Church of England at the close of its most solemn service gives its Peace not as the world giveth — the benediction which had been endeared to him through the long years of his faithful ministrations, every word of which was to him instinct with a peculiar life of its own, a peculiar reflex of his own profoundest feelings. With that benediction let me venture to conclude, in the humble hope that something of his spirit may breathe upon us through this his last legacy — his last message to English Christendom. " The Peace of God, which passeth all understanding, keep our hearts and minds in the knowledge and love of God and of his Son Jesus Christ our Lord; and the blessing of God Almighty, the Father, the Son, and the Holy Ghost, be amongst us and remain with us always."

THE MISSION OF THE TRAVELLER.

April 19, 1874, being the Sunday after Dr. Livingstone's burial.

Other sheep I have, which are not of this fold ; them also I must bring, and they shall hear my voice ; and there shall be one fold, and one shepherd. — JOHN x. 16.[1]

IF a visitant from another planet were to look over the surface of this earth ; nay, if we ourselves cast a glance at the map of the globe, it might seem as if it was a vast system of impassable barriers ; walls of partition mountains high, reaching to the clouds ; rivers which have become the very type of the gulf of death itself ; oceans with their illimitable, "dissociable" expanse of waters — all the varieties of climate, race, customs, which make every change irksome, every step in advance a peril. Add to this the deeply rooted instinct of the human mind, which binds each man to his family and his country, which attaches him to the haunts of his childhood, to the tombs of his fathers, to all the endearing associations and ennobling glories that make "home" one of the most sacred of human words, and patriotism one of the most exalting of human virtues.

Yet, as if to meet these natural difficulties, to enlarge

[1] The Gospel of the day from which this text was taken was John x. 7-16, and the Lessons, which fell in their regular course, were Numbers xxi., describing the wanderings of Israel in the Desert, and Ephesians iii., describing the mission of St. Paul to the Gentile world. The 16th and 23rd Psalms were chosen especially for the occasion, as well as the anthem from the 35th chapter of Isaiah.

these contracted feelings, there is a countervailing instinct planted in the heart of man, which has proved sufficient not only to surmount all obstacles, but, in surmounting them, to give birth to new virtues; to link the human race together by bonds as much stronger than the barriers which keep them asunder as spirit is stronger than matter, as knowledge is stronger than ignorance, as love is stronger than hatred. "Behind these mountains there are also people like ourselves," is the unconscious cry (as expressed in the German proverb), even of the unreasoning savage. "Other sheep I have, which are not of this fold," is the same thought, expressed in the highest form of human and divine compassion. That instinct, in its simplest expression, takes the form of the world-wide ambition of the traveller; in its loftiest development it is the world-wide beneficence of the missionary and the philanthropist. The result of this divinely implanted instinct in the sphere of knowledge is written in the noble sciences of Geography, of Comparative Philology, of Ethnology; in the spiritual sphere, it is the great philosophical and Christian doctrine of the unity of mankind, of the Holy Universal Church, of the gathering of "one flock[1] into one fold under one shepherd."

Let me in a few words trace through its various stages this glorious mission of the Traveller.

I. First, we shall speak of the simple, natural desire of exploring new regions, of visiting famous scenes, of breathing a new atmosphere, of traversing new experiences. Let no one think scorn of this noble passion. Well said the wise man of old, "It is the glory of God to conceal a thing, but the honor of kings is to search out a matter."[2] It is the glory of God to stimulate

---

[1] The word translated "fold" properly means "flock," in the last clause of John x. 16.   [2] Prov. xxv. 2.

search after truth, and enkindle chivalrous enterprise by "determining for the nations their appointed times and the bounds of their habitation." [1]   It is the glory of kings, and kinglike men, to discover the secrets of His Providence, the treasures of His grace, the infinite variety of nature and of man.   Who is there that has not felt at times the glow of that sacred fire, the enthusiasm of that heaven-sent inspiration ?   No doubt the poet spoke truth when he sang —

> Breathes there the man with soul so dead
> Who never to himself hath said,
> " This is my own, my native land ? " —

Yes, but it must also be added, " Breathes there the man with soul so dead " who has not felt a new life within him, when he has for the first time left his native village and seen the great cities of mankind; when he has for the first time crossed the silver streak of sea, and landed on the continent of Europe; when he has for the first time mounted the barrier of the Alps, and descended upon the sunny regions of the South; when he has for the first time passed into the silent pathways of the frozen North, or the ancient splendors of the East, or the teeming activity of the virgin West?   Is it not true (if we may so far enlarge the saying of the Emperor Charles V.) that each one of us becomes a new man not only with every new language he acquires, but also with every new land he traverses?   Who can ever forget, that has once felt it, the exhilarating sense of his first glance at the eternal snows, or his experience of the boundless liberty of the desert, or the sublime solitude of the ocean ?

And if this be so with ordinary travellers, how much more in those nobler spirits in whom it has become a high vocation to unveil the mysteries which none before

1 Acts xvii. 26.

have known? What moment is there of more thrilling interest in the earth's history than when Columbus saw the lights of the New World, of which for years he had dreamed? What purer thirst for knowledge than that which, on the lonely Cape of St. Vincent, or in the exquisite chapel of Belem on the shores of the Tagus, fired the Portuguese voyagers for their manifold discoveries? What more touching proof of devotion to the cause of duty and science combined than the grave of Franklin and his gallant companions in the icy sepulchre of the Polar seas?

Even in this, its simplest form, the glory of the traveller is one of the glories of our race; nay, we may add, one of the glories of our religion. It has its sanction in our earliest sacred associations. Who was the first of the long line of those adventurous spirits who "gat them out of their country and their kindred and their father's house, not knowing whither they went"?[1] It was Abraham, the Father of the Faithful. What was the education of the youth of the Chosen People? It was a perpetual journey, marching and countermarching through a "great and terrible wilderness," through mountain passes, through deep ravines; their leader dying in sight of the good land which he was not to possess — the parable to every subsequent age of the pilgrimage of life, the wilderness of the world, the prelude to the promised rest. Who was it that planned the first voyage of discovery which brought back the sandal-wood of Malabar, the peacocks of Hindostan, the ivory tusks and the apes of Africa, the gold of the unknown Ophir?[2] It was the wise king the son of David. Whose life is it that, as a famous writer expresses it, is one vast itinerary; as another calls it, the Christian Odyssey following on the Christian Iliad; hurrying from continent to

---

[1] Gen. xii. 1; Heb. xi. 8.　　　[2] 1 Kings x. 22.

continent, from island to island, "in shipwrecks often, in journeyings often, in perils of rivers, in perils of robbers, in perils by the heathen, in perils in the city, in perils in the wilderness, in perils in the sea; in weariness and painfulness, in watchings and fastings, in hunger and thirst, in cold and [1] nakedness"? It is Paul of Tarsus, the Apostle of the Gentiles. And what — if we may, with reverence, ask — what was one of the chief aspects of the Foremost Figure of all which our Sacred Books present? It is not of a recluse hermit fixed in the Jordan Valley, nor yet of a teacher stationary in the schools of Jerusalem, with no thought for those beyond the limits of his native land. It is of One whose eye was turned to "the many who should come from the east and from the west, from the north and from the south," [2] before whose glance had once been unrolled, as in a map, "all the kingdoms of the world." [3] It is of One who, in His actual life on earth, was constantly moving to and fro, often not having where to lay His head; a hungry and thirsty wayfarer who, from Galilee to Samaria, from Samaria to Judea, on the hills beyond the Jordan, and on the coasts of Tyre and Sidon, on the snow-clad heights of Hermon, " went about doing good." [4]

> Quærens me sedisti lassus;
> Tautus labor non sit cassus.

> Thou in search of me didst sit,
> Wearied with the noontide heat;
> Oh may all that toil and pain
> Not be wholly spent in vain !

Such is the origin, such, at least in part, the ancestry and likeness that we claim for the noble army of Travellers. And this leads me to speak of the place which

---

[1] 2 Cor. xi. 25-27.   [2] Luke xiii. 29.   [3] Matt. iv. 8.   [4] Acts x. 38.

they fill, or may fill, in the divine economy of the world. I have already glanced at the light which they have thrown on the secrets of the Universe. No one who feels how sacred a thing is this earth, as the handiwork of the Creator, as the expression of His will, can be indifferent to the holy privilege of those who assist in unveiling any part of that handiwork, in revealing any part of that will, to the eyes of men. The whole of it, if we believe in its derivation from one Supreme Mind, hangs together, and so long as any corner of its recesses remains unknown, we have not done our utmost to learn our Father's whole mind toward us. It was the generous expression of a wish, hopeless perhaps to any one individual, that was once uttered by an enthusiastic student of Geography — "I should be miserable, if I thought that there was a single land that I should never visit, or a single language that I should never know." But what in the case of one man is impossible, is possible for the whole race of men, through its more energetic members. There is no land which ought to remain unvisited, there is no language that ought to remain unlearned, if we really desire to follow the true Vestiges of Creation, the true Footsteps of the Creator. "If we take the wings of the morning and dwell in the uttermost parts of the sea, even there shall His hand lead us, and His right hand shall uphold us."[1] But it is not only in the accumulation of knowledge that the Traveller discharges a heavenly mission. It is also in bringing together, and in drawing upwards towards a common centre, "the children of God that are scattered abroad" in every race and clime. The instinct which inspires the adventurous explorer is, in its root, the same as that which inspires the devoted missionary. It is the feeling that Mankind is one; it is

[1] Ps. cxxxix. 10.

the sense of kindred even with the most alien, the most
perverse, the most degraded forms of humanity; it is
the sense that in races most unlike to ourselves there
are capacities of improvement, of superiority, of excel-
lence, of which, till we had seen them, we were almost
unconscious. And as the Traveller by the nature
of the case is almost always the representative of a
more civilized nation, of a more refined religion than
those into whose haunts he wanders, he becomes almost
perforce a missionary — a missionary either for good
or for evil. A missionary it may be for evil. It is
unfortunately true that the liberty of a traveller has
sometimes been the mask of license, that the indifference, the profaneness, the self-indulgence, of the European are the only characteristics of himself which he
by his example imparts. Of all the crimes against our
common humanity, few are deeper in guilt or more
widespreading in their consequences, than that of the
man who thus coming in the guise of an angel of light
transforms himself into an angel of darkness, who
takes to himself the vices of the savage and gives in
return the vices of civilization. But this is not the
true Traveller, this is not the genuine seeker after
truth, this is not the faithful messenger to "the other
sheep that are not of this fold." Far oftener, we would
fain believe, the Traveller rises to the height of his
lofty calling, and awakens to the new responsibility
which his new position lays upon him. The humblest
wayfarer in the far East or the farther South has it
in his power, by fairness, by kindness, by justice, to
leave behind him his stamp on those who in him, perhaps for the first time and the last time, have the
chance of knowing what is meant by a European, by
an Englishman, a Christian. The Explorer, even in
the most purely scientific pursuits, becomes accessible

to the catholic tendencies of pure Religion, to the reverent sense of a watchful Providence, such as men in their ordinary lives can hardly experience. What lessons of faith and wisdom are read to us by that passage in the life of Mungo Park, when, naked and alone in the desert, he was recalled to hope and perseverance by his reflection on the care of God, as displayed in the leaves of the little plant which he saw before him not bigger than his finger's end! And when, to the effects of personal example and personal experience, there is added the assurance that, through every pathway that the Traveller opens, civilization, commerce, and religion will follow, and that thus alone the waste places of the earth can become redeemed and cultivated, — then we see how, as if by an undesigned, or shall we not rather say a designed, coincidence, the special obstacles of lands all but inaccessible are met by the rare faculties of special men. If we may venture to invert the ancient proverb, "God's extremity is man's opportunity." At home, no doubt Charity begins. "He who loveth not his brother whom he hath seen," how can he love the distant savage whom he hath not seen? But, nevertheless, it is the very will and purpose of our Creator, and of our Redeemer, that "His voice shall be heard" even by those most remote from the fold of our own religion, from the fold of our own civilization. It is the very burden of the prophets of old that not only the near, but the far distant, horizon, shall share in the promised regeneration. "The kings of Tarshish and Arabia, Ethiopia stretching out her hands unto God,"[1] were not, in the grand prophetic view of the world, out of mind, because out of sight. They occupied, we may say, the constant background of the picture. It is in the far-

[1] Ps. lxviii. 31; lxxii. 10.

thest and most unlikely regions that the most signal triumphs of truth and goodness were expected to be felt.   Not the crowded city only — not the peaceful hamlet only — but "the wilderness and the solitary place" shall be glad for them: not the garden and the vineyard only, but "the desert shall rejoice and blossom as a rose, and the parched ground shall become a pool, and the thirsty land springs of water, and an highway shall be there, and it shall be called the way of holiness."[1]

II. And now let us turn to the occasion which has led to these thoughts.

I have spoken of the gracious allotment by which the Ruler of the world has brought the inborn sentiment of curiosity and benevolence in the more highly favored parts of the earth to bear on the darkness and isolation of the more remote and obscure.   It would almost seem as if, by a yet further distribution of the same merciful Wisdom, particular tracts of the world had become the vent, the sphere for the energy of particular nations, which have acquired a kind of special parental interest in these neglected lands, these Foundlings, as it were, of the human family.   Such has been the singular lot of Africa.   That vast, impenetrable continent has been, for the last hundred years, the peculiar subject of the inquiry and the philanthropy of England, as in early ages it was to the civilized world of Greece and Rome. The grand secret of geography — the course of that mysterious and beneficent River which has for ages veiled its head, and provoked the curiosity of mankind from Herodotus downwards — has laid a special hold on the imagination of this remote island, of which Herodotus hardly dreamed.   The forlorn condition of the African races has awakened a sympathy in English

[1] Isa. xxxv. 7, 8.

hearts which no Greek or Roman ever knew; and this Abbey teems with the memorials of those who have labored in the cause of the negro and slave.

Such was the sphere to which, in its double aspect, was devoted the life of him who has been adjudged by competent authority the greatest African traveller of all time.

In few men has been developed in a stronger, more persistent form, that passion which we just now analyzed, for penetrating into the unknown regions of the earth. His indomitable resolution has revealed to us, for the first time, that vast waste of Central Africa which, to the contemplation of the geographer, has literally been transformed from a howling wilderness into "the glory of Lebanon." "The parched ground" has, in his hands, "become a pool, and the thirsty land springs of water."[1] The blank of "Unexplored Regions" which, in every earlier map, occupied the heart of Africa, is now disclosed to us, adorned with those magnificent forests; that chain of lakes, glittering (to use the native expression) like "stars" in the desert; those falls, more splendid, we are told, even than Niagara, which no eye of civilized man had before beheld — where, above the far-resounding thunder of the cataract and the flying comets of snow-white foam, and amidst the steaming columns of the ever-ascending spray, on the bright rainbows arching over the cloud, the simple natives had for ages seen the glorious emblem of the everlasting Deity — the Unchangeable seated enthroned above the changeable. To his untiring exertions, continued down to the very last efforts of exhausted nature, we owe the gradual limitation of the basin within which, at last, must be found the hidden fountains that have lured on traveller after traveller, and hitherto baffled

---

[1] Isa. xxxv. 8.

them all. We trust that those way-worn feet now rest not unfitly on the dust of Rennell, the most illustrious of the founders of African exploration. We cannot but rejoice to think how the aged[1] chief of geographical science in our own day, if he could not welcome back alive, would have welcomed back dead to this his last repose the friend in whose existence his own seemed to be bound up.

But there was yet another feeling — deeper than the thirst for knowledge, however insatiable, or the love of adventure, however indomitable — that drew him forth to those distant wilds. There was implanted in him, as there has been from time to time among the sons of men, not merely the love of human kind at large, but the love for that particular race of mankind, which by color, by long oppression, by persistent resistance alike to the inroads and the influence of civilization, has alternately repelled and attracted the more privileged children of Shem and Japheth. "My practice," he said, "has always been to apply the remedy with all possible earnestness, but never allow my own mind to dwell on the dark shades of sin's characters.[2] I have never been able to draw pictures of guilt as if that could awaken Christian sympathy. The evil is there. But all around in this fair creation are traces of beauty, and to turn from those to ponder on deeds of sin cannot promote a healthy state." Most noble and wholesome sentiment — noble and wholesome, not only in Africa but in Europe — not only in heathendom but in Christendom; in dealing both with Christians and with heathens, how often neglected, and yet for any hopeful, energetic action, how indispensable! He loved to dwell on their individual acts of kindness![3] He reiterated

[1] Sir Roderick I. Murchison. [2] Livingstone's *Researches*, i. 200.
[3] *Ibid.* i. 500.

his assurance that their moral perceptions of good and evil are not essentially different from our own.[1]   And out of this sense of his fellowship with them as children of the same Heavenly Father and of the possibility of embracing them within the fold of the same Heavenly Shepherd, there rose, as he wandered on amongst them, the passionate desire, ever mounting to a higher and yet a higher pitch of burning indignation, of fierce determination, to expose and by exposing to strike a fatal blow at that monster evil, which by general testimony is the one prevailing cause of African misery and degradation — the European and Asiatic Slave-trade. He grappled with it, as with the coils of a deadly serpent, and it recognized in him in turn its most formidable foe.   Each strove to strangle each, and in and by that struggle he perished; too soon, alas! for him to know how nearly he had succeeded; not, we trust, too soon for us to secure that his success will be accomplished; and that the work, which in its commencement and its continued inspiration was the brightest side of the name of Wilberforce, shall in its completion shed the chief glory on the name of Livingstone.

Such he was as an Explorer, such as a Philanthropist; what was he as a Missionary?   I have, in part, already answered this question; for all these callings spring from the same root in human nature, from the same inspiration of the Providence of God.   But we should miss one of the chief lessons of the Wanderer's course, if we did not in a few words indicate his peculiar place in the glorious company of those who have devoted their lives to the spread of the Christian faith. It was a peculiar place.   He was a missionary, not only as ordained for that work by the hands of a small group of faithful ministers, some of whom yet live to see how

[1] *Ibid.* i. 158; ii. 277-301.

he followed out the charge which they intrusted to him, but as fashioned for the work by special gifts of the Creator. Preacher he was not, teacher he was not; his was not the eloquence of tongue or pen. His calling was different from this, and by that difference singularly instructive. He brought with him to his task an absolute conviction, not only, as I have said, of the common elements of humanity shared alike by heathen and Christian, but of the common elements of Christianity shared by all Christians. Himself born and bred in one of the seceding communions of Scotland, allied by the nearest domestic ties, and by his own missionary vocation, to one of the chief Nonconformist Churches of England, he yet held himself free to join heart and soul with all others. For the venerable Established Church of his native land, for the ancient Church and Liturgy of this country, with one of whose bishops he labored, as with a brother, through good report and evil; even for the Roman Church of Portugal, and the disciples of Loyola,[1] from whom in theological sentiment he was the furthest removed, he had his good word of commendation. If he freely blamed, he also as freely praised. He remained faithful to the generous motto of the Society which sent him forth. "I never," he said — strange and rare confession — "I never as a missionary felt myself to be either Presbyterian, Episcopalian, or Independent, or called upon in any way to love one denomination less than another."[2] Followed to his grave by the leading Nonconformists of England and the stanchest Presbyterians of Scotland, yet we feel that all the Churches may claim him as their own; that all English-speaking races may regard him as their son; not only those who nurtured his childhood

[1] Livingstone's *Researches*, i. 3, 393, 396, 453, 410, 611, 676.
[2] *Ibid.* i. 6, 118.

and his youth, but those who beyond the Atlantic strove, in his later days, with characteristic energy and with marvellous success, to search out the clew of his wanderings, and to bring back the latest assurance of his lost existence.

Yet, further, he was penetrated, as years rolled on, through and through and more and more with the sense that the work of a missionary is confined to no order or profession of men. As even from his early youth he steadily refused to recognize the opposition between religion and science,[1] so in his later years he hailed the evangelization effected by the trader, the traveller, and the legislator, no less than that effected by the professed evangelist. When, in one of his latest utterances, he expressed with enthusiastic gratitude his conviction that "Statesmen are the best of missionaries," he taught a truth which all Churches, and all societies, not least in our day, may well ponder and plead. But the most powerful missionary agency, as proclaimed both by his teaching and his example, is that of individual character. Most impressive in itself, and in its transparent simplicity, is that testimony which he rendered years ago. "No one ever gains much influence in Africa without purity and uprightness. The acts of a stranger are keenly scrutinized, by both old and young. I have heard women speaking in admiration of a white man because he was pure, and never was guilty of secret immorality. Had he been, they would have known it, and, untutored heathen though they be, would have despised him everywhere."[2]

When he first came among them, he was reverenced as a man born in the depths of the sea; clothed with a lion's mane, controlling the rains of heaven. But, after he had long dwelt among them, he was reverenced

---

[1] Livingstone's *Researches*, i. 4, 5.　　[2] *Ibid.* i. 513, 553; ii. 195.

on far higher grounds. They then learned to appreciate the true above the false supernatural; he was loved
and feared, not as a magician or a spectre, but as a just
and kind benefactor, before whose strong will they
bowed, and by whose faithful affection they were subdued. And when, in after times, the passing stranger
shall look on his grave in this church, and shall be told
that it contains the bones of a wayfaring man who perished in the remote wilds of Africa, that grave itself
will be felt to be the most enduring monument of his
greatness, because the very fact of his burial here, in
the heart of· England, is, as it were, the footmark and
finger-print of the plighted faith and awe-struck veneration which inspired the reverent care alike of heathen,
Mussulman, and Christian around the solitary death-
bed; because it shows, by the most indisputable tokens,
the devotion which must have sustained that small band
of African youths in their arduous enterprise of carrying, through six long months, in spite of all the obstacles of climate, all the inborn prejudices of ancient
superstition, all the machinations of hostile tribes, the
last relics of their departed master.

III. And now one word in conclusion. Those African boys have done their duty. What is ours? We
are told that the last words of the mighty traveller in
his lonely hut were, "I am going home." Home in
both senses — his spirit to the home of his Father which
is in Heaven, his mortal remains, they doubtless felt,
to the home of his fathers in the land of the distant
north. He is come home to us. Cosmopolitan, catholic, almost African as he had become, yet let us not
forget that he was bone of our bone and flesh of our
flesh. He never forgot his Scottish birthplace, or his
English friends. As his predecessor, Mungo Park, be-
guiled the solitary night of travel by repeating the dear

lays of the Border minstrelsy, so David Livingstone delighted to see in the strange scenes of Central Africa an enlarged likeness of the vale of his native Clyde, a reminiscence of the Campsie Hills, and of Arthur's Seat.   He was one of us; he was, if there be amongst my hearers artisans or craftsmen from the loom or the factory, he was especially one of you.   Like Tompion and Graham, like Telford and Stephenson, by whose side he now lies, he was the builder of his own fame and of his own character.   What he was and what he became, that, by God's grace and your own stout hearts, you may be and you may become.   What boy is there that may not be inspired by the example of that vigilant industry by which in his youthful days, amidst the roar of machinery, he picked up sentence after sentence from the book which his spinning-jenny was made to support?   What man is there that may not be at once humbled and encouraged by the record of that patient, almost painful perseverance, with which in declining years, counting the obstacles of time and space for nothing, he toiled, through ceaseless hardship, through ever-multiplying infirmities of body and mind, with the sickening sense of loneliness, desertion, and disappointment, towards the attainment of the work which he had set himself to do, or die?   Who is there that may not be nerved to the performance of duties, high or low, by the sight of the life-long comment on that homely maxim treasured up by him as the family legacy of his rustic ancestor — "Be honest;" or those other words addressed to him from the death-bed of a poor Scottish peasant — "Now, lad, make religion the every-day business of your life, not a thing of fits and starts; for if you do not, temptation and other things will get the better of you."

English lads of every degree, remember that such a

one as yourselves has achieved this famous career —
has won this memorable name. " Strengthen the weak
hands ; confirm the feeble knees. Be strong ; fear not."[1]
Such deeds as these are the Alpine summits and passes
of life ; these are the safety-valves even of our insular
eccentricities. And when we consider the ends for
which his life was given — the advancement of knowledge to the uttermost parts of the earth, the redemption
of a whole continent and race of mankind from the
curse of barbarism and heathenism, and from the curse
of the wickedness of civilized men more hateful than
any savagery or idolatry, then from his grave there
arise not only to us as individuals, but to our whole
nation — I will even say to all the nations of the civilized world — the last prophetic words which, in the
fulness of his vigor, he addressed to that English University which paid special honor to his labor: " I know
that in a few years I shall be cut off in that country
which is now open ; do not let it be shut again. I go
back to Africa to make an open path for commerce and
Christianity. Do you carry out the work that I have
begun. I leave it for you." He leaves it for you,
statesmen and merchants, explorers and missionaries,
to work out the wise fulfilment of these designs. He
leaves it to you, adventurous spirits of the rising generation, to spend your energies in enterprises as noble as
his ; not less noble because they were useful ; not less
chivalrous and courageous because they were undertaken for the glory of God and the good of man.

[1] Isa. xxxv. 3, 4.

CHARLES KINGSLEY.

January 31, 1875.

Watch ye; stand fast in the faith; quit you like men, . . . be strong. — 1 CORINTHIANS xvi. 13.

I<small>T</small> was once remarked to me by a venerable and saintly person, the late Thomas Erskine, of Linlathen, that one of the most striking characteristics of the Psalms was their free, unrestrained appreciation of what we call nature, whether in the moral or the physical world; that they begin with commending the honest, upright man, "the noblest work of God," and they end by calling on every creature, animate or inanimate, to praise the Eternal. This sympathy with the natural man and the natural creation is the more remarkable in the Psalter, because, of all the sacred books of the Old Testament, it is the one which is confessedly the most spiritual, the most intimate in its communion with the Divine. And we learn from this, as from many like characteristics of the Bible, that the modern distinction drawn, from the Middle Ages downward, between nature and grace, between the secular and the spiritual, between the Church and the world, however difficult it may be altogether to avoid such phrases, is not an essential part of the Christian religion, and in no way corresponds to the opposition drawn in the Scriptures between the flesh and the spirit, between the holy and the unholy — is the product of an artificial condition, whether of

214

barbarous or civilized society, which has stunted rather than forwarded the upward growth of the spirit of man towards its Divine original. To these artificial separations the mass of mankind readily accommodate themselves; it is more easy for the worldly to be entirely worldly, and for the religious to be exclusively religious, each in the isolated mediocrity, whether we call it golden or leaden, which tends to produce a false standard of religion and a low estimate of the sphere in which our duties are cast. But it is for this reason that we ought to prize as among God's best gifts any characters, any phenomena, that break through this commonplace level, like mountain crags, and countersect and unite the ordinary divisions of mankind, or, like volcanoes, burst forth at times, and reveal to us something of the central fires within and underneath the crust of custom, fashion, and tradition. Such are those whom we sometimes see, who appear to cynical critics or to superstitious formalists to have chosen a position in life apparently alien to the bent of their inclinations or their antecedents — a religious man, for example, becoming a lawyer or a statesman; a bold, gallant youth, born to be a sailor or a soldier, and led by circumstances into the career of a clergyman. Such, also, are those in whom the inborn flame of genius illuminates, or, perhaps, shatters the earthly vessel which contains it, and, despite of all surrounding obstacles, claims affinity with kindred sparks of light and warmth, wherever they exist.

We all know what and who it is that suggests these thoughts. In that multiplied shadow of sorrow and death which has for the last few months and weeks enlarged its borders beyond usual precedent throughout the land, one brilliant light which shone in our dim atmosphere has been suddenly extinguished: and we cannot allow it thus to pass away without asking ourselves what we have gained by its brief presence amongst us, what we have lost by its disappearance. Others have spoken, and will long speak, on both sides of the Atlantic, of the literary fame of the gifted poet whose dust might well have been mingled with the dust of his brother poets within these walls. Others will speak, in nearer circles, of the close affection which bound the pastor to his flock, and the friend to his friends, and the father to the children, and the husband to the wife, in that romantic home which is now forever identified with his name, and beside which he rests, beneath the yews which he planted with his own hands, and the giant fir trees that fold their protecting arms above. But that which alone is fitting to urge from this place is the moral and religious significance of the remarkable career which has left a spot void, as if where a rare plant has grown, which no art can reproduce, but of which the peculiar fragrance still lingers with those who have ever come within its reach. To the vast congregations which hung upon his lips in this church, to the wide world which looked eagerly for the utterances that no more will come from that burning spirit, to the loving friends who mourn for the sudden extinction of a heart of fire, for the sudden relaxation of the grasp of a hand of iron — I would fain recall some of those higher strains which, amidst manifold imperfections, acknowledged by none more freely than by himself, placed him unquestionably amongst the conspicuous teachers of his age, and gave to his voice the power of reaching souls to which other preachers and teachers addressed themselves in vain.

It has seemed to me that there were three main lessons of his character and career, which may be summed up in the three parts of the Apostolic farewell, which I have chosen for my text — "Watch ye; quit you like men, and be strong; stand fast in the faith."

1. Watch — that is, "be awake, be wakeful;" have your eyes open, the eyes of your senses, the eyes of your mind, the eyes of your conscience.

Such was the wakefulness, such the vigilance, such the devouring curiosity of him whose life and conversation, as he walked amongst ordinary men, was often as of a waker amongst drowsy sleepers, as a watchful sentinel in advance of a slumbering host. The diversity of human character, the tragedies of human life, were always as to him an ever opening, unfolding book. But perhaps even more than to the glories and the wonders of man, he was — far beyond what falls to the lot of most — alive and awake in every pore to the beauty, the marvels of nature. That contrast in the old story of "Eyes" and "No Eyes," was the contrast between him and common men. That eagle eye seemed to discern every shade and form of animal and vegetable life. That listening ear, like that of the hero in the fairy tale, seemed almost to catch the growing of the grass and the opening of the shell. Nature to him was a companion, speaking with a thousand voices. And nature was to him also the voice of God, the face of the Eternal and Invisible, as it can only be to those who study and love and know it. For his was no idle dreamer's pleasure; it was a wakefulness not only to the force and beauty of the outward world, but to the causes of its mysterious operations, to the explanations given by its patient students and explorers. Rarely, if ever, did he join in the headlong condemnation — never in the cowardly fear — of science and scientific men. They seemed to be fellow-workers, and he with them. From this noble confidence in the results of physical research take comfort, O ye of little faith;

open wide your eyes and ears to every breathing of the Divine Spirit, to every accent of the Divine Truth. To you. as to him, let every thing that hath breath praise the Eternal God. Children gathering shells on the sea-shore, fishermen by chalk streams, huntsmen on the bright days of autumn and of winter, watchers of the secret growth of plant and insect, and penetrating stream and shifting soil — fear not to learn and to teach those lessons of holy and innocent enjoyment which awakened in him the constant praise of the Eternal Cause, "for His name only is excellent, and His power above heaven and earth."

When he spoke in his sermons of the "cedars of God," or, "of the lions roaring after their meat from God" — when he spoke in his romance of the tropical skies and forests, which "at last" he saw with the bodily eye, long after he had described them with the imagination of the poet — who does not feel that the contemplation of those wonderful works of God became, as it were, part of the framework and groundwork of his religion, and may, in a measure, become part of ours also?

Who that has heard him speak of the *Benedicite*, the Song of the Three Children, can hear it again without feeling in it that sanctification of science which drew from him such reiterated cries of admiration, regarding it as he did, apocryphal though it be, as the very crown and flower of the Old Testament — the invocation of Nature to bear witness against the idolatry of nature? — "O ye works of the Lord, bless ye the Lord : praise Him and magnify Him forever."

Who, again, can fail to derive a sense of grim consolation — nay, more, of Christian philosophy — as he encounters, even in the bitter, biting blast of our sharp English winter, or yet sharper spring, that moral lesson, that living sermon, breathed into it by those exulting lines which will hardly grow old as long as the east wind blows and the English nation lasts?—

> Welcome, black North-easter,
> O'er the German foam —
> O'er the Danish moorlands,
> From thy frozen home !
>
> .   .   .   .   .   .
>
> Come, as came our fathers,
> Heralded by thee,
> Conquering, from the eastward,
> Lords by land and sea ;
> Come, and strong within us
> Stir the Vikings' blood,
> Bracing brain and sinew —
> Blow, thou wind of God !

2. This leads me to the second part of the Apostolic maxim —"Quit you like men, and be strong," Ἀνδρίζεσθε καὶ κραταιοῦσθε. Surely, if there was any one of our time with whom this precept was associated, even to exaggeration, it was with him who is gone. That famous phrase which he indeed repudiated for himself, but which became inextricably attached to his name, was but the Apostle's word in modern form. No doubt the Bible overflows with sympathy for the sorrowful, the suffering, the feeble ; but it is also full of heart-stirring commands "to play the man," "to be men in understanding," "to quit us like men," and "be strong and very courageous." Christianity, if it is to hold its own and be what it claims to be, must be not only gentle, feminine, and sweet, but masculine, muscular, and strong. But, in fact, the two sides thus represented in the Bible, and certainly as exemplified in him, were not inconsistent ; rather in their best form they are inseparable. No one was more chivalrously respectful towards women, more tender to the weak and suffering. Of all his songs, of all his utterances, that which will

live the longest in the mouths of men is that which is
full, not of the fierce spirit of the Sea-kings, but of the
wailing and weeping cry of simple human pathos —

> O Mary; go and call the cattle home,
> And call the cattle home,
> And call the cattle home,
> Across the sands of Dee.

Even in his rude conflict with the superstitions of
mediæval times half his force was derived from his
kindly appreciation of their nobler side. The "Saint's
Tragedy" would have been to him no tragedy had he
not fully recognized that Elizabeth of Thuringia was
indeed a true Christian saint. And this gave yet more
strength to the determined stand which he made, in
what he deemed an effeminate age, for the vigorous,
courageous, straight-forward aspect of true religion —
the sense that justice and truth and courage were as
essentially saint-like as tenderness, beneficence, and
devotion.

It was this which in his earlier life roused his chivalrous defence of those whom, perhaps in excess, he
thought oppressed and neglected. It was this which
in his later life roused his chivalrous defence of those
whom, also perhaps in excess, he regarded as sacrificed
to popular prejudice. It was this profound feeling
of the rights of the poor and the duties of the rich
that kindled the fiery pages of "Alton Locke" and
of "Yeast."

It was this just impatience of a sickly sentimental
theology which denounced alike the monk of the 13th
century and the fanatical preacher of the 19th. It was
this moral enthusiasm which, in the pages of "Hypa-
tia," has scathed with an everlasting brand the name
of the Alexandrian Cyril and his followers, for their
outrages on humanity and morality in the name of a

hollow Christianity and a spurious orthodoxy. Read, if you would learn some of the most impressive lessons of ecclesiastical history — read and inwardly digest those pages, perhaps the most powerful that he ever wrote, which close that wonderful story by discriminating the destinies which awaited each of its characters as they passed, one after another, "each to his own place."

It was this righteous indignation against what seemed to him the glorification of a tortuous and ambiguous policy, which betrayed him into the only personal controversy in which he was ever entangled; and in which, matched in unequal conflict with the most subtle and dexterous controversialist of modern times, it is not surprising that for the moment he was apparently worsted, whatever we may think of the ultimate issues that were raised in the struggle, and whatever may be the total results of our experiences, before and after, on the main question over which the combat was fought — on the relation of the human conscience to Truth or to authority.

It was this passion for gallant deeds and adventurous daring that created the characters of Lancelot and Thurnall and Amyas Leigh, that revived the heroes of Greece for the young, and the heroes of the Elizabethan age for the old.

And it was this sense that he was a thorough Englishman, one of yourselves, working, toiling, feeling with you and like you — that endeared him to you, O artisans and workingmen of London, to you, O rising youth of England. You know how he desired with a passionate desire that you should have pure air, pure water, habitable dwellings; that you should be able to share the courtesies, the refinements, the elevation of citizens and of Englishmen; and you may therefore trust him

the more when he told you from the pulpit, and still
tells you from the grave, that your homes and your
lives should be no less full of moral purity and light,
that vice and idleness, meanness and dishonesty, are
base, contemptible, and miserable. It is for this that he
speaks to you with especial force, you whom he would
have called the sons of Esau — the frank, the generous,
the self-forgetful; and bids you rise to higher spiritual
spheres. It is for this, also, that the religious world,
the orthodox world, the sons of the believing but yet
timid, wily Jacob, ought to feel that in his presence
they had the best, because the most severe, of monitors,
that in his departure they have lost the most faithful
of friends because the severest of critics.

Quit you like men, and be strong — strong against
your vices as well as your weaknesses, strong in body
and strong in understanding, strong in spirit.

As he lay, the other day, cold in death, like the stone
effigy of an ancient warrior, the "fitful fever" of life
gone, the strength of immortality left, resting as if after
the toils of a hundred battles, this was himself idealized.
From those mute lips there seemed to issue once more
the living words which he spoke ten years ago, before
one who honored him with an unswerving faithfulness
even to the end. "Some say" — thus he spoke in the
chapel of Windsor Castle — "some say that the age of
chivalry is past, that the spirit of romance is dead.
The age of chivalry is never past, so long as there is a
wrong left unredressed on earth, or a man or woman
left to say, I will redress that wrong, or spend my life
in the attempt. The age of chivalry is never past, so
long as we have faith enough to say, God will help me
to redress that wrong, or if not me, He will help those
that come after me, for His eternal Will is to overcome
evil with good. The spirit of romance will never die,

as long as there is a man left to see that the world might and can be better, happier, wiser, fairer in all things than it is now. The spirit of romance will never die, as long as a man has faith in God to believe that the world will eventually be better and fairer than it is now; as long as we have faith, however weak, to believe in the romance of all romances, the wonder of all wonders, in that wonder of which poets have dreamed, and prophets and Apostles have told, each according to his light — that the earth shall be filled with the knowledge of the Lord, that nation shall no more rise in war against nation — that wonder which our Lord Himself bade us pray for, as for our daily bread, and say, Father, Thy kingdom come, Thy will be done on earth as it is in heaven."

3. And this leads me to that clause in the Apostle's warning which I have kept for the last — "Stand fast in the faith." I have hitherto spoken of our lost friend in his natural, God-given genius, not in his professional or pastoral functions. He was what he was, not by virtue of his office, but by virtue of what God had made him in himself. He was, we might almost say, a layman in the guise or disguise, and sometimes hardly in the guise, of a clergyman — fishing with the fishermen, hunting with the huntsmen, able to hold his own in tent and camp, with courtier or with soldier; an example that a genial companion may be a Christian gentleman, that a Christian clergyman need not be a member of a separate caste, and a stranger to the common interests of his countrymen. Yet human, genial, layman as he was, he still was not the less — nay, he was ten times more — a pastor than he would have been had he shut himself out from the haunts and walks of men. He was sent by Providence, as it were, "far off to the Gentiles" — far off, not to other lands

or other races of mankind, but far off from the usual sphere of minister or priest, "to fresh woods and pastures new," to find fresh worlds of thought and wild tracts of character, in which he found a response to himself, because he gave a response to them. Witness the unknown friends that from far or near sought the wise guidance of the unknown counsellor, who declared to them the unknown God after whom they were seeking if haply they might find Him. Witness the tears of the rough peasants of Hampshire, as they crowded round the open grave, to look for the last time on the friend of thirty years, with whom were mingled the passing hunter in his red coat and the wild gipsy wanderers, mourning for the face that they should no more see in forest or on heath. Witness the grief which fills the old cathedral town of my own native county and of the native county of his ancestors, beside the sands of his own Dee, for the recollection of the energy with which he there gathered the youth of Chester round him for teachings of science or religion. Witness the grief which has overcast this venerable church, which in two short years he had made his own, and where all felt that he had found a place worthy of himself, and that in him the place had found an occupant worthy to fill it. In these days of rebuke and faintheartedness, when so many gifted spirits shrink from embarking on one of the noblest, because the most sacred, of all professions, it ought to be an encouragement to be reminded that this fierce poet and masculine reformer deemed his energies not misspent in the high yet humble vocation of an English clergyman; that, however much at times suspected, avoided, rebuffed, he yet, like others who have gone before him, at last won from his brethren the willing tribute of honor and love, which once had been sturdily refused or grudgingly granted.

Scholar, poet, novelist, he yet felt himself to be, with all and before all, a spiritual teacher and guide.

We do not claim for him, what he never claimed for himself, the character of a profound theologian. For the disentanglement of the historical growth of Christian doctrine, so indispensable to the right understanding of its language and its meaning, for the critical researches which have in our time endeavored to trace back to their remote origin the sacred books, and have given new life to their history, philosophy, and poetry —he had little inclination; perhaps he rendered scant justice to those who ventured on that arduous but necessary service of Divine truth, opening the horizon and clearing the path for all who would enter on the sacred ministry of the Word of God, even as the scientific discoveries in which he himself so much delighted did the same for the Works of God.

One fatherly friend and counsellor he followed closely; he felt that to him he owed his own self, and would sometimes playfully say it was enough for him to be to the outside world the interpreter of Frederick Maurice. But with or without that inspiring influence, it was still a noble pastoral function that, amidst all the wavering inconstancy of our time, he called upon the men of his generation, with a steadfastness and assured conviction that of itself steadied and reassured the minds of those for whom he spoke, "to stand fast in the faith." "In the faith." On what special form of the Christian faith did he most insist? In what special fastness and fortress of the ancient Catholic faith of former times, or of our own English Protestant faith, did he plant his foot with this undoubting firmness? Doubtless for him, as for many, the old walls seemed sufficient for the coming strife, and he cared not to repair their breaches; the old vessels seemed to him

strong enough to contain the new wine, and he cared
not to make new vehicles even for the fermentation of
the "yeast" which he himself had stirred. But still
there were two main doctrines — old as eternity, yet
forever needing to be renewed with each age of the
world — which he held with a fervor and tenacity all
his own, with a freshness and a vigor that amounted
almost to the originality of genius — which, in his
teaching, enlightened and controlled and colored even
the most antique and the most trite of the ordinary
teachings of past or present times.

One of these fixed, paramount, over-ruling persua-
sions was the belief, often forgotten, often derided,
sometimes even severely discountenanced, that the
main part of the religion of mankind and of Christendom should consist in the strict fulfilment of the duty
of man, which is the will of God. Alike in the Old
Testament and in the New, he delighted to bring
together the golden passages which exalt the law, the
statutes, the testimonies, the commandments of God;
and he set forth their ancient meaning, for our modern
days, in his own plain, strong English words, which
none can mistake or forget, and which have the rare
merit of being at once perfectly intelligible and perfectly true.

Nothing can be a substitute for purity or virtue.
" Man will always try to find a substitute for it. But
let no man lay any such flattering unction to his soul.
The first and last business of every living being, whatever be his station, party, creed, tastes, duties, is Morality. Virtue, virtue, always virtue! Nothing that man
ever invents will absolve him from the universal necessity of being good as God is good, righteous as God is
righteous, and holy as God is holy."

And this leads me to the other doctrine, which also

shall be stated in his own words, as we heard him from this place, when he delivered his farewell sermon before starting for the American continent, in conclusion of that brilliant and solemn course to which, Sunday after Sunday, the eager multitudes came to hear the new preacher of our Abbey.

"And now," he said, "new friends, and almost all friends unknown, and alas! never to be known by me, you who are to me as people floating down a river, while I, the preacher, stand upon the bank and call, in hope that some of you may catch some word of mine ere the great stream shall bear you out of sight — oh catch, at least, catch this one word, the last which I shall speak here for many months, and which sums up all which I have been trying to say to you of late. Fix in your minds, or rather ask God to fix in your minds, this one idea of an absolutely good God; good with all forms of goodness which you respect and love in man; good as you, and I, and every honest man, understand the plain word good. Slowly you will acquire that grand and all-illuminating idea; slowly and most imperfectly at best; for who is mortal man that he should conceive and comprehend the goodness of the infinitely good God? But see, then, whether, in the light of that one idea, all the old-fashioned Christian ideas about the relations of God to man — whether a Providence, Prayer, Inspiration, Revelation; the Incarnation, the Passion, and the final triumph, of the Son of God — whether all these, I say, do not begin to seem to you, not merely beautiful, not merely probable, but rational and logical and necessary moral consequences from the one idea of an Absolute and Eternal Goodness, the Living Parent of the Universe. And so I leave you to the Grace of God."

So he spoke, standing here as I stand now, as on the

banks of this great river of life. So he speaks to us
still, standing on the farther bank of another vaster,
deeper, darker river, the river of death. Whether he
sees us or not, we know not; whether in that light into
which we trust he has passed, those strong impassioned
words may have become weak and pale; how far, "when
that which is perfect has come, that which is partial in
them shall vanish away," like the half-formed thoughts
and inarticulate utterances of a child, we know not;
but this we cannot and we will not doubt, that as they
were his last message to us at that last parting, so they
contain in substance and spirit the message which he
would have delivered to us down to his last moment
on earth, and, if possible, beyond it. When the shadows of death were closing him round, still, we are told,
the same beatific vision of that which alone makes the
blessedness of heaven was before his failing sight —
"How beautiful," he said, "how beautiful is God!"

Stand fast, O my brethren, stand fast in that faith,
in the faith that God is good, and that man, to be well-
pleasing to God, must be good also. That faith which
is indeed the "Good news of God" to man, "that Name
of the Eternal," was to him "a strong tower, in which
the righteous could take refuge and be safe" — "the
stronghold and the castle to which he would always
resort," from which he derived whatever strength and
force there was in his creed or in his life.

Stand ye fast in this faith, O wavering, perplexed,
anxious souls, and you shall not be shaken by doubt,
nor undermined by superstition. Stand fast in this
faith, O sorrowing, suffering, bereaved friends, who feel
that in the removal of those whom you have loved or
admired the splendor of your life is dimmed, and you
shall not be sorry as men without hope for those that
sleep in Him who is Perfect Grace and Perfect Truth.

Stand fast in this faith, and by it correct, enlarge, enlighten, strengthen, whatever other faith you have.

And not only stand fast in it, but follow it onward
whithersoever it leads you. Be not only "steadfast
and unmovable," but be also "abounding," overflowing
in the ever-increasing "work of the Lord" which lies
before us all, "forasmuch as you know" and have seen
in him that his labor was "not in vain in the Lord."

On his last journey in America, in answer to one who
had wished him long life, he replied: — "That is the
last thing that I desire. It may be that, as one grows
older, one acquires more and more the painful consciousness of the difference between what *ought* to be done
and what *can* be done, and sits down more quietly when
one gets on the wrong side of fifty, and lets others start
up to do for us the things we cannot do for ourselves.
But it is the highest pleasure that a man can have who
has turned down the hill at last (and to his own exceeding comfort) to believe that younger spirits will rise up
after him, and catch the lamp of truth, as in the old
lamp-bearing race of Greece, out of his hand before it
expires, and carry it on to the goal with swifter and
more even feet."

The lamp has fallen from that hand: it is for us, for
you, to hand it on, with increased light, to the generations yet to come.

THE RELIGIOUS ASPECT OF GEOLOGY.

February 28, 1875, after the funeral of Sir Charles Lyell.

The earth was without form and void; and darkness was upon the face of the deep. And the Spirit of God moved upon the face of the waters. — GENESIS i. 2.

THESE words, from the Book of Genesis, of which the lessons are now in our church services drawing to a close, convey a sense wider than their mere literal transcript. They express the transition from that gulf which by the ancient Greeks was called " Chaos," to that grace and order which, under the name of " Kosmos," has been adopted by a famous modern philosopher to describe the system of the universe. The words which portray the formless void of the earth, convey in the original, in the most forcible manner, the image of the old discordant elements of conflict, whilst the word used for the moving of the Divine Spirit on the face of the waters expresses the gentle brooding and yearning as of a parent-bird over the troubled deep.[1] The language, however poetic, childlike, parabolical, and unscientific, yet impresses upon us the principle in the moral and the material world, that the law of the Divine operation is the gradual, peaceful, progressive redaction and development of discord into harmony, of confusion into order, of darkness into light.

To unfold and to exemplify that law is in various

---

[1] " Dove-like sat brooding o'er the vast abyss." — Milton's *Paradise Lost*, Book 1.

degrees one of the chief missions of the nobler souls in whom the Divine Spirit, according to the diversity of its gifts, leads on the human race towards perfection. It has so chanced that within this short month of February, by a most unusual coincidence of mortality, twice have the gates of this Abbey been opened to pay the last honors to two men, widely apart in all else, but alike in the fulfilment of this Divine Law — the one the acknowledged chief[1] of the English musicians of our time; the other, who was yesterday laid in his grave, the acknowledged chief of those who have devoted themselves to the study of our mother-earth.

I. Suffer me before passing to this, the main subject of our thoughts, to say a few words of the first of these two gifted persons; the more so, that his special work was no unapt commentary on the sacred text, no unsuitable prelude to that which shall follow.

Of all the branches of art and letters, none more reveals the hidden capacities of the human soul, or of "the fearful and wonderful" structure of the human frame, than the slow and yet certain process through which from the simplest and the most barbarous sounds that Art, which both heathens and Christians have not scrupled to call Divine, has called into being worlds of melody and harmony, which have entranced the ear, and calmed the heart, and elevated the mind of succeeding generations of mankind, gaining in volume and complexity and force, as time has rolled on. The spirit which brooded over the rude lyre of Orpheus or the rough harp of David, is the same spirit which breathes through the anthems of our great cathedrals or the choral strains of our oratorios; but what a pathos, what a majesty, what a glory, of which David[2] never dreamed,

---

[1] Sir William Sterndale Bennett, who was buried in the Abbey on Feb. 6, 1875.

[2] "I think," said Luther, in the sixteenth century, "that if David

has been inspired into these sounds, by the genius of a Purcell or a Beethoven, a Handel or a Mendelssohn! Some of us may recall the well-known words in which the contrast of this development has been drawn out by one whose insight into the secrets of musical art, and whose complete mastery over the musical cadences of our English tongue are unquestioned, however much we may lament the uncertain tone of his theological trumpet, or wonder at the oblique march of his wayward genius.

There are seven notes in the scale; make them fourteen; yet what a slender outfit for so vast an enterprise! What science brings so much out of so little? Out of what poor elements does some great master in it create his new world! . . . Is it possible that that inexhaustible evolution and disposition of notes, so rich yet so simple, so intricate yet so regulated, so various yet so majestic, should be a mere sound, which is gone and perishes? Can it be that those mysterious stirrings of heart, and keen emotions, and strange yearnings after we know not what, and awful impressions from we know not whence, should be wrought in us by what is unsubstantial, and comes and goes, and begins and ends in itself? No, they have escaped from some higher sphere; they are the out- pourings of eternal harmony in the medium of created sound; they are echoes from our home; they are the voice of Angels; or the Magnificat of Saints; or the living laws of Divine Governance; or the Divine Attributes; something are they besides themselves which we cannot compass, which we cannot utter — though mortal man, and he, perhaps not otherwise distinguished above his fellows, has the gift of eliciting them.[1]

To elicit these marvels, to elevate that glorious art, was the mission of the gentle musician who, three weeks ago, was laid beside those who, in earlier days in this church or nation, in the words of the sacred[2] writers, have " handled the harp and organ," and " found out

rose from the dead, he would wonder much to find how far we have advanced in music."

[1] Dr. Newman's *University Sermons*, pp. 348, 349.

[2] Gen. iv. 21; Ecclus. xliv. 5.

musical tunes;" by such heavenly strains he soothed
his own soul and the souls of others, when they have
sat down "wearied with the journey"[1] of life; and
again and again will his memory be recalled to us, as
we hear the sacred melody on which he has written, as
on waves of light, those Divine words which describe,
as it were, the second creation of the world, which ought
to stand as the principle of all Christian worship — "God
is a spirit, and they that worship Him must worship Him
in spirit and in truth."

II. I have said that this passing allusion to the departed musician, this indication of the latent capacities
for spiritual emotion wrapped up even in abstract and
inanimate things, in elements seemingly without form
and void, is no unfitting prelude to the consideration of
that study of nature, of which he who has just followed
to the same long home was so bright an example. A
celebrated teacher of our age, to whom music was a
sealed book, but to whom objects of natural beauty were
full of enjoyment, used to say, "Wild flowers are my
music;"[2] and so, in like manner, to all students of
nature, earth and sea, with their hidden harmonics, have
indeed a music of their own, which, like the secrets of
of the vocal art, have to be drawn out by the fire of
genius, by the persevering vigilance, by the active search,
of scientific study. In this spirit I propose to call your
attention for a brief space to the religious aspect of
"that noble science of Geology," which a great historian
has called "the boast of our age,"[3] and of which the
words of the text might well, especially in regard to
the work of him whom we now commemorate, be called
the first germ and the abiding motto.

---

[1] *The Woman of Samaria*, by Sir W. Sterndale Bennett.
[2] Arnold's *Life*, p. 185.
[3] Hallam's *Hist. of Literature*, vol. iii. pt. iv. ch. 8.

It is well known that when the science of Geology first arose, it was involved in endless schemes of attempted reconciliation with the letter of Scripture. There were, there are perhaps still, two modes of reconciliation of Scripture and science, which have been each in their day attempted, and have each totally and deservedly failed. One is the endeavor to wrest the words of the Bible from their natural meaning, and force them to speak the language of science. Of this, the earliest, and perhaps the most memorable, example was set by the Greek translators in the time of the Ptolemies — the Seventy, as they are called. They came, in the course of their[1] translation, to that verse of Leviticus[2] containing the well-known stumbling-block which they probably were the first to discern, which speaks of the hare as one of the animals that chew the cud. In the old world, before the birth of accurate observation, that which had the appearance of rumination was mistaken for the reality, and was so described. But, by the time that the Greek translation of the Bible was undertaken, the greatest naturalist of antiquity, the world-famous Aristotle, had already devoted his sagacious mind to the study of the habits of animals, and through his writings the true state of the case had become known in Alexandria. The venerable scholars who were at work on the translation were too conscientious to reject the clear evidence of science; but they were too timid to allow the contradiction to appear, and therefore, with the usual rashness of fear, they boldly interpolated the word "NOT" into the sacred text, and thus, as they thought, reconciled it to science by making the whole passage mean exactly the reverse of that which was intended. This is the earliest instance of the falsification of Scripture to meet the demands of

[1] The *Septuagint* version.   [2] Lev. xi. 6.

science; and it has been followed in later times by the various efforts which have been made to twist the earlier chapters of the Book of Genesis into apparent agreement with the last results of geology — representing days not to be days, morning and evening not to be morning and evening, the deluge not to be the deluge, and the ark not to be the ark. On the other hand, there has sprung up in later times the equal error of falsifying science to meet the supposed requirements of the Bible. Of this, the most signal example was when the discoveries of Galileo were condemned by the Supreme Judge of faith and morals in the Roman Church, and when the Jesuits in their edition of Newton's " Principia " announced in the preface that they were constrained to treat the theory of gravitation as a fictitious hypothesis, because else it would conflict with the " decrees of the Popes against the motion of the earth." This mode of reconciliation has also been tried in our times, at each successive advance of science. Every generation of the ecclesiastical or religious world has been tempted to the hazardous enterprise of denying the voice of God as He speaks to us in His works, and in His laws, and often the plain conclusions of careful observation have been set aside as impious and dangerous.

But there is another reconciliation of a higher kind which, we humbly trust, will never fail — or rather not a reconciliation at all, but an acknowledgment of the affinity, the identity which exists between the *spirit* of Science and the *spirit* of the Bible. And this is of two kinds — first, there is the likeness of the general spirit of the truths of science to the general spirit of the truths of the Bible; and, secondly, there is the likeness of the general spirit of the method of science to the general spirit of the method of the Bible.

1. Let me exemplify both of these in the instance of
Geology, and of the illustrious student of geology who
has just passed away from us.   First, let us see what
is the geological truth which he was the chief instrument in clearly setting forth and establishing on a new
foundation.   It was the doctrine, wrought out by careful, cautious inquiry in all parts of the world, that the
frame of this earth was gradually brought into its
present condition, not by violent or sudden convulsions,
but by slow and silent action, the same causes operat-
ing, as we see operate now, through a long succession
of ages, stretching back beyond the memory or imagination of man.   We have already indicated that there
need be no question raised whether or not this doctrine
agrees with the letter of the Bible.   We do not expect
that it should; for if there were no such scientific researches and conclusions, we now know perfectly well,
from our increased insight into the earlier Biblical records, that they were not, and could not be, literal and
prosaic matter-of-fact descriptions of the beginning of
the world, of which, as of its end, "no man knoweth,"
or can conceive except by figure and parable.   It is
now clear to diligent students of the Bible, that the
first and second chapters of Genesis contain two narratives of the Creation, side by side, differing from each
other in almost every particular of time and place and
order.   It is now certain that the vast epochs demanded
by scientific observation are incompatible both with the
six thousand years of the Mosaic chronology, and the
six days of the Mosaic Creation.   No one now infers
from the Psalms that "the earth is set so fast that it
cannot be moved," or that "the sun" actually "comes
forth as a bridegroom from his chamber" — or that
"the morning stars sang" with an audible voice at the
dawn of the creation.   To insist on these details as

historical or scientific, is as contrary to the style and character of the sacred books themselves as it is to the undoubted facts of science. But when from these we rise to the spirit, the ideal, the general drift and purpose of the Biblical accounts, we feel ourselves in an atmosphere of moral elevation which meets the highest requirements that philosophy can make; we find exactly that affinity which we should expect to find between the most sacred, the most majestic of ancient records (even if we say no more), and the most certain and sublime of modern discoveries.

I have often spoken before of this inner harmony between the highest flights of Scripture and the highest flights of science or genius. Look at the discoveries of Geology in this light, and they will appear to us not only not irreligious, but as filling the old religious truths with a new life of their own, and receiving from those truths a hallowing glory in return. When the historian of our planet points out to us that the successive layers of the earth's surface were formed not by strange and sudden shocks, but by the same constant action of wind and wave, of falling leaves, and silent stream, and floating ice, and rolling stones, that we see in operation daily before our eyes; that there were not separate centres of creation, but one primal law, which formed and governs all created beings; what is this but the echo of those voices which of old declared that "in the beginning the heavens and the earth were created,"[1] not by conflicting deities, but by One supreme and indivisible; which told us that "God's word endureth forever in heaven;" that "His faithfulness continues throughout all generations;" that "as He established the earth, so it abideth;" that "all things continue according to His ordinance;"[2] that "He who

---

[1] Gen. i. 1.   [2] Ps. cxix. 89-91.

laid out the foundation of the world above the waters, for His mercy endureth forever," is the same as He who "daily giveth food to all flesh," for it is the same mercy that endureth forever;"[1] that "He has given a law which shall not be broken." And are we not reminded that long ago there was one who stood in the cave of the cliffs of Horeb, and waited for the sign of the Divine operations,[2] and that it was then borne in upon his soul that the Lord was not in the earthquake, the hurricane, or the fire, but in the still small whispering murmur of the gentle air, and the silence of the desert? Do we not in those deep descents into the ocean gulfs, those subtle transformations of land and sea and all that in them is, discern a reflex of that Presence which has "searched us out and known us;" which "did see our substance yet being imperfect, and in whose book were written all the members" of the human race, and its habitation, "which day by day were fashioned while as yet there was none of them?"[3] And when, further, we contemplate the vast infinitudes of time and space, that long ascending order, that gradual, insensible progress, which Geology demands, do we not feel that much as the Bible may contain of detail and expression and imagery running in another direction, yet its general, though not its uniform teaching, its highest, though not its constant utterances, would encourage us to believe that the world is something deeper and wider than we in our narrow view should imagine it to be; that creation is something which reaches further back and deeper down than our childish and limited notions would suggest to us; that the distance of its first beginning, however remote, melts into a distance remoter still? It is only the doubly doubtful Second Book of the Maccabees[4] which contains the text that the world was made

---

[1] Ps. cxxxvi. 6, 25.   [2] 1 Kings xix. 9-12.   [3] Ps. cxxxix. 1-16.
[4] 2 Macc. vii. 28.

"of things that were not."   The earlier loftier teaching
of the Bible enters into no such metaphysical labyrinth.
There "deep still calls to deep."   There it is still the
"earth without form and void, and darkness gathering
over the face of the deep."   In the Prophets of the
Bible, as in the prophets of Science, there is a sense,
dim and vague, yet strong and earnest, of the infinite
variety of the treasure-house of creation, the infinite
patience and perseverance of the Creator, "A thousand
years in Thy sight are but as yesterday, and one day
as a thousand years." [1]   "My father worketh hitherto
and I work." [2]   "Oh the depth of the riches both of
the wisdom and knowledge of God!   How unsearchable
are His judgments, and His ways past finding out!" [3]
"Where wast thou when I laid the foundations of the
earth? whereupon are the foundations thereof fastened,
or who laid the corner-stone thereof? . . . Hast thou
entered into the springs of the sea, or walked in the
search of the depth?" [4]   "There is one glory of the
sun, and another glory of the moon, and another glory
of the stars.   The first is that which is natural, and
afterward that which is spiritual." [5]

Surely to expressions such as these, however little
they can be pressed into scientific exactness, the cor-
relative theory of science is not that which limits the
duration of earth to the space of a few brief centuries,
but that which expands it to illimitable ages.   Surely
the view which shows the long preparation of the earth
for man gives a grander prelude to his appearance on
this globe, than that which makes him coeval with the
beasts that perish.   Surely the intimations of future
progress, which are suggested by observing the latent
faculties wherewith he is endowed, are more consonant

[1] Ps. xc. 2; 2 Pet. iii. 8.   [2] John v. 17.   [3] Rom. xi. 33.
[4] Job xxxviii. 4–16.   [5] 1 Cor. xv. 41–46.

to the hope of a glorious and fruitful immortality than the view which regards him as a stationary being, knowing at once all that he can ever know, and contented with the narrow horizon that is alone open to him. All honor to the peaceful conqueror who, by years of unhasting, unresting research, annexed these new provinces of thought to the knowledge of man, and therefore to the glory of God! All honor to the herald and archæologist of our race, who has unrolled in all its length and breadth the genealogy of the antiquity of man, and the antiquity of his habitation! All honor to the bold yet reverent touch which, in the Temple of the Most High, not made with hands, rent asunder from the top to the bottom the veil that concealed its full proportions, and revealed its ever-widening, ever-lengthening vistas backward into the farthest past of memory, and forward to the endless future of hope. Not the limitation, but the amplification of the idea of God, is the result of the labors of such a student. Not the descent, but the ascent of man is the final result of his speculations. If, as he used to say, "we have in our bones the chill" of that contracted view in which we had been brought up, yet the enlargement which he effected for the view of the past ought to give a warmth, a fire to our heart of hearts, to our soul of souls, in proportion as we feel that we are not the creatures of yesterday, but "the heirs of all the ages" — even the ages that cannot be numbered, and of worlds that have perished in the making of us; the ancestors, let us trust, of those who, compared with us, shall seem to have attained to "a new heaven and a new earth," wherein "old things shall have passed away, and all things shall have become new,"[1] under the breath of that Spirit which is forever brooding over the face of the troubled universe.

[1] 2 Pet. iii. 13; 2 Cor. v. 17.

2. This leads me to the likeness of the general spirit of the method of the philosophic geologist, and the general spirit of the method of the Bible. If there be any one point in which the whole structure of the Bible and the whole plan of its teaching is a model to the student, whether of nature, of man, or of God, it is the slow "increasing purpose" of Revelation, through " sundry times and divers manners," working as if with the persistence of unconscious instinct and the patience of deliberate will towards the fulness of time, with the constant warning to each succeeding age to have the eyes and ears of its mind open to the reception of Light and Truth. Thus, as in art, so in science, the whole race of mankind, and each individual member of it, must aim to deserve that proud yet lowly title by which the Founder of Christianity called His followers — Disciples, that is, "scholars," learners even to the very end; scholars bent on the attainment of that Truth in all its parts, "to bear witness to which He was born, and for which cause He came into the world."[1]   To invest the pursuit of Truth with the sanctity of a religious duty, to make Truth and Goodness meet together in one holy fellowship, is the high reconciliation of Religion and Science for which all scientific and all religious men should alike labor and pray.   "Sacred, no doubt," said one of the greatest of astronomers, "sacred is the authority of the Fathers; sacred was Lactantius, who denied the earth's rotundity; sacred was Augustine, who admitted the earth to be round, but denied the antipodes; sacred is the authority of the moderns, who admit the smallness of the earth, yet deny its motion; yet, more sacred to me than all these is — TRUTH."   So spoke Kepler.   Yes; more sacred than all things is Truth, next after or along with Good-

---

[1] John xviii. 37.

ness, and therefore to be sought calmly, temperately, deliberately, as in the Holy of Holies and in the presence of the Most High.

Such a union of patient research and reverential piety has been the special glory of the great school of English Geology. Amidst all the alarms of the religious world, and all the embitterments of the scientific world, it has been our just pride in England that the two pioneers of this newborn science, at a time when it had to fight its way against prejudice, and ignorance, and apathy, towards its present hard-won place, were honored dignitaries of the National Church. One was the illustrious Professor of Cambridge, whose generous heart, and brilliant fancy, and heavenward hope enlightened and warmed his whole being, and continued to irradiate a life prolonged beyond the allotted term of man's existence. The other was the eager, indefatigable student, who left his chair at Oxford only to preside over this ancient Church, whose very stones and dust were dear to him, but by him examined and sifted as never before by hand or eye of English layman or ecclesiastic. And now within these walls, beneath the monument of Woodward, the earliest of English geologists, lies the latest of that distinguished group, the friend of Sedgwick and the pupil of Buckland. The tranquil triumph of Geology, once thought so dangerous, now so quietly accepted by the Church, no less than by the world, is one more proof of the groundlessness of theological panics in the face of the advances of scientific discovery.

Of him, who is thus laid to rest, if of any one of our time, it may be said that he followed Truth with a zeal as sanctified as ever fired the soul of a missionary, and with a humility as child-like as ever subdued the mind of a simple scholar. For discovering facts, confirming or rectifying conclusions, there was no journey too distant to undertake. Never did he think of his own fame or name in comparison with the scientific results which he sought to establish. From early youth to extreme old age it was to him a solemn religious duty to be incessantly learning, constantly growing, fearlessly correcting his own mistakes, always ready to receive and reproduce from others that which he had not in himself. Science and Religion for him not only were not divorced, but were one and indivisible. He felt with another eminent votary of science in our time, that this divorce, unhappily so welcome to some on either side, is " a mere pretence," neither true in fact, neither Christian nor philosophic in idea. [1] " The spiritual world and the intellectual world are no more to be separated in this fashion," than are the secular and the religious, the Church and the Commonwealth. The instinct which impels us to seek for harmony between the highest truths of science and the highest truths of the Bible is an instinct far nobler and truer than that which would seek to part them asunder. In this higher instinct, he who has departed fully shared. The great religious problems of our time were never absent from his mind. The infinite possibilities of nature gave him fresh ground for his unshaken hope in the unknown, immortal future. His conviction of the peaceful, progressive combination of natural causes towards the formation of our globe filled him with a profound and ever profounder sense of " the wonder and the glory of this marvellous universe." The generous freedom allowed to religious inquiry in the National Church, the cause of humanity in the world at large, were to him as dear as though they were his own personal and peculiar concern. With that one faithful, beloved, and beautiful soul, who, till within the last two

---

[1] The Duke of Argyll in *The Reign of Law*, pp. 57, 58.

years of his life, shared all his joys and all his sorrows, all his labors and all his fame, he walked the lofty path, "which the vulture's eye hath not seen, nor the lion's whelp trodden "[1] — the pathway of the just, "that shineth more and more unto the perfect day," in which we humbly trust that they are now at last reunited in the presence of that light which they both so sincerely sought.

There is an unusual solemnity in the last thought of one who passes into that Eternal World, on which, as in a shadow or mirror, he had so long and anxiously meditated, in the unknown ages of which he was, as it were, the first discoverer. That "lofty and melancholy Psalm," as a famous historian has called it, which ancient tradition has ascribed to Moses, the man of God, well represents the feeling of one grown gray with vast experience, who here takes his stand at the close of his earthly journeyings, and contrasts the fleeting generations of men with the huge forms of the granite mountains at whose feet they have so long wandered, and contrasts yet more mountains and men alike with the eternity of Him who existed and exists before, above, and beyond them all. "Lord, Thou hast been our refuge, our dwelling-place from generation to generation. Before the mountains were brought forth, or ever the earth and the world were made, from everlasting to everlasting Thou art God."[2] Whether or not it was the funeral hymn of the Lawgiver of Israel, it has become the funeral hymn of the world. And it seems to sum up with peculiar force the inner life of the Christian philosopher, who concluded his chief work with the contrast of "the relations which subsist between the finite powers of man and the attributes of an Infinite and Eternal Being,"[3] who felt persuaded that after all

[1] Job xxviii. 7.   [2] Psalm xc. 1, 2. (See Ewald.)
[3] *Principles of Geology*, ii. 621.

the magnificent discoveries and speculations on mountain and valley, on earth and sea and sky, the religious sentiment still remained the grandest and most indestructible instinct of the human race; strongest, most sublime in those individuals of our race that are most fully and perfectly developed. At such a solemn farewell to the benefactors of mankind, we feel that the True, the Just, the Good is the Eternal Principle and Cause which outlasts and outweighs all outward and visible things. "Before the mountains were brought forth, or ever the earth and the world were made, from everlasting to everlasting Thou art God."

THE RELIGIOUS USE OF WISDOM.

August 1, 1875, being the Sunday preceding the funeral of Connop Thirlwall, late Bishop of St. David's.

Where shall wisdom be found? and where is the place of understanding? — JOB xxviii. 12.

THIS chapter of Job, appointed to be sung for the anthem this afternoon, is not an unworthy glorification of that grace and gift of God, to which sometimes we pay little heed, but which in the Bible occupies so conspicuous a place—the gift of Wisdom—the religious use of Wisdom. Not only the Book of Job, but the Book of Proverbs, the Book of Ecclesiastes, the Book of Wisdom, the Book of Ecclesiasticus, and the character and history of Solomon, which have just been completed in our Sunday services, are full of it. In the old Calendar of Lessons, in this respect perhaps unduly reduced, a larger proportion of Scripture was taken on Sundays from the Book of Proverbs, in the description of Wisdom, than was taken from almost any other book of the Old Testament; more than is devoted to the commendation even of Faith, or Mercy, or Truth, or Love. And one name of Christ Himself, which has given its title to the greatest of Eastern Churches, is the Eternal Wisdom.

I. What, then, is this grace of wisdom, and why is it so highly exalted? Let us take the words of the text. "Where," in the Divine economy, "shall wisdom be found? where is the" religious "place of understanding?"

246

1. First, wisdom, as described in the Bible, is that eager desire of knowledge which rests unsatisfied so long as a corner of darkness is left unexplored; that passion for learning which, like the fleets of Solomon, penetrated into the furthermost regions of the then known world, and brought back from the furthermost shores the stores of natural history, and which asked and answered questions from all the surrounding nations, and which dived, as in the Book of Job, into the mysteries of the creation, " making the weight for the winds, a decree for the rain, a way for the lightning of the thunder;"[1] "entering into the treasures of the snow, and seeing the treasures of the hail," examining "out of whose womb came the ice, and who gendered the hoary frost of heaven."[2] Such a grand inquisitiveness it is which sends out our ships to the Arctic seas, which united in the same tragical and romantic story the beloved chief, the gallant crews, and the devoted and venerable widow, who herself has just departed, and left her memorial behind her in our midst.[3] That joint career alike of husband and of wife was one illustration amongst a thousand of the elevating, inspiring result of efforts after knowledge. It showed how, instead of drying up the heart, or depressing the moral nature, a thirst for truth enkindles and elevates. A spirit of inquiry may, no doubt, become frivolous and useless. But that is not its heaven-born mission, and it was no profane or worldly critic, but the holy author of the "Saints' Everlasting Rest," who commended, by precept as by example, the religious duty of learning all that can be possibly learnt of God, of man, or of

---

[1] Job xxviii. 25, 26. [2] Job xxxviii. 22, 29.

[3] The monument to the memory of Sir John Franklin was erected in the Abbey July 31, 1875, in the week following Lady Franklin's death, and the day preceding this sermon.

nature.   Listen to some of these stimulating injunctions.   "He that can see God in all things, and hath all things sanctified by the love of God, should above all things value each particle of knowledge of which such holy use may be made, as we value every grain of gold."   "Every degree of knowledge tendeth to more; and every known truth befriendeth others; and like fire tendeth to the spreading of our knowledge to all neighbor truths that are intelligible."   "Look well to all things, or to as many as possible.   When half is unknown, the other half is not half known."   Such is the value, the eternal value, of learning.

2. But there is another kind of wisdom — and far the larger part — which, although it may be united with learning, is also often found quite apart from it, and which furnishes most of the elements which go to make up the biblical, the religious, idea of wisdom.   The exercise of "practical judgment and discretion;" "a wise and understanding heart to discern between good and bad;" "largeness of heart" to take in the varying affairs of men; the capacity for "justice, judgment, and equity;" — this also, if the Bible, if human experience, is true, is a heavenly gift of the first magnitude.   No doubt, wisdom is not of itself goodness.   The Proverbs are not the Psalms, Solomon was not David.   But wisdom is next door to goodness, and religion leans upon her.   How many benevolent schemes have been endangered, how many missions foiled, how many bitter controversies engendered and perpetuated, how many wild superstitions encouraged, simply because wisdom has not been allowed to have her perfect work; because men have refused to acknowledge that common sense is a Christian grace; because the children of light have been in their generation less wise than the children of this world; because we have failed to bear in mind for

how many evils the real remedy is to be found, not in ancient precedent, or popular agitation, or resplendent principles, but in a few homely maxims such as those of the Book of Proverbs, a few grains of discretion, sense, and foresight! What a new aspect would be put upon the idleness, the selfishness, the extravagance of youth, if we could be taught to think not only of its sinfulness, but of its contemptible folly, if we could be induced not only to confess how often we were miserable sinners, but also how often we have been miserable fools; what a great security for human welfare if we were to set ourselves not only to become better, but wiser, not only to gain holiness and virtue, but, as Solomon says, to "get wisdom, get understanding;" to pray that He Who giveth liberally and upbraideth not would, in addition to His other blessings, "give us wisdom!"

And now may I exemplify these remarks in the life of one who has this week been removed from amongst us, and who will shortly be laid within these walls, in whom both sides of this Divine gift were shown forth in no ordinary degree? In the opening of that fine recapitulation of the different gifts of God, which we heard in the Epistle of this day, the Apostle says, "To one is given by the Spirit the word of wisdom; to another the word of knowledge by the same Spirit." To the great scholar and prelate who is gone we may truly say that by the same Divine Spirit the word of knowledge and the word of wisdom were given in equal proportions.

II. Let [1] me freely speak to you for a few moments of this patriarch of our national Church in his two ca-

---

[1] The latter portion of this sermon has been already printed as a Preface to the Bishop's *Letter to a Friend*, edited by the late Dean of Westminster.

pacities of a universal scholar and of a wise ecclesiastical statesman.

1. Of that thirst for knowledge in all its parts of which the Bible speaks, of the mastery of all ancient and modern learning, few, if any, have been more wonderful examples than he, who from his eleventh till his threescore and eighteenth year was always gathering in fresh stores of understanding. Of him, as of Solomon, it might be said, " Thy soul covered the whole earth." [1] There was hardly a civilized language which he had not explored both in its structure and its literature. He was the chief of that illustrious group of English scholars who first revealed to this country the treasures of German research, and the insight which that research had opened into the mysterious origin of the races, institutions, and religions of mankind. Many are now living who never can forget the moment when in the translation of " Niebuhr's Roman History " they for the first time felt that they had caught a glimpse into the dark corners of ancient times before the dawn of history had begun. There are many who gathered their knowledge of the Grecian world from the first history which brought all the stores of modern learning to bear on that glorious country and its glorious people, and which still, after all that has been done, remains the only history filled with the continuous sense of the unity of its marvellous destinies in their decline as well as in their rise. Many there are who have never lost the deep impression left by the attempt to trace the refined and solemn irony of ancient tragedy and human [2] fate; many also who in his masterly analysis of the Evangelical narratives first found a key at once to the diversity and unity of Gospel truth, to the structure and the substance of the sacred

---

[1] Ecclus. xlvii. 14.   [2] *Essay on the Irony of Sophocles.*

volume.[1] Such a man is a boon to a whole generation, both by the example of his industry and by the light of his teaching. Even to the very last, even in old age, in blindness, in solitude, he continued with indomitable energy the task of acquiring new knowledge, of adding another and another finish to the never-ending education of his capacious mind; becoming, as he said when at the age of seventy-six he released himself from the cares of his diocese — becoming a boy once again, but a boy still at school, still growing in wisdom and understanding. Hear it, laggards and sluggards of our laxer days! hear it, you who spend your leisure in the things and the books that perish with the using! hear and profit by the remembrance that there has been one amongst us to whom the word of knowledge came in all its force and beauty; to whom idleness, ignorance, and indifference were an intolerable burden; to whom the acquisition of a new language or a new literature was as the annexation of a new dominion, or the invention of a new enjoyment! Well may he rest amongst the scholars of England, beneath the monument of Isaac Casaubon, whom we have of late learnt to know again as if he had lived in our[2] days, in the grave of his own famous[3] schoolfellow, of whose labors in the same field of Grecian history he once said, with a fine union of simple modesty and noble disinterestedness, that to himself had been given the rare privilege of seeing the work which had been the dream of his own life superseded and accomplished by a like work on a larger scale, and in more finished proportions, by the beloved and faithful friend of his early youth.

2. But this was not the half of the wisdom which

[1] Introduction to his translation of Schleiermacher's *Essay on St. Luke*.

[2] *Memoir of Isaac Casaubon.* By Mark Pattison.

[3] George Grote.

will lie buried in that narrow vault.   There is an old English word which has now somewhat changed its meaning, but which was in former times applied to one of our greatest divines, Richard Hooker — the word "judicious."   In its proper meaning it signified exactly that quality of judgment, discretion, discrimination, which is the chief characteristic of the Biblical virtue of wisdom.   Hardly, perhaps, has there been any English theologian, rarely even any professional Judge, to whom this epithet, in this its true sense of *judicial*, *judge-like*, was more truly applicable than to the serene and powerful intellect that has just passed away.   In that massive countenance, in that measured diction, in that deliberate argument, in those weighty decisions, it seemed as though Themis herself were enshrined to utter her most impressive oracles; as if he were a living monument (so said a venerable friend of his own) on which was inscribed "Incorrupta fides, nudaque veritas;" as if he had absorbed into his inmost being the evangelical precept, "Judge not according to the appearance, but judge righteous judgment."   We would not deny — it would be false to human nature, it would be false to himself to deny — that there were occasions when even in his firm hand the scales of justice trembled from some unexpected bias, when his clear vision was dimmed for a time by a glamor which fascinated him the more because its magical influence was so unlike to any thing in himself, when his majestic serenity was ruffled by the irritation of some trivial contradiction or small annoyance.   But for the larger part of his career the even current of his temper, the piercing accuracy of his insight, the calm dignity of his judgment, even when we might differ from its conclusions, remained unmoved and immovable; and thus, when he rose to the Episcopal office, it almost seemed as if in this respect it had been created for him, so naturally did he from it, as from a commanding eminence, take an oversight of the whole field of ecclesiastical events — so entirely did his addresses to his clergy assume the form of judicial utterances on each of the great controversies which have agitated the Church of England for the last thirty years, and thus become the most faithful as well as impressive record of that eventful time. Such a character, moving or standing amongst us, insensibly acted as a constant check on extravagance, a silent rebuke to partisanship, a valuable witness to "the entire dominion which prudence has (to use the words of Burke) over every exercise of power committed to his hands," "especially (again to use the words of the same great statesman) when we have lived to see prudence and conformity to circumstances wholly set at naught in our late controversies, as if they were the most contemptible and irrational of all things." To have beheld such a judgment-seat established amongst us is a warning and a blessing for which we shall often crave in vain now that its oracle is dumb, but which it is for us to reproduce, so far as we can, by the memory of the extent to which we once admired it, and of the strength wherewith it strengthened us.

And there is yet this further lesson : — " Where was it that this wisdom was found ? or where was the place of this wonderful understanding ? " It was on a throne where experience has often told us that it is missing, in a place where we are often cynically warned not to look for it. It was in that sacred calling, which, by the very reason of its sacredness, is exposed more than the other great professions of our country to the fits of sudden fanaticism, to the hurricanes of well-intentioned panics, to the convulsions of blind party-spirit. It was on the . heights of that Episcopal order which, by the very reason

of its eminence, often becomes the prey of timid counsels, unequal measures, and narrow experiences; but
which, when worthily occupied and worthily used, gives
room and scope as no other office, either in Church or
State, to the exercise of that width of view and impartiality of judgment of which the " wisdom " of the Bible
is the Divine expression.

When we sometimes hear it said that in our day there
are fewer attractions for the nobler intellects and the
more gifted spirits to enter the sacred ministry; when
we hear it regretfully said that those who enter often
become demoralized in their highest mental aspirations
by taking holy orders — let us ask what was the experience suggested by the career which is now closed. He
had been destined to another lofty calling, that of the
Bar, where, if anywhere, some of his most peculiar gifts
might have had the fullest development and gratified
the highest ambition. But he found that in the ministrations of the Church of England there was a field for
a yet larger development of his moral and intellectual
stature, for the exercise of a yet nobler ambition. If
from any cause since that time the calling of an English
clergyman has become less congenial to such characters,
if its sphere has become more contracted, if the difficulties placed in the way of embarking upon it have
increased, or the inducements to enter upon it have diminished — it is well for all those who are concerned
to look to it, for few graver evils can befall a Church,
no more formidable prospect threaten its dignity and its
usefulness. And as we so regard the question, let us
think once and again what were the advantages which
he brought to the ministry and hierarchy of the English
Church, and what were the advantages which it offered
to him. He brought to it the assurance that in the
ranks of its clergy there was no reason why the love of

truth and of learning should not abound, why critical inquiry should not pursue its onward course, why the intellectual and spiritual elements of Christianity should not constantly prevail over those which are material and formal. There are those who remember that when he was raised by a courageous statesman to a seat in the English Episcopate, while some trembled with alarm at the entrance of this bold intruder, as he was deemed, others confidently predicted that this intrusion, if so it were, would give to the Church of England a new lease of enduring life. Have not the prophets of hope been justified in their anticipation of good, ten times more than the prophets of fear in their anticipations of evil? Are there any now from one end of the Church to the other who are not proud of the man who has thus adorned their calling, and ennobled the career of the humblest curate of the most secluded hamlet? Are there any who do not feel that English Christianity and English literature would have been the poorer if Connop Thirlwall had become a mere successful lawyer, or remained a mere private scholar, instead of giving by his presence in the Episcopate an example and a guaranty that liberal sentiment, even-handed justice, free research, had their proper sphere in the high places of our Zion? He stood not alone in that former generation of noble students, in those days which " they that are younger now have in their derision." Others there were, perhaps, in their own way, as gifted as he, who certainly left a deeper and wider impress on the writings and the actions of our time, and who were less restrained in their utterances by caution or reticence. But of all that memorable band who found their natural calling in the ministry of the English Church, he was the only one, at least in England, who mounted to its highest ranks, and visibly swayed its counsels. That long and

honored existence bids us not to despair of our Church
or of our Faith ; but it also warns us to keep them at
least on the same level that made his presence amongst
us possible.   It may be that, whatever betides, there
will always be an inducement for the simple enthusiast,
the stirring administrator, the eager partisan, the zealous
dogmatist, to take his place in the ranks of the evangelists or pastors of the Church.   But if there are to be
pillars of the House of Wisdom amongst the clergy like
to him that is gone, there must be something more than
this ; and is it too much to say that one main attraction,
which drew him and like characters to the sacred ministry of our Church, was its national character, and therefore comprehensive, varied, and onward destiny ?   To
nothing short of this, to no meaner service, beneath the
dogmatic or ceremonial yoke of no lesser communion,
would the giants of those days have bowed their heads
to enter.   Other advantages, moral or material, may be
furnished by the separated, disintegrated, or exclusively
ecclesiastical sects or churches of our country.   Many
are the excellent gifts possessed by our Nonconformist
brethren which we lack, and perhaps shall always lack.
But they themselves would confess with us that such as
he of whom we speak would have found, and could have
found, no abiding place in their ranks.   And only, or
almost only, in a national Church — where the permanent voice of the nation, and not only a fraction of it,
takes part in the appointment of its highest officers —
was such an appointment possible, or at least probable,
as that which gave to us the prelate whom we all now
alike delight to honor, and mourn to lose.

Such was the public career of him whom on Tuesday
next we are to lay beneath this roof.   Some perhaps
will lament, with a natural regret, that the prelate who,
of all its occupants, has most conspicuously adorned

through a long Episcopate the ancient see which reaches back to the earliest beginnings of British Christianity, should not have found his last resting-place in the loneliness and grandeur of his own cathedral of St. David's, in the romantic solitude of that secluded sanctuary, beside the storm-vexed promontory that overlooks the western sea. But it was also a natural feeling, in which his own clergy and people proudly share, that one whose fame belonged not to a single diocese, but to the whole Church of England and to the whole world of letters, should claim his rightful place amongst the scholars and philosophers of our country. And in these days of doubt and rebuke there is a satisfaction in the thought that at least one great Churchman by general consent found his way into the innermost circle of the sages of our time; that, on the one hand, there was at least one Greek to whose lofty intellect the religion of Jesus Christ was not foolishness; and, on the other hand, at least one reverent believer to whom its reasonable service, its philosophic depth, its wide-reaching charity, its unadorned simplicity, were not stumbling-blocks.

3. And this brings me to one concluding remark. I have hitherto spoken only of the mental grandeur of him whom we mourn. It is this chiefly which concerns us on this occasion. It is the vindication of the religious mission only of learning and wisdom that I have thus briefly put before you. Yet those who knew the man in his inner life knew well that within that marble intellect, behind that impassive severity, beneath that ponderous eloquence, there was a moral fire which warmed and fused the whole length and breadth of the granite mass through which it breathed. That was no mean sense of duty which constrained him, when in middle life he entered on the Episcopate, to throw his vast linguistic power into the homely and perhaps

ungrateful task of learning, as no English Bishop, I believe, since the Conquest, had ever learnt, the language
of his Cambrian diocese. That was no inconsiderable
effort of moral courage and farsighted justice which led
him on one occasion in his earlier years to vindicate,
amidst obloquy and opposition, the solution of a great
academical [1] difficulty which, since that time, all have
accepted; or, on another occasion in his later years, to
vindicate the solution of a great ecclesiastical [2] difficulty
which all modern statesmen had abandoned, but which
all eminent statesmen of a former generation had combined in urging. That was no cold or callous heart
which found its chief earthly comfort in the faithful
affection of those who grew up around him as his own
children and grandchildren, receiving instruction day
by day from the boundless stores of his knowledge, and
attracted by his paternal care. That was no proud or
hard spirit which lived a life of such childlike simplicity, in the innocent enjoyment of his books or of his
dumb creatures, or in steady obedience to the frequent
call of often irksome duty, or in humbly waiting for his
heavenly Master's summons.

It was an undesigned but impressive coincidence that
during the last days of his life he was employing his
dark and vacant hours in translating, through successive dictations, into Latin, Greek, German, Italian,
Spanish, French, Welsh, the striking apologue which
tells us that, "as Sleep is the brother of Death, thou
must be careful to commit thyself to the care of Him
who is to awaken thee both from the Death of Sleep
and from the Sleep of Death," and which tells us further that "the outward occurrences of life, whether
prosperous or adverse, have no more effect than dreams

---

[1] The admission of Dissenters to the Universities.
[2] The plan of Concurrent Endowment for the Irish Churches.

on our real condition, since virtue alone is the real end
and enduring good." These words, thus rendered with
all the energy of his unbroken mind into those seven
languages, contain, by hazard, as I have said, yet surely
not without significance, the simple, sublime elements
of religion — the two conclusions which, not only in
those closing hours, but in the fulness of his life, penetrated his reason and his faith: unwavering reverence
for the supreme goodness of God, unshaken conviction
of the true grandeur of goodness in man. Suddenly
the summons came. With one call for him who had
been as his own son on earth; with one cry to his Lord
in heaven, Who to his upward gaze seemed yet more
visible and yet more near — he passed, as we humbly
trust, from the death of sleep, and from the sleep of
death, to the presence of that Light in which he shall
see light.

" Where shall wisdom be found? and where is the
place of understanding?"

" Behold, the fear of the Lord, that is wisdom, and to
depart from evil is understanding." [1]

[1] Job xxviii. 28.

THE RELIGIOUS ASPECT OF GOTHIC ARCHITECTURE.

March 30, 1878, being the Sunday after the burial of Sir George Gilbert Scott.

I was glad when they said unto me, Let us go into the house of the Lord. — PSALM cxxiii. 1.

"THE house of the Lord." It is an expression which we at once recognize as figurative. " Behold, the heaven of heavens cannot contain Thee; how much less this house that I have builded!" So it was said even in the Jewish dispensation. In the Christian dispensation it is still more strongly expressed that the only fitting temple of the Most High is the sacred human conscience, or the community of good men throughout the world, or that vast unseen universe which is the true tabernacle, greater and more perfect than any made by hands. Nevertheless, like all familiar metaphors, the expression "the house of God" has a deep root in the human heart and mind. Our idea of the invisible almost inevitably makes for itself a shell or husk from visible things. This is the germ of religious architecture. This is the reason why the most splendid buildings in the world have been temples or churches. This is the reason why even the most spiritual, even the most Puritanical, religion clothes itself with the drapery not only of words, and sounds, and pictures, but of wood, and stone, and marble. A Friends' meeting-house is as really a house of God, and therefore as decisive a testimony to the

260

sacredness of architecture, as the most magnificent cathedral. The barbaric artificers of the tabernacle in the desert were as really inspired in their rude manner, as the Tyrian architects of the temple of Solomon. Who is there that does not feel a glow of enthusiasm when coming back after long absence — it may be like him who addresses you to-day — or long illness, he finds himself once more in the old familiar, venerable sanctuary, which has become the home of his affection, the outward and visible sign of his country's and of his own hopes and duties? Who is there that having grown with the growth and strengthened with the strength of an institution like this, does not feel that it is part of himself, that its honor or dishonor is his own glory or his own shame? That which a humorous saying usually ascribed to the witty Canon [1] of a neighboring cathedral, treated as an impossibility, is in fact the simple truth. We who live under the hull or framework, the vaults or the dome of a building like Westminster Abbey or St. Paul's, are conscious of a thrill of satisfaction when the hand of an approving public is placed on our outward shell; a thrill which penetrates to our inmost souls, because we within, and that superb shell without, constitute but one and the same living creature. It is the consciousness of this intimate connection between the spiritual and the material temple, between the grandeur of religion and the grandeur of its outward habitation, which gives a living interest to the thought which I would this day bring before

[1] It is told of Sydney Smith that he once said to a child who thought that it was pleasing a tortoise by stroking the shell, "You might as well hope to please the Dean and Chapter of St. Paul's by patting the dome." (*Memoirs of Sydney Smith*, vol. i. 324.) It would seem, however, that the story had an earlier origin. The remark was made, in the first instance, or at least simultaneously, by the present Sir Frederick Pollock to his brother.

you — the religious aspect of the noble science and art of the architect. We yesterday laid within these walls the most famous builder of this generation. Others may have soared to loftier flights, or produced special works of more commanding power; but no name within the last thirty years has been so widely impressed on the edifices of Great Britain, past and present, as that of Gilbert Scott. From the humble but graceful cross, which commemorates at Oxford the sacrifice of the three martyrs of the English Reformation, to the splendid memorial of the Prince who devoted his life to the service of his Queen and country; from the Presbyterian University on the banks of the Clyde, to the college chapels on the banks of the Isis and the Cam; from the proudest minster to the most retired parish church; from India to Newfoundland — the trace has been left of the loving eye and skilful hand that are now so cold in death. Truly was it said by one, who from the distant shores of a foreign land rendered yesterday his sorrowing tribute of respect, that in nearly all the cathedrals of England there must have been a shock of grief when the tidings came of the sudden stroke which had parted them from him, who was to them as their own familiar friend and foster-father. Canterbury, Ely, Exeter, Worcester, Peterborough, Salisbury, Hereford, Lichfield, Ripon, Gloucester, Manchester, Chester, Rochester, Oxford, Bangor, St. Asaph, St. David's, Windsor, St. Alban's, Tewkesbury, and last, not least, our own Westminster, in which he took most delight of all buildings in all the world — are the silent mourners round the grave of him who loved their very stones and dust, and knew them to their very heart's core. But it is good on these occasions to rise above the personal feelings of the moment into those more general lessons which his career suggests.

I. It was the singular fortune of that career that it coincided with one of the most remarkable revolutions of taste that the world has witnessed. That peculiar conception of architectural beauty which our ancestors, in blame and not in praise, called Gothic, was altogether unknown to Pagan or Christian antiquity. It was unknown alike to the builders of the Pyramids and the Parthenon, to the builders of the Roman Basilica, and the Byzantine Sta. Sophia. Born partly of Saracenic, partly of German parentage, it gradually won its way to perfection by the mysterious instinct which breathed through Europe in the Middle Ages. It flourished for four centuries, and then died as completely as if it had never existed. Another style took its place. By Catholic and Protestant it was alike repudiated. By the hands of English or Scottish prelates, no less than of English or Scottish Reformers, its traces wherever possible were obliterated. Here and there a momentary thrill of admiration was rekindled by the high-embowed roof, or by the stately pillars of our ancient churches, as in the "Penseroso" of Milton, or in the "Mourning Bride" of Congreve. But as a general rule it was regarded as a lost art, and our poets of the sixteenth century make no more allusion to it than if they had been born and bred in the new world of America.

Look through the popular writers of the sixteenth century, the unconscious exponents of the sentiments of the age that followed the Reformation, examine the writings of Spenser, for instance, and Shakspeare, the many-sided, to whom all the tones of thought of all ages seem to have been revealed and familiarized, of Chapman and Marlow and the rest, and I question whether you will find a line or a word in any one of them indicating the slightest sympathy with the æsthetics of ecclesiastical architecture, which exercise such a fascination over ourselves. Not one line, not one word, I believe, of the charms of cloistered arcades and fretted roofs, and painted windows, and the dim religious light of the pensive poets of our later ages. No wail of despair, no murmur of dissatisfaction reaches us from the generation that witnessed the dire eclipse in which the labor of so many ages of artistic refinement became involved. Their children have betrayed to us no remembrance of the stifled sorrows of their fathers. As far as regards its taste for ecclesiastical monuments, the literature of Elizabeth might have been the production of the rude colonists of the Antilles or of Virginia.[1]

Here and there an antiquarian, like Gostling at Canterbury or Carter at Westminster, allowed the genius of the place to overpower the tendencies of the age. And if a protest against the indiscriminate disparagement of mediæval art came at last from Horace Walpole, it was more in deference to his rank, than from conversion to his sentiments, that the authorities in Church and State consented to preserve what else they would have doomed to destruction. At last in the first half of this century a new eye was given to the mind of man. Gradually, imperfectly, through various channels — in this country chiefly through the minute observations of a Quaker student — the visions of the strange past rose before a newly awakened world. The glory and the grace of our soaring arches, of our stained windows, of our recumbent effigies, were revealed, as they had been to no mortal eyes since the time of their erection. To imitate, to preserve this ancient style in its remarkable beauty was the inevitable consequence, we might say the overwhelming temptation, of this new discovery. The hour was come when the ecclesiastical architecture of the past was to be roused from its long slumber, and with the hour came the man. We do not forget that splendid if eccentric genius who gave himself, though not with undivided love, to the service

<hr />

[1] Sermon preached at Harrow, on the Founder's Day, Oct. 10, 1872, by Charles Merivale, D.D., Dean of Ely.

of another communion. We cannot but remember the gifted architect who raised the stately halls and the commanding towers of the palace of the imperial legislature, and who was laid long years ago — in fit proximity to his own great works — within these walls, where he has been followed by him of whom I now would speak. For there was one who, if younger in the race, and at the time less conspicuous than either of them, was destined to exercise over the growth of Gothic architecture in this country a yet more enduring and extensive influence.

When in this Abbey the first note of that revival was struck by the erection of Bernasconi's plaster canopies in the place of the classic altar-piece, given by Queen Anne,[1] a boy of fourteen years old was in the church watching the demolition and the reconstruction with a curious vigilance, which from that time never flagged for fifty years. That was the earliest reminiscence which Gilbert Scott retained of Westminster Abbey; that was the first inspiration of the Gothic revival which swept away before its onward progress not only the plaster reredos of this Abbey, but a thousand other crudities of the same imperfect period. He impersonated the taste of the age. Antiquarian no less than builder, he became to those fossils of mediæval architecture what Cuvier and Owen have been to the fossils of the earlier world of nature. It may be that others will follow on whom the marvellous bounty of Providence shall bestow other gifts of other kinds. But meanwhile we bless God for what we have had in our departed friend and his fellow-workers. The recovery, the second birth, of Gothic architecture, is a striking proof that the human mind is not dead, nor the creative power of our Maker slackened. We bless alike the

---

[1] *Memorials of Westminster Abbey*, p. 530.

power which breathed this inspiration into the men of old, and that which even from their dry bones has breathed it once again into the men of these latter days.

II. But it is not enough to rejoice that a great gift is resuscitated or a great style imitated. We must ask wherein its greatness consisted, and in what relation it stood to the other gifts of the Creator. There are many characteristics of the inediæval architecture, as of the mediæval mind, which have totally perished, or which ought never to be revived; which represent ideas that for our time have lost all significance, and purposes which are doomed to extinction. The Middle Ages have left on the intellect of Europe few, very few, enduring traces. Their chronicles are but the quarries of later historians; their schoolmen are but the extinct species of a dead theology. Two great poems and one book of devotion are all which that long period has bequeathed to the universal literature of mankind. But their architecture still remains

"Of equal date
With Andes and with Ararat,"[1]

and the reason of this continuance or revival is this, that in its essential features it represented those aspirations of religion which are eternal. As in mediæval Christianity there were elements which belonged to the undeveloped Protestantism of the Western Churches, so also in mediæval architecture there are elements which belong to the churches of the Reformation as well as to the churches of the Papal system. Its massive solidity, its aspiring height, its infinite space, these belong not to the tawdry, trivial, minute, material side of religion, but to its sobriety, its grandeur, its breadth, its sublim-

[1] Emerson.

ity. And therefore it was that when this revival of Gothic architecture took place, it was amongst the Protestant churches of England, rather than in the Catholic churches of the Continent, that its first growth struck root. The religious power of our great cathedrals has, as has been well remarked,[1] not lost, but gained, in proportion as our worship has become more solemn, more simple, more reverential, more comprehensive. There is a cloud of superstition doubtless which, with the latter half of the nineteenth century, has settled down over a large part of the ecclesiastical world; but the last places which it will reach will be the magnificent architectural monuments which defy the introduction of trivial and mean decorations, or, if introduced, condemn them for their evident incongruity with other portions of the buildings. The great antiquaries, the great architects of this century, are but too well acquainted with the differences between the loftier and the baser aspects, between the golden and the copper sides of their noble art, to allow it to become the handmaid of a sect or party, or the instrument of a senseless proselytism.

III. And this leads me to one more point of the marvellous revival of which he who lies in yonder grave was the pioneer and champion. For the first, or almost for the first time in the history of the world, the architecture of the nineteenth century betook itself, not to the creation of a new style, but to the preservation and imitation of an older style. With perhaps one exception,[2] every age and country down to our own has set its face towards superseding the works of its predeces-

---

[1] Dean Milman's *History of Latin Christianity*, vol. vi. p. 91.

[2] The continuance of the Pharaonic style in Egypt under the Ptolemaic princes and Roman emperors. There are also a few examples in Mediæval Architecture, such as the completion of the nave of Westminster Abbey. — See *Memorials of Westminster Abbey*, chap. iii.

sors, by erecting its own work in their place. The
Normans overthrew the old Romanesque churches of
the Saxons. Henry III. in this place "totally swept
away, as of no value whatever," the noble Abbey of
the Confessor. Henry VII. built his stately Chapel in
marked contrast to all the other portions of this building. The great architects of the cathedrals of St. Peter
at Rome, and St. Paul in London, adopted a style varying as widely from the mediæval, which they despised,
as from the Grecian, which they admired. But now,
in our own time, the whole genius of the age threw all
its energies into the reproduction of what had been,
rather than into the production of what was to be. No
doubt it may be said that there is; in the original genius
which creates, something more stimulating and inspiring. Yet still the very eagerness of reproduction is
itself an original inspiration, and there is in it also a
peculiar grace which, to the illustrious departed, was
singularly congenial. If one had sought for a man to
carry out this awe-striking retrospect through the great
works of old, to gather up the fragments of perishing
antiquity, it would have been one whose inborn modesty used to call the color into his face at every word
of praise, whose reverential attitude led him instinc-
tively to understand and to admire. And yet in him
this very tendency, especially in his maturer age, took
so large and generous a sweep as to counteract the
excesses into which, in minds less expansive and less
vigorous, it is sure to fall. Because the bent of his own
character and of his own time led chiefly to the restoration of mediæval art, he was not on that account insensible to the merits of the ages which had gone before, or
which had succeeded. With that narrow and exclusive
pedantry which would fain sweep out from this and
other like buildings all the monuments and memorials

of the last three centuries, he had little or no sympathy. He regarded them as footprints of the onward march of English history, and whilst feeling a natural regret for the inroads which here and there they had made into the earlier glories of the Plantagenet and Tudor architecture, and willing to prune their disproportionate encroachments, he cherished their associations as tenderly as though they had been his own creations, and would bestow his meed of admiration as freely on the modern memorial of Isaac Watts as on the antique effigy of a crusading prince or a Benedictine abbot. It was this loving, yet comprehensive care for all the heterogeneous elements of the past, this anxious, unselfish attention to all their multifarious details, which made him so wise a counsellor, so delightful a companion, in the great work of the reparation, the conservation, the glorification of this building, which, amidst his absorbing and ubiquitous duties, it is not too much to say was his first love, his chief, his last, his enduring interest.

Such is the loss which the whole Church and country deplore, but which we of this place mourn most of all. We cannot forget him. Roof and wall, chapter-house and cloister, the tombs of the dead and the worship of the living, all speak of him to those who know that his hand and his eye were everywhere amongst us. But these very trophies of what he did for us must render us more alive to do what we can for him. His memory must stimulate us who remain to carry on with unabated zeal those works in which he took so deep a concern: the completion of the Chapter-house by its long-promised and long-delayed windows of stained glass; the northern porch, which he desired above all things to see restored to its pristine beauty; the new cloister, which he had planned in all its completeness as the link for another thousand years between the illustrious dead of the generations of the past, and those of the generations of the future. So long as these remain unfinished, his grave will continue to reproach us. When they shall be accomplished, they will be amongst the noblest monuments of him whose ambition for his glorious art was so far-reaching, and whose ideas of what was due to this national sanctuary were so exacting.

IV. But there is yet a more sacred and solemn thought which attaches to the immediate remembrance of so faithful a servant of this State of England, of so honored a friend of this church of Westminster.

It has been sometimes said that it was by a strange irony of fate that the great leader in the revival of mediæval architecture should have been the grandson of that venerable commentator who belonged to the revival of evangelical religion. Yet in fact, from another point of view, it was a fitting continuity. It is always useful to be reminded that the revival, or, as we may better put it, the increase, of sincere English religion, belongs to a generation and a tendency long anterior to the multiplication of those external signs and symbols of which our age has made so much; and in the deep sense of that inward religion, that simple faith in the Great Unseen, the grandson who multiplied and disclosed the secrets of the visible sanctuaries of God throughout the land, was not an unworthy descendant of the grandfather who endeavored, according to the light of 'his time, to draw forth the mysteries of the Book of books. We in this place, who knew him and valued him, who leant upon him as a tower of strength in our difficulties, who honored his indefatigable industry, his childlike humility, his unvarying courtesy, his noble candor, we who remember with gratitude his generous encouragement of the students of the rising generation, who know how he loved and valued the best that we also have loved and valued — we all feel that in him we have lost one of those just, gentle, guileless souls who in their lives have lifted, and in their memories may still lift, our souls upwards. And when we speak of the work which such a career bequeaths to those that remain, let us remember that although, as we said at the beginning of this discourse, the shell, the framework, of a great building like this, is an inestimable gift of God, its creation and preservation one of the noblest functions of human genius and national enterprise, yet on us who dwell within it, to whose charge it is committed, depends in no slight manner its continuance for the future, its glory and its usefulness for the present. There are some eager spirits of our time, in whom the noble passion for reform and improvement has been stifled and suspended by the ignoble passion for destruction, who have openly avowed their desire to suppress all the expressions of worship or of teaching within this or like edifices, and keep them only as dead memorials of the past — better silent with the solitude of Tintern or of Melrose, than thronged with vast congregations or resounding with the music of the psalmist or the voice of the preacher. It is for us so to fulfil our several duties, so to people this noble sanctuary with living deeds and words of goodness and of wisdom, that such dreams of the destroyer may find no place to enter, no shelter or excuse from our neglect or ignorance or folly. The grave of our great architect is close beside the pulpit which he erected to commemorate the earliest establishment of services and of sermons in the nave, which then for the first time were set on foot by my predecessor, and which have since spread throughout the whole country. That reminds us of the kind of support which we, the guardians and occupants of abbeys and cathedrals, can give even to their outward fabric.

It has been well said by a gifted author, who, if any of his time, has been devoted to the passionate love of art, that in the day of trial it will be said even in those magnificent buildings, not "See what manner of stones are here," but "See what manner of men." [1] Clergy, lay-clerks, choristers, teachers, scholars, vergers, guides, almsmen, workmen — yes, and all you who frequent this church — every one of us may have it in our power to support it, by our reverence and devotion, by our eagerness to profit by what we hear, by our sincere wish to give the best that we can in teaching and preaching, by our honest and careful fulfilment of the duties of each day's work, by our scrupulous care to avoid all that can give needless annoyance or offence, by our constancy and belief, by our rising above all paltry disputes and all vulgar vices. In the presence of this great institution of which we are all members, and in the presence of the Most High God, whom it recalls to our thoughts, and in whose presence we are, equally within its walls and without them — every one of us has it in his power to increase the glory, to strengthen the stability, to insure the perpetuity of this abbey. That is the best memorial we can raise, that is the best service we can render, to all those, dead or living, who have loved, or who still love, this holy and beautiful house, wherein our fathers worshipped in the generations of the past, and wherein, if we be but true to its glorious mission, our children and our children's children shall worship in the generations that are yet to come.

[1] Ruskin's *Lectures on Art*, p. 118.

THE LATE PRINCESS ALICE.

December 22, 1878.

She that hath borne seven languisheth; she hath given up the ghost;
her sun hath gone down while it was yet day. —JEREMIAH XV. 9.

IT is impossible for me, in this ancient sanctuary of
the joys and sorrows of English Princes, not to say a
few words on the mournful event which, since I last
entered these walls, has cast another and a deeper
shadow on the day already thrice linked with the lives
and deaths of the Royal House. Even as a domestic
calamity in a private family it would strike a pang
through many hearts to hear of a husband suddenly
left desolate — himself hardly rescued from the gates
of death; the seven children, of whom we are reminded,
in the words of the English poet, that, though two
of them had gone before to their rest, they "still are
seven;" the wife and mother falling a victim to her
vigilant care for those she loved, the sudden termina-
tion of a brilliant career in the midst of unclouded
brightness — these thoughts combine to make this event
almost literally a reproduction of the grief which the
prophet selected as the type of the heaviest misfortune.
But there is a sense in which even the cynical critic
will acknowledge that this private sorrow bears something of a national aspect; and therefore on this occasion, as we take a last look at the sepulchre which has
closed on so much happiness and usefulness; on this
day — when the shadow of mourning still rests, not

only on the British Isles, but on the remotest extremities of the earth where the English language is spoken;
even amongst the children of that New England beyond the sea, now parted from the English Crown, but
mingling their sympathy for that Crown while they
celebrate, as it happens on this day, their own national
birthright — it may not be unfitting to ask what permanent lessons we here may carry away with us from
the event which has left so deep an impression on palace
and cottage, abroad and at home, wherever the tidings
have reached.

The lesson which we may carry away is two-fold.
The first is a homely lesson, but not unimportant for
us to remember, the universality and identity of human
suffering and human affection. We all feel this shock,
because we all know what it is. We know that the
mourners in this case are mourners like the mother,
husband, and children in every household throughout
the land. We know that the tears which flow from
them, and for them, flow from the same fountain of
grief that exists in every human heart. We know that
the parental love which ended in this heart-stirring
world-felt sorrow is the same which sustains the home
of every private circle. When we hear the funereal
music; when we read of the solemn service over the
dead; when we see rival statesmen suspending their
fierce strife for a moment in order to render their
touching tribute to the self-sacrificing love of a mother
for her child, or the simple, manly affection of a brother
to a much loved sister; we are touched with the depth
and the grandeur of those pure domestic feelings of
which we sometimes think too little, but which, at such
moments as this, we acknowledge to be the very life-
blood of families and of nations. Every man, woman,
and child, as they feel for the untimely loss of this de-

voted parent, faithful sister, and affectionate daughter, may well be reminded that they, each in their place, can be and ought to be what she was. The more we recollect that circle of good children, to whose culture and education so much care was given by her whom they have lost, so much more each of us should feel the responsibility of the burden which every parent bears in the little souls that God has intrusted to our keeping. The more we learn of the elevating and softening effect which sorrow had already wrought on the mind and heart of the mother mourning over her dear first lost child, so much the more should we each of us know that through the dark hours of bereavement and misfortune an unseen hand may be leading us upwards to some higher and wider life. Our Christmas homes will not be the less happy if they are lightened with the holy thought that our permanent home is not here; and that there is a brighter and better world even than the brightest and the best that we have known on earth.

There is another lesson. I have hitherto spoken of that experience which is common to all the sons and daughters of men ; but the very fact that this domestic grief is a likeness of that which befalls us all, reminds us that there is another class of reflections aroused, not by the equalities but by the inequalities and varieties of the human race. It is one striking result of the creation and growth of those high offices which break the level monotony of human existence that they bring before us common things and common feelings in a concentrated, personal, and yet public form. A Royal personage or an exalted character is — we none of us need to be told it — one of the same flesh and blood as ourselves. But the fact that by historical tradition, and by the inextinguishable sentiment of mankind, they are necessarily marked out from their fellow-men, gives to all that they do or suffer a power for good or a power for evil beyond that which belongs to those who live and die unknown. The "mute, inglorious Miltons," the undeveloped Plantagenets, Cromwells, or Washingtons in our country churchyards may have been, in themselves, as precious in the sight of God, and as excellent in their dealings with their neighbors, as the greatest and most favored of mankind. But Providence has so ordered it that conspicuous eminence is and can be given only to a few; and those few who stand on their eminences are as a city set upon a hill.

"That fierce light which beats upon a Throne"

reveals lessons and gives opportunities which escape notice in the homelier or obscurer corners of the life of men. This is the second lesson conveyed to us by the event which we are now considering. It was not only that she who is gone discharged those ordinary duties which belong to every wife and mother, but that she was aware of the moral power and of the large responsibility with which her high position of necessity invested her. The active kindness, the gracious attention, the wise interest in benevolent objects which would be useful in every one were, as she well knew, intensified in usefulness by coming from one in her place. Her rank, her name, were used by her not for purposes of selfish indulgence or pleasure, but for beneficence and enlightenment. Those external advantages were, as she felt, special talents committed to her trust for the good of mankind; and as such she used them. It is this use — this good use — of the talents committed to each of us that we would now urge on all. We do not need to be of Regal rank, or to possess a world-wide fame, to have special opportunities intrusted to us. Nor do Regal rank or world-wide fame insure that such opportunities shall be rightly used. But wherever, and in proportion as, they are not used, every institution, or rank, or place, which furnishes them, loses one large part of the object for which, in the order of Providence, it exists; and wherever, and in proportion as, these opportunities and talents are used, there not only is the welfare of society increased, but the existence of the institutions themselves is justified; because it then becomes apparent that they are the vantage grounds, without which the benevolent intentions and the beneficent works of individuals would often lose the fulcrum and the stimulus which every effort for good in this difficult world so much needs. Those who, in any important station, fulfil the duties of that station well; those who make it a matter of conscience to reward unquestionable merit and to advance the obscure deserving; those who make a stand against an evil fashion, or a selfish luxury, or the degraded vices of our age, not only render a service to their immediate generation, but they render a still more enduring service to the generations that are yet to come by helping to preserve the institutions which shall, in future times, be the standing ground whence others may diffuse like benefits hereafter. Those, on the other hand, who in important stations see only the means of encouraging low tastes, foolish fashions, miserable aims; who abuse their power of trust and patronage, or live a life of selfish ease, as if there were none to care for but themselves — these, in proportion as they do this, are not only useless or mischievous in their own time, but are traitors to their country and destroyers of its future hopes. Those who, in whatever station, high or low, make use of their spare moments or their peculiar gifts and graces to diffuse light and

happiness in their immediate neighborhood, are walking
in the steps of the most princely benefactors of mankind, simply because they are employing to the uttermost the gifts that God has lent to them.   There is a
saying of our Lord not recorded in the four Gospels,
but full of meaning — "Be ye trustworthy bankers; be
ye like banks that will not fail."   If this sacred saying falls with a keener edge on the ears of those who,
during the last few months or weeks, have watched the
wide-spreading calamities that have flowed from the
want of giving heed to this solemn duty in its most
literal sense, yet none the less is the saying always true
in that more extended meaning, in which doubtless it
first was used.   "Be ye trustworthy guardians;" such
must have been the meaning of the phrase — "Be trustworthy guardians of the sacred trust of the time, the
health, the influence, and the rank committed to you."
Give to every effort for good that wider usefulness
which your position can furnish.   Sift, test, discrim-
inate every plan or purpose or part intrusted to your
keeping.   Forget not the gracious smile, the generous
word of compassion which comes with so much larger
power if it proceeds from those who are in any way
raised above their fellows.   Grudge not the cheering
welcome, the hearty laugh, the delightful encouragement which the feeble or the helpless so doubly value
from the stronger, or the younger from the elder — or,
it may even sometimes be, the elder from the younger;
which matured genius or saintly wisdom can bestow on
the struggling inquirer or the returning penitent.   So
let us labor; and then, though we also perchance may
pass away in the prime of our existence, though our
sun may go down while it is yet day, yet "honorable
age is not that which standeth in length of time, nor
that which is reserved for length of years."   He or she

who pleases God, and is "beloved of Him, . . . being made perfect in a short time, has fulfilled a long time."[1] This day is the turn of the year, when the days begin to lengthen, when the darkness begins to shrink, and the light begins to spread. May it be so with the mourners for whom the darkest hour has passed! May it be so with the distress and perplexities of sufferers throughout our land at this trying season! May we, each and all of us, learn to rejoice always as we cherish the glimpses of a better world which come to us, at least, through these two lessons on which we have endeavored to dwell — the sacredness, the everlasting sacredness, of human affections; and the sacredness of opportunities for public duty and private kindness!

[1] Wisdom of Solomon, iv. 8-13.

AN INDIAN STATESMAN.

July 6, 1879, being the Funeral Sermon of Lord Lawrence, late Governor-General of India.

Be strong and of a good courage: for unto this people shalt thou divide for an inheritance the land which I sware unto their fathers to give them. Only be thou strong and very courageous, that thou mayest observe to do according to all the law, which Moses My servant commanded thee: turn not from it to the right hand or to the left, that thou mayest prosper whithersoever thou goest. — JOSHUA i. 6, 7.

THERE are few more saddening experiences of human life than the sight of great opportunities offered and lost, of characters suddenly breaking down, of the ruin effected by want of vigilance and firmness. We look back over the fields of history; we see what the actors of those events could not see, or only saw imperfectly; how on the weakness and the wavering of men who knew not what depended on their efforts all depended, and all was lost. We see, in times past and present, the calm before the tempest, when reform was still possible and revolution might still have been averted. We see in great political and ecclesiastical emergencies how truly it has been said that the timidity of the horse which will not leave his stable lest he should run into the fire, is as dangerous as the rashness of the moth which flies into it. We see how the moral cowardice of those who shrink from responsibility is often more calamitous than the physical cowardice which shrinks from pain and death. We see the panic

280

in armies, when the boldest lose their heads, and, from some bewilderment and confusion, precious lives or noble causes are thrown away. We see in churches the waste of days, and weeks, and years in discussion on the most trivial questions, whilst the weightier considerations of removing stumbling-blocks, and enlarging liberty, and strengthening the mental and moral resources of the whole institution, are passed by as though they did not exist. We see in the cases of individuals a splendid birthright, a great position, a new opening of life coming into view. We see how in some religious experience, such as a confirmation and first communion, or a fresh awakening of serious thoughts, a crisis comes that might change the whole character of the man and the boy, that might develop his usefulness, awaken his disposition, purify the whole atmosphere in which he will live. It comes, the crisis comes ; and perhaps through his own weakness, perhaps through the folly and weakness of others, it fleets away unheeded, and through that weakness a soul is embittered and ruined, a life is mis-spent, a wide circle of light extinguished.

But in proportion to this grief at the sight of great occasions wasted — which an ancient writer calls the bitterest of all griefs — is the delight of seeing opportunities seized and filled ; characters under the stress of misfortune, or danger, or temptation, tried and tested, and not giving way ; the disclosure of moral forces such as, perhaps, may always have existed, but never would have had an occasion of displaying themselves at all except under some urgent pressure. We rejoice in the appearance of such characters on the scene, as the compensation for all the wear and waste of the toil and struggle of life. We rejoice to think that there are times when circumstances give full employ to "hands which the rod of empire might have swayed." We are roused to a new sense of the value of great institutions and high offices when we see that they call forth virtues which before we hardly knew; but which, when called forth, are at once a vindication of those offices and institutions, and also diffuse their own savor far and wide instead of being buried in obscurity. This is what the Apostle means when he speaks of "the earnest expectation of the creature waiting for the manifestation of the sons of God," the "manifestation," or, as perhaps we ought more properly to say, "the revelation," "the unveiling," of those god-like characters which only in adversity are fully recognized, which only by trial are fully perfected. This application of our existing knowledge to the anxious problems of human life; this unflinching determination to see things as they really are, and to act independently of what is thought or said of us by others; this perception at the right moment of the right thing to be done and the right word to be said; this presence of mind, which can bring all the faculties to bear on the very danger by which they seem most likely to be dispersed and dissipated, in the accidents of fire and ship-wreck, in the sudden alarms of revolutions — these are the qualities which, in some measure, the humblest of us should strive to attain, and which the most gifted of us should beware of losing or squandering. It is the sense of these manifestations of unexpected strength which gives a zest and charm to those famous scenes of fiction where Achilles suddenly breaks out from the Grecian camp, or Ulysses throws aside his rags and stalks with his dreadful bow across the threshold of the suitors. These are the qualities which blaze forth in the first and finest description ever given of a soldier-statesman which I have selected for my text from the

Book of Joshua. "Be strong and of a good courage."
That is the first, second, and third requisite of a leader
of men; the courage which makes a man master of
himself and master of those around him; the strength
inherent in the will which is determined not to turn
aside to the right hand or to the left from the duty
which is placed in front of him. And the same passage
further describes the inspiring stimulus which turns
the soldier into the statesman and the statesman into
the soldier, and both into the man of God. "For unto
this people shalt thou divide for an inheritance the
land which I sware unto their fathers to give them;"
that is to say, the greatness of the mission intrusted
by the providence of God to the hands of men is the
measure and motive of indomitable and devoted energy. And the reason of this courage and confidence
is, "For the Lord thy God is with thee whithersoever
thou goest." That is to say, we must have the assurance that eternal justice and goodness are with us —
an assurance sufficient to sustain us through good
report and evil, through failure and through success,
through ruin and through victory. "Joshua was no
teacher or prophet: he was the simple, undaunted,
straightforward warrior. He was known always by
his spear or javelin, slung beneath his shoulders or
stretched forth in his hand. His character was drawn
out of obscurity by the great task placed before him.
It was the command to conquer and to retain the land
of promise that first set his soul on fire. From that
purpose he never swerved; but at the head of the
hosts of Israel he went forward from Jordan to Jericho, from Jericho to Ai, from Ai to Gibeon, from Beth-
horon to Merom. He was here, he was there, he was
everywhere, as God called him. He had no words of
wisdom except those that were dictated by shrewd

common sense and a strong public spirit. To him the
Divine revelation was made, not on the solitary heights
of Horeb, nor in the still small voice, nor in the courts
of temple or tabernacle, but as the Captain of the
Lord's host, with a drawn sword in his hand; and that
drawn and glittering sword was the vision which went
before him until all the kings of Canaan were subdued
beneath his feet." [1]

Such a character, such a mission, was that whose
earthly close we yesterday commemorated. Let us
first speak of the mission which moulded the character.
It was like that of Joshua — if not to found, yet to
save an Empire. The Indian Empire! In that name
what an inheritance has been handed down from our
fathers to us! India, the new world, which Alexander
the Great first revealed to Europe; India, the seat of
the earliest traditions and languages of the civilized
races of mankind, the birthplace of the most widely
spread faith that has dawned upon the earth; India, the
scene of the mighty conflicts between the most absolute
Monotheism and the most elaborate Polytheism in the
world, the scene of the desperate struggles by which a
handful of our countrymen built up our own portentous Empire, illuminated by the dubious yet dazzling
splendor of the genius of Clive and Hastings, by the
purer lustre of the beneficence of statesmen like Bentinck; sanctified by the missionary zeal of Martyn and
Schwartz, of Duff and Wilson, by the enlightened wisdom of prelates like Heber and Cotton; India, alike by
its natural grandeur, and its long historic recollections,
inspiring the imagination of Burke and of Macaulay
with their finest bursts of enthusiastic eloquence;
endeared to many of us as the second home of our
childhood, as the scene of our youthful fortunes; en-

[1] See *The Jewish Church*, vol. i., Lecture X.

deared by graves far away, but not less beloved, beneath the shadow of the Himalayan heights, or in the
bed of the rolling Ganges, or by the surf-beaten shores
of Madras, or the swarming thoroughfares of Bombay.
This is the land we have inherited. Into this we have
in part transfused, and it is our business to transfuse,
the soul and mind of Christian England. For this we
have received in return the wealth and power "showered
upon us by the gorgeous East with richest hands."

And this Empire, thus fearfully and wonderfully
formed, is the mightiest instrument which God has
placed in the hands of any nation for the purification
and the regeneration of Asia.

It was this vast fabric which, twenty years ago, suddenly tottered to its ruin. Never, perhaps, in history
had a larger demand been made on the efforts of individual responsibility; never had so much depended on
the instant, energetic efforts of a few. But in that
dark hour, from behind the veil of ignorance which so
often separates the mind of the English people from the
affairs of India, there appeared character after character
— let us say, hero after hero — who by the strength of
individual purpose and of unwavering consciousness
in the goodness of their cause, not only warded off the
world-wide calamity which had burst upon them, but
also disclosed to the minds of Englishmen a host of
warriors and statesmen such as we hardly knew that
we possessed. It was the very darkness of that crisis,
the overclouding of the brightness of the fortunes of
England, that enabled us to see, as we could not have
seen in broad daylight, the constellation of brilliant stars
that adorned the courts and camps of India. Some of
them still live amongst us; most of them are gone to
their reward; and it is of these last only that I now
speak. There were the two Viceroys of India, present

and future, who met in Calcutta at the very crisis of its fate; the one who lies in the northern transept of this church, who in all that city showed " the only face un- blanched by fear," as afterwards almost the only judg- ment unmoved by the cry for vengeance; the other, whose self-sacrificing magnanimity relinquished for the safety of India the troops that were to have secured his own success in China. There was Nicholson, who, for his stainless purity and awful integrity, was not only beloved with passionate love by the soldiers amongst whom he fell, but was worshipped even with Divine honors by the surrounding natives. There was Ed- wardes — whose monument, also, is amongst us here — who by the sole magic spell of his own brilliant and winning character kept in check at that critical time the wild, untamable tribes beneath him in defence of our frontier. There was Havelock, the stern Puritan, whose march to Lucknow this whole country followed with the eagerness of unparalleled anxiety, crowned by the mingled exultation and lamentation with which almost at the same hour we heard of the relief of the beleaguered city and the death of its deliverer. There was Outram, the Bayard of our Indian warfare, whose chivalrous soul made over to his less-known comrade the chance of winning the glory of that great achieve- ment, even as in his earlier days he refused to receive any profit or pay for his successful guidance of a war of which he did not approve. There was Clyde, the veteran of a hundred fights, who from the day when, as a mere boy, in his youthful, unstained uniform, he scaled the hostile fortress, rose through every vicissitude of the successive wars of our country to the heights of military fame. Side by side, those two rival chiefs sleep together in the nave of this church, which has so often before mingled together in its sepulchral chambers those who were in life estranged. And now, himself laid at the feet of these mighty soldiers, as they also at the feet of their predecessor in the early wars of Afghanistan, there comes the last and greatest of all, the survivor of the two heroic brothers, of whom it is not too much to say, that during the moments of that terrible crisis they bore on their Atlantean shoulders the whole fabric of English existence in India. Of the elder I will only say that the name of Henry Lawrence can never be parted from the name of John Lawrence as long as the history of our Eastern Empire is told. Although in death they were far divided; although even in their several careers difference of character and policy at times held them asunder, yet they were both alike "lovely in their lives," and "terrible as an army with banners." It is of the younger of this splendid pair (and, in saying this, we do not forget the two who are still amongst us) that we now would speak.

It was his happy fortune, let us rather say, our happy fortune, that he survived to make his countrymen at home familiar with his form and features, with his soul and character. He belonged, indeed, to that type of men of which the English race — I trust we may say it without boasting — is so grand a representation. It was with good reason that when an illustrious artist wished to depict in the stately hall of one of our greatest palaces of justice the signing of the Magna Charta, he selected the stern, rugged countenance and magnanimous, manly bearing of John Lawrence as the likeness of the chief among the barons of England who, by their uncompromising independence, won for us our liberties against King and Pope. English, yet also, as has been truly said, Scotch and Irish both by race and character; Irish in that wild, generous, impulsive boldness which belongs more or less to all the sons of Erin, and not least to those who have been nurtured in the traditions of the historic city of Derry; Scotch also in the Scottish blood which of old gave such a steadfastness to that refuge of our Imperial race, when it stood there at bay against the overwhelming odds of siege and famine; English and Scotch together, alike in the caution and in the independence which he inherited both from his Scottish descent and also, let us say, from his Yorkshire birthplace on the beautiful banks of the Swale. Some one since his removal spoke to me in quaint expressive phrase of "his great, deedful life." "Deedful," indeed, it was, full of daring deeds which belong rather to a soldier than to a statesman, deeds which will make the hearts of Englishmen beat for many a long day to come as they read of the retention in his iron grasp of the province of the Five Rivers, the Punjab, with which his name is forever united, and of that tremendous march of thirty miles a day under the burning heat of the summer sun, which, by his absolute reliance on the power of that grasp, he alone organized and made possible, and by which, if by any one single measure, the Indian Empire was preserved.

But on an occasion like this we would rather dwell not so much on the outer deeds as on the inward spirit which lightened and thundered through them; the inward spirit, which is as much needed by England as by India; which is, perhaps, especially needed in the generation through which we are passing. It is in no indiscriminate eulogy that we would indulge. He had, no doubt, his failings of judgment and his faults of character, but so much the more conspicuous for warning and encouragement are the traits which those who knew him best have communicated to me in such a form as to enable me to use their very words. We sometimes hear it said that ostentation and luxury are gaining ground

on the "plain living and high thinking" of former times.
It may be so: at least, if it is so, let us recall, as a
counteractive and antiseptic to these corrupting influences, the example of that Spartan simplicity, carried
sometimes to excess, but rooted in a genuine modesty
and granite solidity, which, if we could not always
imitate or commend, we could not help admiring. We
hear, also, in these modern days that the responsibility
of great officials in our distant dependencies is of necessity relaxed and enervated because of the increasing
control exercised from the central source of power. It
may be so: it may be inevitable: but, nevertheless, there
will always be a lesson of profound instruction in the
example of a man who had the foresight to discern what
needed to be done and the boldness to do it without
fear of consequences and without regard to his own
fame and fortune. We often hear it said, also, that to
the cause of party all other interests must be subordi-
nated; that for the sake of keeping a party together no
interests are too sacred or too enlightened to be spared;
that, in deference to its claims, appointments must be
made regardless of the fitness of the man to the place
or the place to the man. But to India that distortion
of party bias never reaches. Whatever else may be the
faults of its governors, it is the welfare of India, and
not the personal disputes of English politics, that sway
their minds. No such thought, still less any thought
of selfish aggrandizement, entered into the noble soul
which has passed away. Doubtless in this, as I have
said, he stood not alone; yet it is worth remembering
how, in this conspicuous example, we have had amongst
us a spirit permeated through and through by the rare
virtue of unshaken impartiality, and fruitful of that
class of good deeds which, as regards their effects on
human happiness and virtue, rank almost the very high-

est, that which the Emperor Alexander Severus placed as amongst the chief graces of the early Christians, that they gave away their offices to the best men without respect of persons.

Again, stern as he was in action and forward in decision, it was action and decision depending on the knowledge that he had acquired. If in England he failed in some of his undertakings, it was, as he himself felt, from the want of sufficient knowledge; but if in India he was confident of success, it was from the fulness of knowledge which gave him the power to do with all his might whatsoever his hand found to do. He strove to the utmost to make himself acquainted with all forms and varieties of the native races which he was called to govern. He was a fine example of the value — the inestimable value — of India as a school of training for the bringing up of a race of civil and military administrators, in whom it is ingrained, not as a theory, but as a duty, to study those complex forms of human character so unlike ours and yet so deeply instructive for us to contemplate, even without regard to the usefulness of such a study for their effective governance. It was this wide circumspection which made every word of rebuke or reproof from him, whether to Englishmen or to natives, come with such peculiar force. There is a story worth repeating as an instance of his lofty dealing with inferior minds. During his conduct of some important cause for a young Indian Rajah, the Prince endeavored to place in his hands under the table a sack of rupees. He answered at once, "Young man, you have offered to an Englishman the greatest insult which an Englishman can possibly receive. This time, in consideration of your youth, I excuse it. Let me warn you from this experience never again to perpetrate so gross an offence against an English gentleman." How many are there who will never forget the moral effect produced upon themselves by his indefatigable, untiring industry so long as health and eyesight were left to him, and his profound contempt for the idle, lounging, loitering habits by which so much of human existence in our time is expended and destroyed! He worked, we are told, morning, noon, and, in the literal sense of the word, night, as well as day. He was free to receive communications of all sorts from all sorts of people. If a murder, or party fight, or flagrant robbery was reported to him, he was at once in the saddle and away to any part of his district, regardless of sun or tempest. If a dispute about land was threatening the public peace, he flew at once to the spot, with the proverb ever on his tongue, "Disputes about land must be settled on the land," — a homely proverb, full of truth on many other questions than that of land, and in many other countries than India.

Such virtues and graces as I have spoken of may, perchance, be thought too homely, too far removed from the burning and thrilling atmosphere of inspired genius or brilliant wit or impassioned piety to deserve the tribute of honor awarded to him by a sorrowing nation. But it is the very homeliness of these gifts and graces that makes them so instructive for a mixed congregation or for a whole nation to contemplate. He was, indeed, a hero even after the manner of the heroes of his favorite Plutarch, or of his favorite Walter Scott; but he became a hero through the means of those quiet, intelligible, and, so to speak, ordinary virtues which are not beyond the reach of the youngest or the humblest of those who hear me. It was, as has been said, by reason of those heathen, often-despised yet cardinal and most Christian virtues of justice, for-

titude, temperance, and prudence, exercised by him on
a grand scale, that the Empire of India was sustained.

Yet one step farther. We may be allowed to penetrate beyond the manifestation of great deeds, behind
the manifestation of great qualities. Any one who
saw him felt at once in his presence a certain majestic
dignity, a calm repose, which made us confident that
with him, under whatever emergency, we were safe.
He was not only a leader of men, but a leader on
whom men could rely without the apprehension of
those sudden weaknesses and betrayals by which some
of the most gifted among the human race have diffused
around them a sense, not of security, but of mistrust.
We were reminded, when we saw him, of that passage
in the Book of Isaiah, which says, "Who among us
shall dwell with the devouring fire? who among us
shall dwell with everlasting burnings?" That is to
say, in the true sense of the passage, "Who shall
endure the scorching flames of temptation, or trial, or
danger, or pain, in order to gain that supernatural
strength which bids defiance to the wrong-doings of
earth?" And the answer of the prophet is the only
true one: "He that walketh righteously, and speaketh
uprightly; he that despiseth the gain of princes, and
that shaketh his hands from the holding of bribes,
and that stoppeth his ears from hearing of blood, and
shutteth his eyes from seeing evil;" that is to say, he
who scorns to do wrong; he who would not go against
his conscience for any advantage; he who has no eyes
to see, and no ears to hear the allurements to evil —
he, and he only, will be certainly prepared for every
thing that can come upon him. We ask yet further,
Why and how is this? What is it, whether in the
ordinary trials of everyday life, or the sterner trials of
the State or the Church, that gives us this security?

The prophet's next words give the reply: " He shall dwell on high; his place of defence shall be the strong rocks; his bread shall be given him; his water shall be sure." That is to say, he shall be like a man in an impregnable fortress; though the castle be wrapped in a circle of flames, he will look down on the raging sea of fire without the fear of its reaching his soul; his provisions will certainly hold out; there is within his citadel a perennial well of water.

This is exactly the description of the upright Christian man, whether martyr or missionary, whether statesman or soldier. He looks down as from a mountain cliff. He looks down on pain and weakness as contemptible. This is the very intention of calling such a man a man of high soul, of high mind, of high principle. He is lofty; he is in the "munitions of rocks." He has his own resources in himself. He has the bread and water which shall not fail, the food of noble thoughts, of inspiring recollections, and devout prayer. He has that well of living water, an undefiled conscience, a pure heart, clean hands, communion with the invisible world.

Such, or something like this, was, we may believe, the inner character which formed the spiritual basis of that mountain of moral strength. We know that in the narrower sense of the word religion, he was never ashamed or afraid to profess his belief in those simple truths of Christianity which he found enough for his soul's support. To societies for the diffusion of the Bible, or for promoting missionary efforts, he gave his sincere and public adhesion. In the welcome rendered to the unfettered faith of the Indian Reformer, Chunder Sen, outside the pale of every church, he cordially joined. But it is not these more external expressions of Christian belief that bear the best witness to his

religious life.   It is the fact that his whole conduct
was grounded on the assurance that he was working
with and for Eternal Righteousness and Love.   Those
virtues of which we have spoken — of just dealing and
indomitable industry — were touched by the light as of
a better world, were purified and softened as time went
on.   "He only feared his fellow-men so little" — I
quote the words of one who knew him well — "because
he feared his God so much."   In early days, his friends
used to call him "Iron John."   Their feeling towards
him was more, perhaps, of respect and awe than of
affection; but as years advanced, and his solid character yielded more and more to religious and domestic
influence, his gentler nature was developed.   Those
who enjoyed his intercourse more and more perceived
a gracious pleasantness which was rather commended
by his outward ruggedness and sternness.   There was
a touching magnanimity brought into relief by the
entire resignation with which, regardless of suffering
and weakness, he submitted to the privations and trials
— alas! how severe to him and to us all — of failing
powers and failing eyesight.   Each year he seemed to
those around him to become more prepared for that
great change which has now suddenly overtaken him.

Farewell, great pro-consul of our English Christian
Empire!   Where shall we look in the times that are
coming for an abounding knowledge and disinterested
love of India like his?   Where shall we find that resolute mind and countenance which seem to say —

> —— this rock shall fly
> From its firm base as soon as I?

He has gone; but he has not been amongst us in vain,
and we have not lost him altogether, if he has left behind
him a standard of integrity to which every Indian ruler

can look back — an example for every Englishman and every English boy of what an Englishman and a Christian may be, a true servant of the English State, a true servant of our Lord Jesus Christ. In that touching prayer found in the handwriting of the young French prince whose untimely death this country is so sadly mourning, there are these most true and significant words, which come home to every bereaved heart and every bereaved nation: "If I forget those who are departed, I shall in my turn be forgotten. May I never give way to the sad suggestion that time effaces every thing! Grant that there may sink deeper and deeper into my heart the conviction that those who are gone are witnesses of all my actions. My life shall then be worthy to be seen by them. My innermost thoughts shall then be such as will never cause me to blush for them."

That, in a narrower or a further degree is the feeling which, more or less, we ought, all of us, to entertain of the dead. They, in their blest estate, are witnesses to us of what they would have us to be. Their memory is a standing rebuke, or a cheering call, in the hours of failure, and temptation, and sorrow. From the grave of such a one as he whom we have lost there comes up the message of his life, not only to the nation at large, but to the weary and heavy laden, the desolate and the afflicted: "Be strong and of a good courage: be not afraid, neither be thou dismayed; for the Lord thy God — the Eternal Truth and Mercy — is and shall be with thee in this world and in the next whithersoever thou goest."

THOMAS CARLYLE.

February 6, 1881, on the occasion of the death of Mr. Carlyle.

The kingdom of heaven is likened unto a man which sowed good seed in his field. —MATTHEW xiii. 24. .

THE Gospel of this day starts with a comparison of the kingdom of heaven to a sower. It is the same as that with which the more celebrated parable begins, "A sower went forth to sow." They both fix our minds on the manner in which God's kingdom — the kingdom of truth, beauty, and goodness — is carried on in the world. The kingdom of all that is good is fostered, not so much by direct and immediate plantation, or grafting, or building, or formation of any kind; but rather by the sowing of good seed, which in time shall grow up and furnish a rich harvest.

It is so with regard to the truths of the Bible. They are sown in the world; the good which grows up after them is never in outward form like the truth which came from the actual source. Institutions spring up. They may derive their vitality from the " corns of wheat which fall into the ground and die;"[1] but they cannot be the very thing itself. There is not a single form or a single doctrine of Christendom of which the outward shape is not different in some way from the principle of life which gave it birth.

There is only one instance in the whole Bible of a

---

[1] John xii. 24. .

ready-made scholastic doctrine, and that has been long known to be spurious. It is not the verse of the three witnesses, but the parable of the Good Shepherd, the poetry of the Prodigal Son, the pathetic story of the Crucifixion that have been the true seeds of the Christian life. In this way it is that the Divine origin of these truths proves itself. The bright and tender words can never grow old, because they are not flowers cut and dried, but seeds and roots, which are capable of bearing a thousand applications.

Again, this is the ground of our looking forward with a hope which nothing can extinguish towards the transformation, the renewal of the human life, for a moment perishing, to re-appear, we trust, in some future world instinct with the capacities for good or evil with which it was endowed or which it has acquired in the world that now is. "The seminal form within the deeps of that little chaos sleeps," which will, we trust, in the Almighty Providence of God, restore that chaos of decayed and broken powers into conditions more elevated than now we can dream of.

Again, characters appear in the world which have a vivifying and regenerating effect, not so much for the sake of what they teach us, as for the sake of showing us how to think and how to act. What Socrates taught concerning man and the universe has long since passed away; but what he taught of the method and process of pursuing truth — the inquiry, the cross-examination, the sifting of what we do know from what we not know — this is the foundation, the good seed, of European philosophy for all time. What St. Paul taught concerning circumcision and election or grace is among the things hard to be understood, which the unlearned and the unstable may wrest to their own destruction, or which, having served their generation, may be laid asleep; but what he taught of the mode and manner of arriving at Divine truth, when he showed how "the letter killeth and the spirit maketh alive;" when he sets forth how charity is the bond of all perfectness; when he showed how all men are acceptable to God by fulfilling, each in his vocation, whether Jew or Gentile, whether slave or free, the commandments of God — when he said these things he laid the true foundation of Christian faith; he planted in the heart of man the seed, the good seed, of Christian liberty and Christian duty, to bear fruit again and again amidst the many relapses and eclipses of Christendom. When Luther dinned into the ears of his generation the formulas of transubstantiation and of justification by faith only, this was doomed to perish and "wax old as doth a garment;" but his acts, his utterances of indignant conscience, and of far-sighted genius, became the seed of the Reformation, the hope of the world. When John Wesley rang the changes on the well-known formula of assurance, it was the word of the ordinary preacher; but his whole career of fifty years of testifying for holiness and preaching against vice — that was the seed of more than Methodism; it was the seed of the revival of English religious zeal. Such seeds, such principles, such infusions, not of a mechanical system, but of a new light in the world, are not of every-day occurrence; they are the work of a few, of a gifted few; and it is therefore so much the more to be observed when any one who has had it in his power to scatter such seeds right and left passes away, leaving us to ask what we have gained, what we can assimilate of the peculiar nourishment which his life and teaching may have left for our advantage. Few will doubt that such a one was he who yesterday was taken from us. It may be that he will not be laid, as might have been expected, amongst the poets and scholars and sages whose dust rests within this Abbey; it may be that he was drawn by an irresistible longing towards the native hills of his own Dumfriesshire, and that there, beside the bones of his kindred, beside his father and his mother, and with the silent ministrations of the Church of Scotland, to which he still clung amidst all the vicissitudes of his long existence, will repose all that is earthly of Thomas Carlyle. But he belonged to a wider sphere than Scotland; for though by nationality a Scotchman, he yet was loved and honored wherever the British nation extends, wherever the English language is spoken. Suffer me, then, to say a few words on the good seed which he has sown in our hearts.

In his teaching, as in all things human, there were no doubt tares, or what some would account tares, which must be left to after times to adjust as best they can with the pure wheat which is gathered into the garner of God. There were imitations, parasitic exaggerations, of the genuine growth, which sometimes almost choked the original seed and disfigured its usefulness and its value; but of this we do not speak here. Gather them up into bundles and burn them. We speak only of him and of his best self. Nor would we now discourse at length on those brilliant gifts which gave such a charm to his writings and such an unexampled splendor to his conversation. All the world knows how the words and the deeds of former times became in his hands, as Luther describes the Apostle's language, "not dead things, but living creatures with hands and feet." Every detail was presented before us, penetrated through and through with the fire of poetic imagination, which was the more powerful because it derived its warmth from facts gathered together by the most untiring industry. Who can ever, from this time forward, picture the death of Louis XV., or the flight of the king and queen, without remembering the thrill of emotion with which, through the " History of the French Revolution," they became acquainted with them for the first time? Who can wander amongst the ruins of St. Edmund's at Bury without feeling that they are haunted in every corner by the life-like figure of the Abbot Samson, as he is drawn from the musty chronicle of Jocelyn? Who can read the letters and the speeches of Cromwell, now made almost intelligible to modern ears, without gratitude to the unwearied zeal which gathered together from every corner those relics of departed greatness? What German can fail to acknowledge that not even in that much-enduring, all-exhausting country of research and labor — not even there has there been raised such a monument to Frederick the Second, called the Great, as by the simple Scotchman who, for the sake of describing what he considered the last hero-king, almost made himself for the time a soldier and a statesman?

But on these and many like topics this is not the time or place to speak. It is for us to ask, as I have said, what was the good seed which he sowed in the field of our hearts, and in what respects we shall be, or ought to be, the better for the sower having lived and died among us.

It was customary for those who honored him to speak of him as a "prophet." And if we take the word in its largest sense he truly deserved the name. He was a prophet, and felt himself to be a prophet, in the midst of an untoward generation; his prophet's mantle was his rough Scotch dialect, and his own peculiar diction, and his own secluded manner of life. He was a prophet most of all in the emphatic utterance of truths which no one else, or hardly any one else, ventured to deliver, and which he felt to be a message of good to a world sorely in need of them. He stood almost alone among the men of his time in opposing a stern, inflexible, resistance, to the whole drift and pressure of modern days towards exalting popular opinion and popular movements as oracles to be valued above the judgment of the few, above the judgment of the wise, the strong, and the good. Statesmen, men of letters, preachers, have all bowed their heads under the yoke of this, as they believed, irresistible domination, under the impression that the first duty of the chiefest man is not to lead but to be led, the necessary condition of success to ascertain which way the current flows, and to swim with it as far as it will bear us. To his mind all this proved an insane delusion. That expression of his which has become, like many of his expressions, almost proverbial in the minds of those who like them least, will express the attitude of his mind — his answer to the question, "What are the people of England?" "Thirty millions — mostly fools." The whole framework and fabric of his mind was built up on the belief that there are not many wise, not many noble minds, not many destined by the Supreme Ruler of the universe to rule their fellows; that few are chosen, that "strait is the gate and narrow is the way, and few there be that find it." But when the few appear, when the great and good present themselves, it is the duty and the wisdom of the multitude to seek their guidance. A Luther, a Cromwell, a Goethe, were to him the born kings of men. This was his doctrine of the work of heroes; this, right or wrong, was the mission of his life. It is, all things considered, a fact much to be meditated upon; it is, all things considered, a seed which is worthy of our cultivation.

There is another feeling of the age to which he also

stood resolutely opposed, or, rather, a feeling of the age
which was resolutely opposed to him — the tendency
to divide men into two hostile camps, parted from each
other by watchwords and flags, and banners and tokens
which we commonly designate by the name of party.
He disparaged, perchance unduly, the usefulness, the
necessity, of party organization or party spirit as a
part of the secondary machinery by which the great
affairs of the world are carried on; but he was a signal
example of a man who not only could be measured by
no party standard, but absolutely disregarded it. He
never, during the whole course of his long life, took an
active part — never, I believe, even voted — in those
elections which, to most of us, are the very breath of
our nostrils. For its own sake he cherished whatever
was worth preserving; for its own sake he hailed whatever improvement was worth effecting. He cared not
under what name or by what man the preservation or
the improvement was achieved. This, too, is an ideal
which few can attain, which still fewer attempt; but it
is something to have had one man who was possessed by
it as a vital and saving truth. And such a man was the
Prophet of Chelsea. But there was that in him which,
in spite of his own contemptuous description of the
people, in spite of his scorn for the struggles of party,
endeared him in no common degree even to those who
most disagreed with him, even to the humblest classes
of our great community. He was an eminent instance
of how a man can trample on the most cherished idols
of the market-place if yet he shows that he has in his
heart of hearts the joys, the sorrows, the needs of his
toiling, suffering fellow-creatures. In this way they
insensibly felt drawn towards that tender, fervid nature
which was weak when they were weak, which burned
with indignation when they suffered wrong. They felt

that if he despised them it was in love; if he refused to follow their bidding it was because he believed that their bidding was an illusion.

And for that independence of party of which I spoke, there was also the countervailing fact that no man could for a moment dream that it arose from indifference to his country. He was no monk; he was no hermit dwelling apart from the passions which sway the destinies of a great nation. There is no man living to whom the thrift, the industry, the valor of his countrymen was so deeply precious. There is no man living to whom, had it been possible for him to have been aroused from the torpor of approaching death, the news would have been more welcome that the Parliament of England had been in the past week saved from becoming a byword and reproach and shame amongst the nations of the earth. And all this arose out of a frame of mind which others have shared with him, but which, perhaps, few have been able to share to the same extent. The earnestness — the very word is almost his own — the earnestness, the seriousness with which he approached the great problems of all human life have made us feel them also. The tides of fashion have swept over the minds of many who once were swayed by his peculiar tones; but there must be many a young man whose first feelings of generosity and public spirit were roused within him by the cry as if from the very depths of the heart, "Where now are your Hengists and your Horsas? Where are those leaders who should be leading their people to useful employments, to distant countries — where are they? Preserving their game!" Before his withering indignation all false pretensions, all excuses for worthless idleness and selfish luxury fell away. The word which he invented to describe them has sunk perhaps into cant and hollowness; but it had a truth when first he uttered it. Those falsities were shams, and they who practised them were guilty of the sin which the Bible, in scathing terms, calls hypocrisy.

And whence came this earnestness? Deep down in the bottom of his soul it sprang from his firm conviction that there was a higher, a better world than that visible to our outward senses. All who acted on this conviction — whether called saints in the middle ages, or Puritans in the seventeenth century, or what you like in our own day — he revered them, with all their eccentricities, as bright and burning examples of those who "sacrificed their lives to their higher natures, their worser to their better parts." In addressing the students at Edinburgh he bade them remember that the deep recognition of the eternal justice of heaven, and the unfailing punishment of crimes against the law of God, is at the origin and foundation of all the histories of nations. No nation which did not contemplate this wonderful universe with an awe-stricken and reverential belief that there was a great unknown, omnipotent, all-wise, and all-just Being superintending all men and all interests in it — no nation ever came to very much, nor did any man either, who forgot that. If a man forgot that, he forgot the most important part of his mission in the world. So he spoke, and the ground of his hope for Europe — of his hope, we may say, against hope — was that, after all, in any commonwealth where the Christian religion exists, nay, in any commonwealth where it has once existed, public and private virtue, the basis of all good, never can become extinct, but in every new age, and even after the deepest decline, there is a chance, and, in the course of ages, the certainty, of renovation. The Divine depths of sorrow, the sanctity of sorrow, the life and death of the Divine man — these were to him Christianity. We stand, as it were, beside him whilst the grave has not yet closed over those flashing eyes, over those granite features, over that weird form on which we have so often looked, whilst the silence of death has fallen on that house which was once so frequented and so honored. We call up memories which occurred to ourselves. One such, in the far past, may perchance come with peculiar force to those whose work is appointed in this place. Many years ago, whilst I belonged to another cathedral, I met him in St. James's Park, and walked with him to his own house. It was during the Crimean War; and after hearing him denounce with his vigorous and perhaps exaggerated earnestness the chaos and confusion into which our Administration had fallen, and the doubt and distrust which pervaded all classes at the time, I ventured to ask him, " What, under the circumstances, is your advice to a Canon of an English Cathedral?" He grimly laughed at my question. He paused for a moment and then answered in homely and well-known words; but which were, as it happened, especially fitted to situations like that in which he was asked to give his counsel — " Whatsoever thy hand findeth to do, do it with all thy might." That is no doubt the lesson he leaves to each one of us in this place, and also to this weary world — the world of which he felt the weariness as age and infirmity grew upon him; the lesson which, in his more active days, he practised to the very letter. He is at rest; he is at rest; delivered from that burden of the flesh against which he chafed and fretted! He is at rest! In his own words, " Babylon, with its deafening inanity, rages on, innocuous and unheeded, to the dim forever." From the " silence of the eternities " of which he so often spoke, there still sound, and will long sound, the tones of that marvellous voice.

Let us take one tender expression written three or four years ago, one plaintive yet manful thought which has never yet reached the public eye. " Three nights ago, stepping out after midnight, and looking up at the stars which were clear and numerous, it struck me with a strange, new kind of feeling — Hà ! in a little while I shall have seen you also for the last time. God Almighty's own theatre of immensity — the infinite made palpable and visible to me — that also will be closed — flung to in my face — and I shall never behold that either any more. The thought of *this* eternal deprivation (even of *this*, though this is such a nothing in comparison) was sad and painful to me. And then a second feeling rose upon me, What if Omnipotence that has developed in me these pieties, these reverences, and infinite affections, should actually have said, Yes, poor mortal, such as you who have gone so far *shall* be permitted to go farther? Hope, despair not! — God's will. God's will; not ours if it is unwise."

God's will, not ours, be done. Yes, God's will be done for us and for him. The Lord gave and the Lord taketh away.

THE DAYS OF OLD.

February 13, 1881, the Sunday following the death of Lord John
Thynne, Sub-dean of Westminster.

I have considered the days of old : and the years that are past. —
PSALM lxxvii. 5 (Prayer-book version).
I have considered the days of old, and the years of ancient times. —
Ibid. (Bible version).

THE Psalmist is in a state of deep depression ; he
wonders whether the Eternal will absent Himself forever ; he asks whether His mercy is clean gone forever, and His promises come utterly to an end for evermore. We know not the special causes of this anxiety, but we see in the Psalm the manner in which
his troubled spirit was composed, and the thoughts in
which he took refuge. He dwelt on the days of old ;
on the history of the years that were past. He remembered the wonders that God had wrought in old time ;
he thought of all His works ; he went back especially
to the days long ago when the people of Israel were
brought up out of the land of Egypt ; he seemed to see,
almost as in a vision, the passage which they accomplished through the Red Sea ; the storm of the strong
east wind that drove the waters back, the thunder
which shook their souls with dread, the lightning which
illuminated the darkness of that memorable night, the
earthquake which caused the ground beneath them to
tremble, the mysterious pathway through the great
waters, the inscrutable footsteps of the Most High in

the waves of the Red Sea, and the leading of the people like a flock of terrified sheep by the hand of their venerable rulers, Moses, the mighty Prophet, and Aaron, the sacred Priest.

Such a backward view towards the past is still one chief remedy for times of despondency. It is true that to look forward is the best of all remedies. The belief that in the progress of mankind there is a hope of ultimate perfection was the prevailing sentiment of the highest spirits in the Jewish race. The Jewish race itself had, as has been said, its golden age not in the past but in the future. The same thought has descended to Christian times. The Apostle forgot those things that were behind, and reached forward to those things which were before. The whole creation, according to him, was constantly reaching forth its hand in the earnest expectation of the manifestation of some future glory in the sons of God. But this prospective glance is not the only consolation. At any rate, without a retrospective look into the times that we have already known, the forward apprehension of what is to be becomes unsteady and unstable. A great statesman,[1] whose monument is in this church, has combined the expression of the two feelings in a motto which is now engraven upon the pedestal — *Per ardua stabilis*, that is to say, constantly ascending the most arduous and adventurous precipices, yet still never losing his footing. It is written under the mountain goat, which, climbing constantly, and yet firm in its hold on the rock, is the emblem of the house of Russell — but also the emblem of every wise statesman. That hold, that footing, is best preserved by having an anchor, so to speak, in the thoughts and memories of the past.

There are two special lessons which this study of the

---

[1] The late Earl Russell.

days of old enforces upon us. First, in face of the temptation to which we are all liable of regarding ourselves as "the foremost in the files of time," it is the natural corrective to be from time to time reminded that there have lived "famous men" in old time — that there have been the "fathers that begat us" — that, as the Roman poet sings, "there were mighty men who lived before Agamemnon," and who, perchance, have only fallen out of our knowledge because there was no bard to trumpet forth their praises, or because we are so ignorant as not to know what they did or what they thought. "Art thou the first man that was born, or wast thou made before the hills?" Such a belief is very common at the present time. It shows itself in many ways; it shows itself in a mode of feeling widely diffused, as if Christianity had been born into England about thirty years ago, or at least as if the revival of religious life in England dated from a modern movement of yesterday. Without going back to the earlier times of the eighteenth century, which, whatever drawbacks it may have had, yet produced the solid, massive, enduring faith of Butler, Burke, Johnson, and Paley, and embraced the whole of the splendid career of John Wesley and his followers — without going back to that period, there was, in the beginning of this century, a general awakening of the deeper and higher life in a thousand quarters, breathed into the world by the seriousness which was the natural outgrowth of the great events subsequent to the French Revolution. Of these convulsions it may well be said in the words of the Psalm from which the text is taken: "The waters saw Thee, O God, the waters saw Thee, and were afraid: the depths also were troubled. The voice of Thy thunder was heard round about. The lightnings shone upon the ground: the earth was moved and shook withal. Thy way was in the sea, and Thy paths in the great waters, and Thy footsteps were not known." This seriousness expresses itself in many forms — in the profound poetry of Wordsworth, in the heart-stirring romances of Walter Scott, in the deep earnestness of Thomas Carlyle, in the thoughtful philosophy of Coleridge, in the stimulus given to religious education by Arnold, in the practical fervor of Wilberforce and of Simeon, in the more sober but not less effective energy of laymen like Joshua Watson, and clergymen like Blomfield and his compeers on the Episcopal Bench. These were all in full operation before the first growth of that movement which claims to itself in the present day the exclusive privilege of having enlightened and purified the country. All honor to those who in our time, by any means in their power, whether by the adornment of worship, or by throwing life into old forms and light into old truths, have carried on the work which their fathers began for them! But not the less is the first honor due to those who in the early years of this century awoke to the duties of their position, and fulfilled its high calling. And if, as was the case, they performed their duties and fulfilled their task with the more difficulty because they were the first to attempt it; if they did good not for the sake of glorifying themselves or the party to which they belonged, but simply for the sake of doing good, and of rendering the best service to the Church and Commonwealth in which their lot had been cast, so much the more praise is due to them in their often thankless and unrewarded mission.

Again, the study of the past teaches us the intrinsic value of qualities which we do not possess. The young are always apt to believe that in their sanguine, lively, forward imaginings there is something superior to the

wisdom and experience of old age. Doubtless each
generation must learn not only from that which has
gone before but from that which is coming after it.
The rising generation has grasped some truth which
the older generation may have failed to apprehend.
Even a child can instruct its elders by good example, by innocent questions, and by simple statements.
Elihu, in the Book of Job, was " very young," and the
three friends were " very old," yet to the younger and
not to the elder was intrusted the message of pointing
out the answer to the difficulties which had perplexed
them. " I am wiser than the aged," says the Psalmist,
" because I keep Thy commandments." This is a truth
which we must bear in mind in dealing both with men
and with nations. But nevertheless reverence for age
is a duty of all times and all places. Diffidence and
modesty are the virtues which ought to belong to youth
alike in the East and in the West. There is a kindred
.nation across the Atlantic which, with all its excel-
lences, has not possessed in any eminent degree this
modesty of thought or action. That is chiefly because
it has, or thinks it has, no venerable ancestry at its
back, and no long traditions to hold in reverence. The
respect due to age is founded on the qualities which
long experience brings with it, and the wide and comprehensive view of human affairs which, unless it falls
grievously below its calling, is unquestionably its own.
I have frequently mentioned, and will yet again mention, that most touching of all the expressions of auto-
biography, the reminiscences in which Richard Baxter,
at the close of his long and eventful life, sums up the
points in which the excesses and the crudities of his
youthful opinions were checked by the moderation and
the calmness and the charity of old age. From such
counsellors every one may pause in the hurry of life to

learn the lessons of a truth which is not our own, and a wisdom which, if not from above, is at any rate not of this world. "Reverence is the angel of the world" —so said the great master of the human heart. So remarked upon the words the oldest and one of the wisest of our statesmen the other day, before he sank to his long rest, "Reverence is what softens, elevates, refines, the minds of men."

You will have perceived what is the thought that has suggested these reflections. A long and venerable career in this Abbey has just closed. A link — almost the only surviving link — which united us with the earlier years of this century has been snapped asunder. That stately figure, those courtly manners, that high bearing, that grand form and fashion as of the antique world, will no more be seen amongst us. For nearly fifty years has the second office in this collegiate church been in the same hands, and the continuous tradition of six decanal reigns has been summed up in the existence which has passed away.

He was one of those on whom were poured some at least of the beneficent influences of the opening years of the nineteenth century. He was one of those of whom I spoke, to whom belongs the singular merit of having been an unconscious reformer before the time when reform became so fashionable; one who, while himself a stanch adherent of ancient usage and established custom, nevertheless saw the possibility and the necessity of purifying them of their ingrained abuses. He did this at a time when such work was difficult in proportion to its novelty. He found this Abbey infected with maladies which the negligence or the altered circumstances of preceding years had introduced into its very core. The free admission to its sacred walls, which had been debarred by tolls and im-

posts at almost every entrance, he forced on the reluc-
tant authorities, regardless of the panic fears which
would have protected the building at the cost of rendering it useless. Down to his time nave and transepts
were alike closed to the wayfarer and the worshipper
in London. All these restrictions were done away;
and if there still remain some obstacles to the full and
free enjoyment of every part of the Abbey, it will be
following in the footsteps of his policy to sweep them
away when time and opportunity shall permit. The
vast congregations which now assemble Sunday after
Sunday are enabled to enjoy free air and free hearing,
by the courage and confidence with which, under his
sanction, the wooden screens were thrown down on
either side, which cut off all communication between
the choir and the transepts. The reredos, with its
mosaics and its statues, may have been arranged and
designed by other hands and other minds, but its whole
form and fabric is owing to his active watchfulness
and foresight, as was also the pulpit from which the
preacher speaks. The bald walls of the Jerusalem
Chamber, from a like source, have resumed something
of their original splendor, and the tapestries which
adorn them are chiefly gifts from the stores of his ancient home. The services which have gathered thousands within the sound of the preacher's voice on
Sunday evenings were first inaugurated by him when,
in the year of the Great Exhibition, multitudes from
all the ends of the world were congregated in this
metropolis, and many heard, for the first and last time
from an English pulpit, in his own French language,
the words of a vigorous preacher,[1] now no more. The
whole architecture of this Abbey received a new life
from the introduction, under his patronage, of that

[1] Dr. Jeune, afterwards Bishop of Peterborough.

famous architect whose name is identified with almost
every Gothic church in England. The choral service,
with all its arrangements, was by him rescued from the
neglect and disorder into which for many years it had
fallen. The addition of a Great Cloister, which should
extend the glory of the Abbey, and provide for the
future interment of the eminent men of our country,
was never absent from his mind. His wish still remains unfulfilled; but if there should revive in the
nation or its rulers any thing of the munificent spirit
of former times, it will be remembered that the idea
first arose with him, and was by him encouraged and
fostered at every turn, with all the fondness of a parent for a long-expected child.

In earlier times, it may be, from the gradual steps of
the increase in the population around it, the Abbey of
Westminster had taken but little heed of the multitudes
which at last pressed upon it with an intolerable burden. He was the first who recognized the fact that to
this vast neighborhood the Abbey had a duty to perform. Long ago, before any public attention had been
called to the need, he urged the wants of the surrounding parishes on those concerned; and it was owing to
his incessant exertions that thousands were given to
the support of churches which are now the standing
witnesses of his energy. He was the zealous assistant
of his colleague, the present estimable Bishop of Lincoln, in starting that fund for relieving the spiritual
destitution of the people of Westminster which long
preceded the agencies since set on foot for the same object. The times have moved, the special work is accomplished; but the originators ought not to be forgotten,
and the enterprise then set on foot has still to be carried on, though the head and the heart which first
planned it have been chilled by age and infirmity, and
are now cold in death.

And far away from Westminster, in Somersetshire and Cornwall, there are many who will remember the good works which, whether in his own peculiar field or in the wider sphere of the rising wants of the Church, he fostered and favored by bringing to bear upon them his administrative ability and his honest intentions. May I mention two instances of this? One shall be the effect which he produced on Nonconformists. In the western parish in which he long labored there was a colony of the Society of Friends. Separated from them by every feeling, political and ecclesiastical, he was yet so drawn to the good Quakers by their singular purity and piety, and they were so drawn to him by his singular straightforwardness and uprightness, that a steady friendship resulted, never broken, and which lasted to the very end. The other example will endear his memory to many of my own profession. He was the virtual founder of the first of theological colleges — nearly the first in time, and absolutely the first in importance — the college at Wells. There is no doubt much to be said for and against theological colleges, much to be said in favor of the larger, more generous, education that young men receive at the two ancient Universities. But there can be no doubt that there was room for at least one such college; there can be no doubt that a real want was supplied by the institution which sprang up in that loveliest of all cathedral precincts, in that beautiful Vicars' Close, under the shade of that stately palace and that exquisite cathedral, which had once been the home of Ken. Not a few will trace back their rescue from frivolous pursuits, their sense of a deeper religious earnestness, to the parental counsels of the good old man whom he chose as its chief, and whose snow-white head and benignant face will be remembered by every student in the college as the

sign and symbol of all that was venerable and lova-
ble.[1]

"I have considered the days of old, and the years of
ancient times." For half a century he has been part of
this Abbey — almost like one of its own massive pillars,
unchanged while all around has changed, with the air,
the manners, the aspirations of another age. He, of all
our body, most united us with the days, as it were, be-
before the flood — before the flood of stir and change
broke in upon us in the far-off age of the first Reform
Bill. He most faithfully represented the time when
the nobles of the land were not ashamed to bear office
in the high places of the English Church. As these
changes whirled and wheeled around him he acknowledged their power, although he never shared their influence. Like the aged poet, whom a younger bard
celebrates —

> He grew old in an age he condemned;
> He looked on the rushing decay
> Of the times that had sheltered his youth;
> Felt the dissolving throes
> Of a social order he loved.[2]

In that long succession of Deans, to whom he acted
as vicegerent, of Canons, to whom he acted as colleague, there were varieties of character which might
well have vexed, and which doubtless did vex, his un-
bending nature. But, nevertheless, he well knew his
position as in one of the most national and all-embracing institutions of our national and all-embracing
Church. He did not shrink from companionship with
the widely tolerant and multifarious learning of Milman. His aged heart warmed at the fiery enthusiasm

[1] The Rev. John H. Pinder, first principal of the Theological College, Wells.
[2] Matthew Arnold on Wordsworth, in *The Youth of Nature*.

of Charles Kingsley. He delighted to work with the
bold geologist who for a time ruled over us. He delivered over the powers that he had long enjoyed with
chivalrous gallantry to the accomplishments and graces
of my honored predecessor. And, last of all, he bore
with one who must have sorely tried his endurance,
and who would fain take this occasion of expressing his
heartfelt gratitude for a loyal and generous forbearance,
never to be forgotten.

As years rolled on he faded away from our sight, but
we still remained in his thoughts. The time drew near
for the term of residence, which with unshaken fidelity
he had kept for fifty years. He came as usual. Like
an ancient warrior, he would still, so long as life was
granted, be found at his post. But on the threshold
the Angel of Death met him, and he passed away in
the sacred cloisters endeared by the recollection of his
beloved partner, whose loss had taken away so much of
the brightness of life — passed away in the effort to dis-
charge the last remaining relic of duty which was left
to him, and amidst the family to whom his patriarchal
presence and domestic virtues were so long an example,
a support, and a delight.

The shades have closed thick upon us — "fast falls
the eventide," — sorrow after sorrow, parting after
parting, has "rent our sheltering bowers." Not only
ourselves but the times are changed; tasks new and
unknown lie before us. But our duty and our hope
remain the same. That maxim which I quoted last
Sunday from the old prophet and sage of Scotland[1] is
still our motto : "Whatsoever thy hand findeth to do,
do it with all thy might." That was what he whom
we have lost from among us, so long as strength was
granted him, did, according to his light and according

---

[1] Carlyle. See *Sermon*, p. 263.

to his capacity. He persevered in what was often a thankless toil ; he set a falling house in order ; he laid the solid foundation whereon we must build. All of us. through all our degrees, have to do the work of edifying, beautifying. elevating, enlarging the Church of England, through this its most august and character-istic edifice. All of us have a high calling before us, which every difficulty, every obstacle, ought to stimu-late us to fulfil. The voices of the dead, the claims of the living, the greatness of England, the far-reaching future of the everlasting Gospel of Christ our Lord, entreat us not to be weary or faint. The last of an ancient race is gone from us. Let us do our best rightly to honor the trust which was once committed to him, and which he and his generation have handed down to us.

> Something ere the end,
> Some work of noble note may yet be done . . .
> 'Tis not too late to seek a newer world, . . .
> Made weak by time and fate, but strong in will,
> To strive, to seek, to find, and not to yield.

THE EARL OF BEACONSFIELD.

May 1, 1881.

So the dead which he slew at his death were more than they which he slew in his life. — JUDGES xvi. 30.

THESE words describe the death of Samson. A grim satisfaction breaks out of the sacred narrative as it records the circumstances of the hero's end. The vigor with which this feeling is expressed has given to the words a sense far more general than they bear in their immediate context. They rise above themselves — as is the fashion of words inspired by the feeling of men or by the Spirit of God — into regions far more exalted than they originally embraced. It has even been the custom, by a strange excess of exaggeration, to apply them to the greatest of all deaths, that of our Lord and Saviour Jesus Christ. But they have also been frequently applied to the deaths of men, on all occasions where advantages arise from dwelling on death and its concomitants. It has been felt to be so in cases where the manner of the death has redeemed the faults of an imperfect life; as when King Charles the First by his execution awakened a feeling which had been extinguished by his many faults, but was revived by the tragical nature of his end. As was nobly sung by the poet[1] of his enemies : —

> He nothing common did, or mean,
> Upon that memorable scene,

[1] Andrew Marvell, *Horatian Ode upon Cromwell's return from Ireland.*

> But with his keener eye
> The axe's edge did try;
> Nor call'd the gods with vulgar spite
> To vindicate his helpless right —

not, as he was called, a martyr, but still an example of the effect which an impressive death may have in recti-fying the mistakes of a life, rallying round himself and his cause a tender sentiment which had become almost extinct, but which, reviving from his blood, restored the fallen Church and monarchy. Sometimes it has been that the death has been such as to give a seal to the life, and be accordant with it, crowning and carry-ing it on to the end. Such have been the deaths of martyrs, according to the well-known saying of the seventeenth century, "The blood of the martyrs is the seed of the Church." Sometimes the effect has been produced by the last words of dying men, those swan-like strains which have in them a kind of prophecy, like music sweetest at its close, and which all the world afterwards delights to gather up as expressing a sense which no words in life would have equally conveyed. Sometimes it has happened in the case of eminent and gifted men that only their deaths have revealed to us their true value, and the value, or the failure, of our judgments respecting them. Not once or twice only within our own experience have we acknowledged too late the genius, the goodness, the intellect, of those whom in life we disparaged, neglected, or attacked. Not once or twice only has death converted many a bitter enemy, caused, we may almost say, a nation to do penance by the graves of those who were recog-nized at last, when they were passed beyond the reach of human praise and blame. Again and again have misrepresentations been explained by death more completely than ever could have been done by life.

This application, mingling more or less with the others, is suggested by the singular tribute of respect and grief which throughout England and Europe has attended the death of the celebrated statesman who has in the past week been laid in his quiet grave. It is not my intention to pronounce a funeral discourse upon the qualities which by universal consent rendered his career so remarkable. Such a treatment has been precluded by the circumstance of his not receiving the sepulchral honors within this Abbey to which in the judgment of his mighty rival and of a consentient country he was entitled. It is also rendered unnecessary by the eloquent words which on last Sunday were spoken to the vast congregation assembled within these walls.

But dismissing all thought of the judgments which may have been framed at the different points of his long and varied career, or of the religious and political questions which his life in its different parts suggested, I wish, before the shadow of the event has passed away from our recollection, to fix your thoughts for a few moments on the permanent lessons to be drawn from a sympathy so general as that which followed, not without surprise, on the close of this eventful life. It was a sympathy, not indeed to be named as equal, either in kind or degree, to that which accompanied to his grave the great warrior of our age some thirty years ago, but it is remarkable that, beyond doubt, it approached more nearly to that sentiment than any other which we have since witnessed, and as such is commemorated in that funeral anthem which has not been, and could not have been, repeated on any other occasion since the time when it was first composed for the funeral of that great man to whom I just now referred. " And the king himself followed the bier; and the king lifted up his voice and wept at the grave, and all the people wept."[1] These words at any rate correspond in some degree to the feeling which has now been roused, and they have on the whole corresponded to none other within the present generation. Let us see what we may learn from the expression of a grief which, whether right or wrong, whether well-grounded or ill-grounded, whether it pass away with the moment or whether it endure for posterity, is not unworthy of consideration in a Christian Church and in a national edifice.

First, there is something in the character of such a sentiment which is of itself ennobling. It is true that there was nothing sudden or striking in the departure of which we speak. It was not like the deaths to which I referred just now of Charles the First or of the early martyrs, nor yet did it bear any resemblance to the dreadful shock produced by the terrible murders of kings and emperors. It was a death, expected and prepared for, of one who was gathered like a full shock into the garner, passing away calmly and peacefully in the grasp of dear and faithful friends. But for this very reason there is something in it which appeals to our common nature, to our ideal of what we desire for ourselves and our children. There is in the great National Museum of France a touching likeness, from an Egyptian monument of four thousand years ago, representing the soul of the departed, clothed in the white garments of the grave, being led with calm and unmoved features into the unseen world by the strange and dark divinity who, with tender embrace, draws the dead man onwards into the presence of the impartial and awful Judge. What that image represents to us in outward form and in the earliest ages of the world, is

[1] 2 Sam. iii. 31, 32. Composed by Sir John Goss, Mus. Doc., for the funeral of the Duke of Wellington in St. Paul's, November 18, 1852.

the true figure of what the thought of death in its natural and constantly recurring shape suggests to every
son of Adam. Death, whenever it appears on the grand
stage of the world, must have a solemn and impressive
aspect. The end of a peasant is equally mournful and
equally significant to those of the little circle who assist
at the last hours; but when on an occasion of this kind
the curtains of the sick room are withdrawn and the
last scene is described to hundreds and thousands of
human beings in all parts of the civilized world, it is
then, in the words of our greatest living orator, though
in another sense, as if the Angel of Death passed near
to every one of us, as if the beating of his wings were
felt in every household, and the shadow of the sepulchre embraced us all within its precincts. The flashing eye is quenched, the commanding voice is silent.
Each one is reminded that there is an end of human
things, and a beginning of things eternal, inconceivable
yet certain.

Secondly, there is a natural sentiment in the human
heart, by which, in the presence of death, not only all
rancorous and ignoble feelings die and wither away, but
there is an irresistible tendency to view the dead for the
moment as transfigured by the light of his better qualities, and to dwell, not on the points wherein we widely
differ, but on the points wherein we closely agree. I
dwelt on this aspect of such events some weeks ago,
when speaking on another subject; but what I then
said has since received a striking and unexpected commentary in the unanimity of expression by which even
the severest judgments of the departed have been controlled, and the bitterness of alienation has been transformed into affectionate remembrance. I will not ask
how far this alienation or that severity were deserved
or undeserved, how far this kindly feeling was justified

or not justified; but we may all ask which of the two
sentiments is the more elevated, the more worthy of
rational human beings, the more becoming to Englishmen and to Christians. If such a sympathetic sentiment is in itself superior to the common expression of
an acrimonious hostility, it may be worth while to ask
whether we could not afford a little more, on one side
and the other, to introduce such a noble tone of thought
and feeling into our political and ecclesiastical strife,
whether after all there is not a more excellent way than
the constant interchange of fierce recriminations and
angry personalities. This may seem a chimerical
dream. It may even appear a condition of our existence which is not to be sought after; it may even commend itself to the light of reason and of Christianity
that the darker elements of human nature, the eager,
impetuous denunciation of what we deem wrong, must
have always their full sway, that rage and indignation
are the only true parts of eloquence, the only safe-
guards of right against injustice. One cannot help believing that, however just this may be for the time, yet
there is such a thing, even in this sphere, as striving
after Christian perfection. In the glimpses of a higher
state of feeling which now and then flash upon us in
moments of loftier sentiment and purer devotion, there
is brought before us something of that condition which
the Gospel describes to us, of the higher and the lower
state, in which Martha, the busy, incessant, indefatigable, uncontrollable worker, is cumbered about many
things, whilst Mary, her eye fixed on the brighter,
nobler aspect of sorrow, on the far-off intimations of
the Divine, has chosen the better part which shall not
be taken away from her. If any of us now look back
with satisfaction on the thought that in former days
they acknowledged in the departed the conscientious

endeavor to accomplish the duty of an English statesman, is not this a proof that such expressions were in
themselves admirable, and that, at the time, we were
fortunate to have given them vent? Or if, on the
other hand, we have used expressions which any of us
now regret, if we were so immersed, confined, cribbed,
and cabined within our own narrow views as to have
no eyes for what we now admire, is it not something to
have had a wider horizon opened before us in which
human characters appear as they will appear in the
presence of the All-just and the All-merciful?

Thirdly, there is another reflection akin to this. I
have several times spoken from this place of the hollowness of what are called popular judgments, of the futility of seeking after popularity, from whatsoever side
it comes. Sometimes popular judgments are generous,
sometimes they are ungenerous; sometimes they are
wise, sometimes they are foolish; sometimes they rest
on foundations which after ages may approve, sometimes they rest on absolutely no foundation at all.
But whether generous or ungenerous, wise or foolish,
groundless or well grounded, they are in all cases
worthless themselves. They are echoes, and not voices.
They breathe indeed an atmosphere round them, which
may be turned to good or evil account by those who
have the control of human affairs. But they have over
and over again been proved to shift with every gust of
feeling and fashion. Witness the rapid changes in the
French Revolution; the hero of to-day, the rejected of
to-morrow; the heresy of yesterday, the fixed principle
of to-day. Witness the changes that have taken place
with regard to persons and systems in our own time
and country. Such were in very great measure the
varying opinions respecting him who is gone. There
was the expression of strong approval some years ago;

there was the expression of no less strong disapproval a year ago; there is again the strong expression of sympathy now, almost universal. We do not venture to pronounce which of these various judgments most nearly corresponds with the truth. What is certain is that this popular voice has represented in this instance, as in a thousand other instances, widely opposite sides, and that it is to other than popular judgments that we must refer for our final decision on the characters or the events that come before us. We feel now, as it were, the breath of genial spring, the disappearance of a cutting wind. He on whom the favoring breeze now blows would have rejoiced in its gentle airs, but not the less did he bravely bear the blast when it came from an opposite quarter, and was black with storm and whirlwind. So it must be always. Like the Fortune of the poet, we do well to cherish the popular voice whilst it goes with us, we do well to bask in the good-will of our fellow-men and our fellow-citizens whilst it gives its great and often just impetus to our natures. But we should be not the less aware of its fleeting transitory value; we should be able to puff it away without a sigh, and be content with that only judgment which is truly beyond dispute, the judgment of our own conscience, the judgment of Almighty God, who judges not as man judges, and who trieth the very secrets of the heart.

Fourthly, those of us who lament over the departed, those also who do not lament over him, must nerve ourselves to do what in us lies, on one side or the other of political life, to supply the qualities which we imagine ourselves to have lost in him. It was said on the occasion of the death of the last great statesman who was cut off in the prime and vigor of life that the darkest side of the calamity was that we "*bitterly* thought of the morrow." There is beyond question a great gulf and void created, whenever we lose one who has filled a vast space in the eyes of our own and other countries. It disturbs the balance of power and parties, it changes the hopes and the fears of almost every class. And it is not only in the camp to which the departed statesman belonged that this sense of a vacancy is felt. The great statesmen, the acknowledged leaders of parties, are by that very fact raised above those parties themselves. They are, in fact, much more nearly allied to each other, in purpose and principle, than the ordinary common-place herd who form the rank and file of their supporters would suffer us to believe. The great natures of Pitt and Fox, widely different in a thousand points, were yet bound together by a closer kindred in largeness of soul, in genuine patriotism, than either the one or the other could allow in their lifetime. And in like manner the great twin brethren of our own day, though in all their varied endowments the very opposite of each other, yet each supplied what the other needed ; of each it might be said that

> Never on earthly anvil
> Did such rare armor gleam.

Each, though coming from widely differing hosts, will, we may hope, be acknowledged by posterity to have fought for what he deemed the right in the cause of England's empire and England's commonwealth. As was finely said of them some years ago, Castor and Pollux were both indispensable to us, the one as much as the other, and both have left the print of their immortal hoofs on the rock of the Capitol. If one was more dexterous in training his forces, and the other was more distinguished in attack, both will be recognized to have had qualities which raised them into a region above the ordinary strife, and made their combat worthy the combat of giants, their union, in that which is highest and noblest, worthy of the union of gods. It is these godlike qualities we can all of us admire; it is these qualities which some of us perchance may feebly imitate. It is these gifts which in the departed (I speak for a moment only) rose above every narrow section of political life. Moderation where moderation was possible, the genius which knew when to give way and when to resist, the passionate love of the honor and greatness of England; these are virtues which belong to no party, which may at times be exhibited more by one than the other, but which are in themselves wholly independent of the artificial lines that divide party from party, and which they who can most truly claim the name of English citizens and Christian patriots will most truly honor, and, when gone, most deeply lament.

These are some of the reasons why the mourning of the Sovereign and of all the people for the great man who has fallen in Israel may bear fruit in every class, whether high or low, whether agreeing or disagreeing. He rests not here. A tender and generous feeling, the expressed wish of her who had been most·near and dear, drew him to the spot where he now reposes. But his name will live amongst us here to remind us in future days of the extraordinary career which led the alien in race, the despised in debate, the romantic adventurer, the fierce assailant, the eccentric in demeanor, by unflagging perseverance, by unfailing sagacity, by unshaken fidelity, by constantly increasing dignity, by larger and larger breadth of view, to reach the highest summits of fame and splendor.

In the intricate entanglements of strife and thought, in the ever-shifting fortunes of our country, so great yet so little, so far reaching in its aims yet so confined in its immediate action, it is hardly possible to forecast in any degree the future which is in store for us, perhaps gloomy with disaster and shame, perhaps bright with the promise of unknown glory. The words with which Milton concludes his poem on the death of that Jewish warrior with whose name I began this discourse, are still the best consolation and the best instruction for us to bear away from the contemplation of one of whom, as of Samson, it may be said in the widest sense that the dead which he slew at his death were more than they which he slew in his life : —

> All is best, though we oft doubt
> What the unsearchable dispose
> Of Highest Wisdom brings about,
> And ever best found in the close.
> Oft He seems to hide His face,
> But unexpectedly returns.
>
> .   .   .   .
>
> His servants He, with new acquist
> Of true experience from this great event,
> With peace and consolation hath dismiss'd,
> And calm of mind, all passion spent.

CHRISTIAN FRATERNITY.

St. Andrew's Day, November 30, 1874, appointed as the day of interces- sion for Missions, preparatory to the Lecture on "The Universal Religion," delivered in the nave of the Abbey, by the Very Rev. John Caird, D.D., Principal of the University of Glasgow.

He first findeth his own brother Simon. — JOHN i. 41.

IT has been vehemently contested whether St. An- drew's Day was a fitting day to choose for the anniver- sary of missions. There is, however, one characteristic of the Apostle which brings out one aspect of missions peculiarly interesting in our time, and on which I will venture for a few moments to fix attention.

It is the characteristic contained in the text — what we may call the principle of Christian Fraternity; of Fraternity not in that indiscriminating sense in which the word has been used by our brilliant neighbors in their times of revolution — a sense in which a country- man [1] of our own has severely and forcibly criticised it — the sense of confounding all differences of institution, family, rank, country, under one unmeaning compliment. Not in this sense, but in the almost contrary sense of the word — the sense of recognizing, first and foremost, before all other ties, the bond of brotherhood, of neigh- borhood, of likeness and homogeneousness of charac- ter and principle. "He first findeth his own brother Simon." Andrew, the first Evangelist, was before all else a good brother. In the great church [2] at Rome,

[1] *Liberty, Equality, and Fraternity.* By J. Fitzjames Stephen.
[2] St. Andrea della Valle.

330

which is dedicated to him, no other inscription could be found suitable, except " Andrew, the brother of Peter." Before casting his nets here and there on Jew or Gentile, on priest or publican, he first bethought him of the one fellow-creature who was near to him by the ties of home and family. " Blood is thicker than water " in sacred as well as in social life. " If a man cares not for his own household, how shall he care for the Church of God ? " " If a man loves not his brother " — his nearest and dearest — his brother, whom he sees every day — "how can he love God " or God's scattered children, " whom he has not seen ? "

This is a principle which has often been quoted as an argument against missions altogether. It is a principle which certainly needs to be constantly re-asserted as a corrective of the excesses of the missionary or proselytising spirit ; but on the present occasion I propose to show how it also contains within itself some of the best methods of the true conversion of the outside world, even whilst it seems at first sight to withdraw us from it. This may be seen under three separate aspects of the subject.

1. It exemplifies the undoubted truth that the best, the most permanent mode of diffusing Christianity in the world is by enlightening, purifying, Christian nations and Christian families at home, by converting our own countrymen, our own brethren, who have settled abroad. It has been well said that the chiefest missionary of the Apostles, he who was especially the Apostle of the Gentiles, in every case made his own Jewish countrymen the nucleus round which the heathen converts were to be gathered. Of all the Epistles of St. Paul, there is not one which is addressed exclusively to Gentiles. In every city he first found his own brothers, the sons of Israel. In every church that he founded, it is to them

that the chief of his arguments are addressed. It was part of what we may call the Providential preparation for the propagation of Christianity, that these centres of light were already created, by the vast dispersion of the Jewish settlers in every province of the Roman Empire. This is a practical lesson for all of us in respect of foreign missions. Every English settler in a distant land is already, by his good or evil conduct, a missionary for God or for the devil; nay more, every country in Europe, according as it holds up Christianity in a repulsive or an attractive form, repels or attracts the outside world from the light of the Gospel. It is said that some of the Japanese envoys who lately visited the nations of Europe and America had come with the predisposition to establish Christianity in Japan on their return, but that after witnessing its actual fruits they in disappointment relinquished the project. The story may be true or false, but it conveys a warning which we should do well on this day to take to heart. If they had seen our best institutions, our best hospitals, our best schools, our best colleges; if they had been led to regard our splendid literature, our ancient liberties, our continuous progress, as products of our religion; if they had been led to admire the most disinterested, most generous, most truthful characters that Christendom has produced — then we cannot but think that, in spite of all our failures, they might perhaps have felt that it would be worth while to try, in their distant empire, the great experiment which has here produced such magnificent results. But if they had been present at one of those miscalled holidays, when so large a part of our population is given up to drunkenness or degrading vice; if they had read the rancorous animosities of our so-called religious journals; if they had witnessed, throughout Europe, the obstacles thrown in the way of education, of peace, of progress, by theological passion and prejudice; if they had heard in our own country of the fierce controversies which have raged on the shape of a vestment, the direction of a face, or the placing of a table — we could hardly be surprised at their doubting whether it was worth while to transplant into their own country a religion which, by its own adherents, was identified with such noxious or trifling matters. No: let us first find and convert and elevate our own brethren and our own kindred, and we shall then go with clean hands to convert the Jew, the Turk, the heretic, and the infidel. This is a missionary enterprise in which every man, woman, and child who hears me can bear a part. Find each of you thine own brother —each of you is his brother's keeper, his brother's guardian — make thy brother better than thyself, as good as thyself. Be good thyself, that thy brother may learn good from thee, if from no one else. In this way the Home Mission becomes the mother of all missions; in this way the humblest may contribute his mite to this day's solemnity.

2. But the same principle which thus fixes our main attention on our own immediate circle, also points out to us the best access to the hearts and minds of the unknown strangers of heathen lands. There, too, are to be found our own brothers, not merely in that general sense in which sometimes, with indiscriminate generality, all mankind are called our brothers — but in that more specific sense indicated by the natural affection with which Andrew first found his own brother Simon. In every heathen country, in every savage tribe, there are those whom we may call our own brothers, for the nobler qualities which raise them above their fellows, and bring them nearer to the civilized and the Christian type. In every heart, or

almost every heart, that God has placed in the human breast, there are sentiments which correspond to ours, and which make us feel that those to whom we speak are our fellow-men in the sight of God, our fellow-scholars in Christ Jesus.   Often, indeed, this fraternal sympathy has been rendered impossible on the one hand by the impurities, the cruelties, the follies of heathen nations, on the other hand by the pitying scorn, or the iniquitous dealing, with which the European, the Christian, even the missionary, has looked down on what are called, in one sense truly, the inferior races of mankind.   But happy, thrice happy, are those Englishmen, those missionaries who have taken a more generous view of their calling; who have made it a point first to find their own brothers in those strange faces.   Such was the philanthropic spirit of the long line of English statesmen and governors whom, for this reason, David Livingstone hailed as the best of missionaries — statesmen who labored for the welfare of forlorn and distant tribes as if for their own countrymen, governors who have felt that there were moments when their brothers were discerned, not in the stronger party that cried for vengeance, but in the weaker that entreated for mercy.   Such was the spirit of that prince of missionary travellers whom I named just now, and who lies beneath the floor of this Abbey; who was never tired of repeating that he found amongst the native races of Africa the same feelings of right and wrong that he found in his own conscience, and that needed only to be enlightened and developed to make the perfect Christian.   Such an one was that martyr Bishop of Polynesia,[1] who won the hearts of his simple converts by treating them as his children, his brothers, his friends, detecting the Christian beneath the heathen,

---

[1] Bishop Patteson.

the civilized man beneath the savage. Such an one (if I may for a moment speak of one who in this respect, whatever else we may think of him, stands in the foremost rank of living missionaries) is that South African Bishop [1] who, of all those who have been sent to that distant land, has given to it the fullest and largest share of his laborious life; who was amongst the first of the Colonial Bishops to translate the Holy Scriptures into the native language of those whom he was sent out to instruct; who, by dealing with his simple converts not as inferiors, but as companions and fellow-scholars, had the grace to learn from them with a new force some old truths, which, though sometimes pushed to excess, have been, in essential points, almost accepted at home; who stands conspicuous amongst the missionaries of our time in the noble self-forgetfulness with which he has sacrificed his dearest prospects and several valuable friendships, cemented by the most trying circumstances, in order to vindicate the rights of a barbarous tribe,[2] which (whether truly or not, I do not here pronounce) he believed to have been unjustly treated through the misapprehension or the misjudgment of his fellow-colonists. Such a sacrifice, made fearlessly and freely, whilst others, from whatever motive, either kept silence, or swelled the popular panic, is an example of missionary enterprise and of Christian chivalry which, wholly apart from any question of theological opinion, the Church of England is justly proud to claim, and ought on this day (when we call over as it were, the roll of missionary martyrs and confessors) to commend to the honor which it deserves on earth, and which it will, we humbly trust, receive in the sight of Him who seeth not as man seeth — in the

[1] Bishop Colenso.
[2] *Langalabalele and the Amahlubi Tribe.* By the Bishop of Natal.

judgment of Him who has said of any kindness done to the friendless stranger, even though he be an African savage, "Inasmuch as ye have done it unto the least of these my brethren, ye have done it unto Me."

3. There is one further application of the principle of Christian fraternity, of choosing first our own brothers as fellow-disciples. I refer to the duty, obvious, though often neglected, of seeking for our co-operators in this, as in all good works, not those who are far away, but those who are close at hand. There is in this congregation at this moment a venerable stranger from distant parts — the Syrian Patriarch of Antioch who has been received with all courtesy and respect by the authorities of our Church, but with whom the difference of manners and customs and language precludes us from holding any other than the most outward and formal intercourse. Most Christian, most becoming was the welcome which has been given to that aged representative of an ancient Church, a kindred branch of which had excited sympathy centuries ago in the heart of the Saxon Alfred, and which, in our own day, wakened a spark of enthusiasm in the poetic soul of Reginald Heber. Most Christian, most becoming has been his simple yet profound reply to his English hosts — "I was a stranger, and ye took me in." Nevertheless we cannot but feel that this and all like manifestations of sympathy must be, comparatively speaking, transitory and external. The chiefs of far-off communions, whether in the Eastern or the Latin Church, can be co-operators with us only in a remote and secondary sense. Let us cultivate by all means a friendly intercourse with them, as with all Christian people throughout the world. But an intimate, organic union can only be with those who are near at hand, or of the same race and nation and culture as ourselves. The

divergence of sentiment, language, geographical limits, outweighs a hundredfold any apparent ground of union supplied by the retention of a form of the Christian ministry, which in name only, or hardly in name, resembles that which is retained by ourselves. Like Andrew, we must first find out our brother Simon, those who are our own brothers by national kinship, by common liberties, common traditions, by neighborhood, by language, by inheritance of the same glories of the British name, the same aspirations breathed into us by the Protestant Reformation. It is because the work of evangelizing the heathen has a direct tendency to bring all English Christians together that this day is doubly blessed; blessed alike in what it gives and in what it receives. It lays upon us the duty of finding first our own brethren of the same flesh and the same blood, to carry on the task which no others can equally well execute together, because with all our divisions we understand each other better than we understand any one else.

Let us first find those of our own communion; let us try to make the most of all the various schools and shades of thought which make up our national Church; remembering that each supplies something which the other lacks, and that only by their joint co-operation can the Church attain the likeness of that great Apostle who was all things to all men. Our differences may be wide and deep, but they are not wider or deeper than those which have always existed in every civilized Church, not so wide or deep as they are at this moment in that portion of Western Christendom (the Roman Church) which has been accustomed the most to pride itself on its outward unity. Let our first effort, therefore, be, before we go far and wide for other fellow-workers, to make the most of the fellow-workers we have at hand in our own Church — our own laity, our own clergy, our own bishops, through all the various shades of English feeling and thought.

But next to our own Church, and before any combinations with foreign Christians, however estimable, let us find out our own brethren in the British Islands, who, however parted from us, through the misfortune or the misconduct of their ancestors or ours, are yet heirs of the same national traditions and of the same inspiring future. Such are our brethren amongst the Nonconforming communions of England, whose praise for their missionary zeal, even if sometimes not according to knowledge, is in all the Churches; whose sympathy in this, as in all good works, is dear to every Churchman; whose " watchful jealousy," if so it be, it is ours to disarm by frank generosity and straightforward courtesy and equal dealing.

And yet once more. Foremost amongst those who, being thus divided from us, yet are one with us, let us name the sister Church of Scotland; like our own, the Church of the nation; like our own, a Church recognized both in solemn prayer and legislative enactments; like our own, if I may venture so to magnify ourselves, abounding in works of active charity, of enlightened faith, of Christian tolerance. On this day, St. Andrew's Day, the day of Scotland's national saint, whose bones, according to the ancient legend, were believed to have drifted without oar or sail to the rocky headland which now bears his name; the cross of whose martyrdom on the shores of Achaia is still emblazoned on the escutcheon of the northern kingdom; on this day, which in both Churches is observed for the same sacred missionary cause, I have thought that I should best be acting in accordance with the principle which I have endeavored to set forth, and with the exigencies of the times in which we live, by invoking the assistance of the wisdom and the learning of the chief of the greatest Scottish University, the first preacher and theologian of the Scottish national Church. As last year we listened to the voice of the distinguished German scholar [1] who had explored the depths of heathen religions and of primeval language, so this year we shall hope to listen to the voice of our own countryman,[2] who has explored as few else in this island, on the one hand, the " Religion of Common Life," and on the other hand, the links which bind together Philosophy and Christianity in that indissoluble unity which can alone win for the glad tidings which we profess to carry throughout the world a solid basis and a permanent triumph — the promise of the life that now is and of that which is to come.

[1] Professor Max Müller.
[2] The Very Rev. John Caird, D.D., Principal of the University of Glasgow.

DIVERSITY IN UNITY.

St. Andrew's Day, November 30, 1877, being the day of intercession for Missions ; preparatory to an Address on "Missions" in the nave, by the Rev. John Stoughton, D.D., Professor of Historical Theology in the Independent College, Hampstead.

*In the midst of the throne, and round about the throne, were four "living creatures," full of eyes, before and behind. And the first "living creature" was like a lion, and the second "living creature" was like a calf, and the third "living creature" had a face as a man, and the fourth "living creature" was like a flying eagle. —*REVELA-TION iv. 6, 7.

THERE is an argument often used against Christian Missions which is supposed to be fatal to their effect. It is said that the natives of heathen countries are disturbed by the various forms under which Christianity is presented to them, and that it is, therefore, difficult for them to accept as true what appears under such diverse and sometimes rival aspects.

It is an argument which is also used at home in favor of suppressing these different forms, as far as possible, and substituting for them some one system which shall supersede all the others.

This objection, if sound, would strike at the very root of all missions as they now exist, and it may, therefore, be worth while to meet it; and the more so as the statement of the counter principle is full of edifying reflections.

So far from its being the case that a uniform or absolutely homogeneous statement of the truth is necessary

340

for all times and circumstances, the whole structure of
the Bible is a direct testimony to the contrary position; namely, that there are, as St. Paul says, diversities of gifts, of ministrations, of operations, through
which the same Father reigns, the same Lord is served,
the same Spirit works; that Divine light can only be
received in the world through the refractions, as St.
Peter says, of "many colors and many shapes" — delivered, as the author of the Epistle to the Hebrews
says, in "many parts and in many fashions" — represented, as St. John represents it, by the widest diversity of figures that the prophetic imagination could
conceive; image upon image, metaphor upon metaphor; not one lamp, but seven; not the throne only,
but the rainbow; not the sight only of sapphire or of
emerald, but the sound of thunder and trumpet, and
the roar of many waters; the Supreme Unity encom-
passed and surrounded by venerable sages, and strange
animals, and ten thousand times ten thousand heavenly
messengers.

Amongst those figures, that which I have chosen for
my text has been consecrated by the long usage of the
Church to the special subject of the evangelization of
mankind. The four Living Creatures which surround
the throne of God have, fancifully perhaps, yet not
without a profound meaning, been appropriated by
early tradition to the four Evangelists. In ancient times
there was no fixed appropriation of these several images, each to each. It was only the general fact of the
fourfold figure that suggested the comparison. The
man, the lion, the calf, and the eagle, so entirely unlike
each other in form and aspect, have been assigned in
varying degrees to St. Matthew, St. Mark, St. Luke,
and St. John. But this diversity truly represents the
divergence of the four delineations which the Gospels

contain of the Saviour's life and character. It might
have been that they should all have been fused into
one; it might have been that the peculiar traits or
ideas represented respectively in the four Evangelists
should have been altogether suppressed, that so the
world might have been saved the perplexities and
stumbling-blocks which the strange contradictions and
varieties of the several accounts have left to trouble
the mind of Christendom. But it was not so ordered;
and in spite of these momentary difficulties, we may
well be thankful that the fourfold picture has been
allowed to remain, and that the world has been left to
explore and to reconcile, as best it may, these widely
differing reports.

What is thus exemplified in the case of the four
Evangelists has more or less continued in the work of
evangelization ever since. Vehement as have been the
attempts to reduce into one single system the various
modes by which Christian doctrines or Christian institutions have been developed, human nature and Divine
grace have been too strong to be bound in any such
artificial restraints; and those portions of mankind
which lie outside the Christian pale have no just cause
to complain of the sameness of the points of view from
which the message of the Gospel has been conveyed to
them.

In the seraphic hymn which in the services of the
Eastern Church forms one of the most solemn parts of
the Communion office, the words in which praise is expressed have, by the singular richness of the Russian
language, been represented by four phrases, which, whilst
they all contain the same common idea of thanksgiving,
enable the hearers, as it were, to catch, through the con-
cordant music, sounds as of the roaring of a lion, as of
the scream of an eagle, as of the bellowing of an ox, and

as of the speech of a man. This well explains to us the general effect which may be, which ought to be, and which to a large extent has been conveyed to the world, by the diversity and the unity of Christendom.

No doubt to a mere childish or barbarian intellect the idea of such complexity is difficult to grasp; but after all, in presenting to uncivilized or half-civilized nations the truths of a religion, which, if it be any thing, ought to correspond with the results of the highest civilization, we must be content to trust ourselves in some degree to the common sense and common reason of mankind, which, even in the most barbarous races, is not wholly extinguished; and, when such an objection is brought forward, it must be met, as many other objections are to be met, not by acquiescing in the stupidity or perversity of those we address, but by appealing to the highest light that is in them, and drawing the lessons which they themselves might acknowledge in their common experience.

The fact is, that the offence given in the eyes of heathen nations by the differences of Christendom, is in great measure occasioned not by the mere fact of those differences, but by the fierce rivalries, and unhallowed jealousies, and overleaping ambitions by which different phases or forms of Christianity have attacked and endeavored to absorb each other in the race of proselytism. These inhuman passions are justly calculated to alienate the unsophisticated consciences, whether of civilized or of savage heathendom; but they would be equally odious even though there were not a single heathen to be converted. They are amongst the vices of Christian society, like drunkenness, gambling, impurity, such as we have been told have in our Australian colonies provoked an army of Brahmin missionaries to the good work of endeavoring to convert our benighted fellow-countrymen — in these respects truly benighted — to a better and purer life. But these are quite another matter from the innocent divisions which have parted Churches from each other. "It is not," as was well said by an excellent Nonconformist, who was educated within these walls two centuries ago, "it is not the actual differences that do the mischief, but the mismanagement of those differences." In point of fact it has been found that Christian missionaries in heathen parts do for the most part forget their divisions in the face of the heathen. It was the testimony of the Report presented to both Houses of Parliament in 1872, that, "from the nature of their work, and from their isolated position, they co-operate heartily together, and that, with few exceptions, it is a fixed rule among them that they will not interfere with each other's converts or each other's spheres of duty."

We propose, therefore, to guard against the growth of these exceptions, and to uphold this fixed rule; to show that, so far from such a diversity being contrary to the genius of Christianity, it was involved in the religion of our Divine Founder from the very beginning; that so far from its being a reasonable obstacle in the way of its reception, it ought to be one of the chief commendations of it to the reception of those to whom it is addressed.

Let me illustrate this position by several great examples in the history of Christian missions.

(1.) Let us first take the diversity of creeds. When we consider how variously constituted are the powers of human apprehension, how mixed are the ingredients out of which any human representations of truth are composed, it is an almost inevitable result that every creed and confession of faith which Christendom has produced must partake of that mingled, complex, and imperfect character which belongs to human speech and human thought. No one creed or confession can claim absolute truth; or, even if it does claim absolute truth, it cannot claim to represent the exact form of truth which will be most opportune for each varying country.

There are, no doubt, some truths so divine, so transparent, so universal, that even the imperfections to which we have referred can hardly obscure their brilliancy; there are some falsehoods so absurd, so mischievous, so narrow, that even the most uneducated conscience might be expected to reject them if they stood alone; but what has usually happened is, that these truths and these falsehoods, though not in the same proportion, have become inextricably mixed together, and thus the imperfection of one creed is almost of necessity rectified by some countervailing clause in another. To use a homely proverb, "It is not safe to put all our eggs into one basket." This is a maxim of common life: it is not less a rule for the evangelization of the world. And how remarkably is this borne out if we look on a large scale at the conversion of mankind!

Who was it that evangelized our ancestors, the Gothic tribes of Northern Europe? It was Ulfilas, an Arian bishop; a missionary, that is to say, who adhered to a particular form of the Christian faith which, at the time when he lived, was denounced with the severest penalties, both civil and ecclesiastical, by the then rulers of the Catholic Church, and which has long ago become extinct in every part of the world. But from him was derived the first translation of the Scriptures into our own mother tongue — the precursor of the versions of Wycliffe, of Luther, of Tyndale, and of our own present English Bibles. He was the Moses, as he was called, the leader and deliverer of our Gothic ancestors; the precursor of Augustine and Boniface and Adelbert.

And who was it that established the first missions through the whole of Central Asia, the great exception to the usual lethargy of the Eastern Church? It was the Nestorian Christians, the Christians who clung to the faith of the once persecuted, exiled, and detested Nestorius.

And who was it that in later days conveyed the first germs of the Christian faith to the vast tribes of India and of China? Whose name is it that is still invoked, as I am told, by the boatmen of Madras as they dash through the perilous waves which encircle their surf-beaten shores? It was Francis Xavier, the representative, not merely of the Roman Church, but of that most repulsive and offensive phase of the Roman Church, the Society of Jesuits.

And who was it that first undertook the colonization and Christianization of Greenland, with its unpromising races, its ungenial climate, its dark future? It was the simple-minded Moravians, whose principles and whose tenets were even more different from those of Ulfilas, or of Francis Xavier, and of the Nestorians, than any of these from each other.

And yet, not only did these several agencies succeed in presenting Christianity in a shape which more or less struck root in these diverse countries; but as we look back on their distant labors — distant both in time and space — we must acknowledge that they were severally the fountain-heads from which the native Christianity of Europe, of Asia, and of North America, has received the fullest streams of Christian life.

(2.) Again, let us leave the question of the diversity of creeds, and look at the diversities of organization. From very early times, Episcopacy was regarded as the one outward channel through which the evangelization as well as the ordinary government of the Church was to be carried on. Baptism, preaching, marriage — noth-. ing could be done without the bishop. But it was not long before immense exceptions began to be, as it were, scooped out of the Episcopal system.

In a large part of Europe the chief work of proclaiming the Gospel, and its concomitant message of civilization, to the unconverted or half-converted races, was conducted, not by bishops, but by presbyters — by those presbyters who, under the name of abbots and monks, carried on their work, not only irrespectively, but independently of, and above, the Episcopate. Such was Columba, the apostle of Scotland. Such, during the larger part of his missionary career, was Cuthbert of Lindisfarne. Such was Columbanus, the apostle of Burgundy. Such was St. Gall, the apostle of Switzerland. Such was St. Benedict, the founder of that great Benedictine order which was for centuries the chief nurse of learning and culture in Europe.

In like manner in our own later days, in the Churches of the Reformation, the first attempt to evangelize our heathen dependencies was maintained and executed, not by the regular Episcopal system, so well suited as it is to our wants at home, but by the great societies, called by diverse names, through which, irregularly, perhaps, but not with any greater irregularity than the system of Columba or Benedict, the light of Christian truth was handed on by a succession of noble-minded torch-bearers, whose torches flamed not the less brightly because they were shaken in the winds of a wide and unlimited field, and not confined within the more restricted limits of a constant supervision.

Those who knew India in former days used to tell us that, great as were the advantages produced by the more complete organization introduced through the foundation of the Anglo-Indian Episcopate, yet still there was a fire and a fervor enkindled by the wandering lives of Schwartz and his contemporaries, which we vainly seek for in our more orderly generation. We would not for a moment disparage the benefits conferred on English Churchmen settled in those regions by the establishment of a regular, unfailing supply of pastors and chief pastors, whose function was specially to raise up and foster in our English settlers those who, after all, must, by their lives and examples, be the true missionaries of Christianity to the heathen. We do not underrate the blessing of prelates, who, by the winning grace of a Heber, or the long-continued devotion of a Wilson, or the wise and fatherly counsel of a Cotton, or the indefatigable zeal of a Milman, became, as it were, the patriarchs of Indian missions of whatsoever persuasion. But still, any attempt to disparage, overrule, and override the efforts of those societies which have performed in our time a work corresponding to that effected by the great monastic orders in the Middle Ages, implies, not merely a want of evangelical largeness of heart, but an ignorance of those ecclesiastical principles which acted so large a part in the conversion of modern Europe.

(3.) Again, there is an analogous difference of organization with which we are more familiar at home, but which must be allowed to play freely its part also in the distant countries of the world. There has been in this country, since the Reformation, an acknowledged divergence in the mode of disseminating truth which may be described, if I may use the expressive language of a highly valued brother ecclesiastic, as "the public and the private way." "The public way" is that whereby the nation has taken advantage of an organization which has come down with much continuity, although with much discontinuity, from the earliest times of our history; which is controlled by national laws, which is guarded by national principles, which is regarded as on the whole the exponent of the national faith. This is the system which by various names is called the Established Church, the National Church, the Church of England. But, side by side with this, there is another "way" in which individuals fired with peculiar zeal, or endowed with peculiar gifts, have taken advantage of the liberty gradually and increasingly left by the nation to those who deviate from the more public and established system; a way in which, partly by their own special energies, partly by founding new organizations, which have themselves in the course of time become a mixture of the more public and the more private systems, they have filled up the deficiencies and increased the usefulness of that larger and more comprehensive institution intended to cover the whole nation.

By these two channels the flood of Christian doctrine and civilization has forced its way through our own land. On one side we see, as it were, a majestic river, swollen with many tributaries, bearing on its bosom stately fleets, feeding populous cities which else would languish, fertilizing large tracts which else would wither and die; on the other side we see foaming torrents penetrating through rocks which perchance nothing else could break, attracting attention by the roar of cataracts which arouse the most heedless ear, forcing their way into devious corners which lie outside the main current of the larger stream. And what has been productive of such beneficent results at home, cannot but, we believe, be capable of like results abroad. Wherever the two systems come into contact, it is surely the dictate at once of Christian wisdom and of Christian charity, that each should use the other as its best and indispensable ally.

In former times it was the temptation of the public national form of religion to repress and suppress by legislative enactments the private utterances of Nonconformity. In our times it is the temptation of the Nonconforming elements of religion to endeavor to repress, and suppress by legislative enactments, all expression of the public and national form. The means adopted in the two cases are different, but the end sought is the same. In either case, the error was and is equally impolitic, equally illiberal. Let us hope better things for the age that is coming. Let us remember, both at home and abroad, the speech of Abram to Lot — "Is not the whole land before thee? If thou wilt take the left hand, then I will go to the right; or if thou depart to the right hand, then I will go to the left." Let us remember the same maxim translated into the language of the Apostle — "We will not boast in another man's line of things made ready to our hand." "Every way, whether in pretence or in truth," whether, we may add, by a public or a private way, "Christ is preached; and I therein do rejoice, yea, and will rejoice." "Why, when both organizations exist," so it has been pertinently asked, "why should one of the two be taken from us?" In point of fact, the contributions to missions, so far as we can judge from statistics, bear out this conclusion, that not by repression of variety, but by encouragement of variety, is the chief result produced.[1]

In the British dominions, the largest amount is contributed by the Church of England, that is to say, the communion in which, our enemies themselves being our judges, the largest diversity of thought exists and is allowed. It is 500,000*l*. The next largest contribution

[1] "Church and Dissent," in *Quarterly Review*, cxxx. 452, ascribed to the Dean of St. Paul's.

is that of the Nonconformists, who are also a very mixed body. It is nearly 400,000*l.* But the contributions from the Roman Catholic Church, which refuses to acknowledge any such diversity, throughout the whole world amount only to one-quarter of what is collected by the various Protestant Churches and societies within the United Kingdom alone, and the sum collected from British churches of the Roman persuasion does not amount to 7,000*l.*[1]

No doubt the Church of Rome and the Protestant Churches have each their separate grooves. But in the generous efforts for the cause of missions, it would seem that the freedom of the Reformation has been far more potent than the authority of the Papal See. It would seem further that if either the Church of England were destroyed, according to the wishes of some ardent Nonconformists, or Nonconformity absorbed, according to the wishes of some ardent Churchmen, the cause of Christian missions would grievously suffer.

(4.) There is yet one further exemplification of the principle, which lies behind all the others; namely, the effect of the differences, deeply rooted and ineradicable, of human character and pursuits. The fierceness of the lion, the rapidity of the eagle, the strength of the ox, the intelligence of the man, are not more strongly impressed on the differences between Arian and Catholic, Greek and Latin, Roman and Protestant Churchmen and Dissenters, than they are on the deep lines of demarcation which divide the studious scholar, the soaring philosopher, the bold warrior, the zealous pastor, each from each; and yet every one of these distinct characters may, through the one Divine Spirit working in each, be brought to bear on the world of sin and

[1] *British Contributions to Foreign Missions in the year* 1876, by the Rev. W. A. Scott Robertson, M.A.

ignorance, as confidently as though each one existed by itself. The barbarian, the heathen, the Mohammedan, the Hindoo, are not distracted by these divergencies of character. They are rather drawn towards the central fire which gives to each of them its life and energy.

And it is this necessity of the joint action of the most diverse elements of character which throws such a power and such a responsibility on all of us. No one, whether in England or in foreign countries, can say that he is freed from any concern in missionary influence. Every one, prince or peasant, soldier or settler, has his own influence, even although he may never have opened his lips as a preacher. I have seen pictures of a distinguished English ruler, Sir Donald M'Leod, I have heard of another of a gallant soldier, General Nicholson, in which the Hindoos represent them, with their British costume, and with their genuine English features, in the attitude of their own divinities, to whom they are offering worship and sacrifice. And what was it that won for them this adoring respect, that made these poor heathens feel that these Englishmen were superior beings — messengers of heaven? It was simply this: they knew them to be thoroughly just, thoroughly truthful, thoroughly chaste. Who is there that cannot help in producing this holy, this Divine impression? Is there any one, however far removed by office or character from ordinary clerical or missionary life, who cannot strive by stainless honor and purity to convince the heathen "of sin, of righteousness, and of judgment"?

These, then, are some exemplifications of the manifold grace of God in the work of evangelization.

The Proteus of human nature, as Lord Bacon happily allegorizes the ancient fable, and as it has been finely drawn out of late by an eminent physician, will go through many shapes before he will speak at last the words of the heaven-sent seer. But this is the Divine message which he is commissioned to speak. We must be patient with him, we must watch for him, but at the last he will tell us what we want to know, not the less because his unity of purpose has been veiled in such immense diversity of action.

In all these various forms of approach there is no need for sacrificing our convictions that one is superior to the other. We may believe that Athanasius was more sound than Ulfilas; that the Protestant is better than the Jesuit; that the Episcopate in the long run has been a more useful agency than the monastic orders; that the comprehensive system of the National Church is more efficient than the more limited systems of individuals or sects; that Mary, who sat at Jesus' feet, chose a better part than Martha, who was cumbered with much serving. All this may well be; but what we wish to show is, that there has been, that there is, that there will be to the end of time, room for the weaker as well as for the stronger, for the lower as well as for the higher, for the eagle as well as for the ox, for the man as well as for the lion, in the vast and complex work of the regeneration of the world.

(5.) And now may I, as on former occasions, ask your attention to the mode in which, year after year, I have endeavored to make St. Andrew's Day in some measure serve to vindicate this principle?

On the first occasion you were invited to hear the words of a world-renowned scholar of another country; on the second occasion you heard the discourse of the most eloquent orator of the Northern kingdom; on the third you listened to the homely address of the patriarch of British missionaries; on the fourth to the close reasoning of a minister of the Church of Ireland, parted from ours by a recent convulsion, yet not without affinities derived by long connection. I now invite you to attend the teaching of one who, belonging to one of those great organizations which I have already described as growing up outside the Established Church of this country, has proved himself, by a long pastoral life and by studies which traverse one of the most distracted portions of our ecclesiastical divisions, capable of understanding both the excellencies of his own communion, and also the excellencies which belong to the larger system of the Church of England. Others before our time have written histories of the Puritans, in which we hear of nothing but the glories of the Puritans; others have written histories of the Church of England, in which we hear of nothing but the glories of the Church of England. He who will address you this evening is the first who has written of both with equal candor, and courtesy, and gracious appreciation. He will speak to you in the name of those illustrious dead, whose characters he has so well portrayed; of Chillingworth, Jeremy Taylor, and Cudworth, on the one side, of Baxter, Howe, and Owen on the other side, whose voices were once heard within these walls, and of which the echo, we trust, will be prolonged this evening. He will, in the same kindly and truthful spirit, endeavor to set before you, as in a fourfold vision, some of the diversities of human character and Christian culture by which, in various fields of missionary labor, the kingdom of God has, in these our latter days, been advanced.

And if, perchance, the record of what he has said under this venerable roof shall reach those distant regions for which we this day pray, it will be to them, I trust, not a stumbling-block or cause of offence, but rather a proof and example of the Divinity and Universality of the Faith which we profess — an exemplification of those beautiful lines which he has himself quoted with fervent admiration from a Christian [1] philosopher of the seventeenth century :

> But true Religion sprung from God above,
> Is like her fountain — full of charity;
> Embracing all things with a tender love,
> Full of good-will and meek expectancy;
> Full of true justice and sure verity,
> In voice and heart; free, large, even infinite;
> Not wedged in strait particularity,
> But grasping all in her vast active spright —
> Bright Lamp of God! that men would joy in thy pure light!

To this Divine Light may God in His mercy lead us all !

[1] Henry More.

THE CLOSE OF THE MISSION SERVICES
ON ST. ANDREW'S DAY, 1879.

St. Andrew's Day, 1879, prior to the Lecture by the Rev. Principal Tulloch, of St. Andrew's University, Scotland, delivered in the Abbey on the same day.

The field is the world. — MATTHEW xiii. 38.

IN the grounds of a secluded college amidst the hills of North America, is a pillar which marks the spot where four young Presbyterian students bound themselves by a solemn vow to found missions for the propagation of the Gospel in distant countries. It was the first awakening of that missionary spirit amongst the Americans which has issued in such extended enterprises, and which only this year drew from the lips of the ruling statesmen of this country unwonted expressions of eulogy. On that pillar are written the words —

"THE FIELD IS THE WORLD."

I have said that this monument commemorates the first revival in the New World of missionary zeal to the distant regions of the earth; but it followed upon and was part of the like zeal which arose for the first time in all Protestant Churches at the close of the last century and the beginning of this.

The ancient mediæval Church, at the time of the settlement of the barbarian tribes, had no doubt conceived the noble ambition of extending the frontiers of Christianity beyond the empire which it had already converted; and the same tradition was continued in

356

the later Roman Church in the splendid adventures on which the Society of the Jesuits embarked in China, in India, in Canada, and in South America. But these missions have on the whole left but feeble traces, and the contributions of the whole Roman Church at this moment to the missionary cause do not amount to one-third of what is contributed by the Protestant communions of Great Britain alone.

It was in those Protestant communions, after a long apathy, for which various causes may be assigned, that the ancient fire of missionary ardor was rekindled towards the close of the eighteenth century.

The Church of England and the English Noncon-formists then began to feel that they had a duty to the heathens within or without our dominions, such as before they had only acknowledged towards our own race, or possibly the races immediately dependent upon us. In the Church of Scotland the question was form-ally discussed in its General Assembly, and was all but extinguished by the philosophic arguments of one of the distinguished ecclesiastical leaders of that time, had it not been for the sudden and vehement appeal, which I have once before quoted from this place, made by a zealous minister to the Holy Bible, as it lay on the table before the seat of the Moderator.

The principle on which that appeal and all like appeals are founded, is contained in the sacred words which I have chosen for my text, " The field is the world." There are no limits to the advance of truth and goodness, and therefore no limits to the advance of Christianity, save those which are interposed by the extremities of space that bound the habitable globe.

Whatever may be the failings in the methods of missionary enterprise, however much they need to be transformed from age to age, yet that enterprise rests in all its forms on these two fundamental truths, That all, or almost all, branches of the human race are capable of moral improvement; and That the Christian religion is sufficiently wide to comprehend, and take its part in, every form of moral improvement of which the human race is capable.

Such are the grounds on which, from time to time, I have advocated, on the successive anniversaries of this solemnity, the cause which the Primate of All England has commended to our attention at this season of the year. This is the last occasion on which I shall have an opportunity of bringing the subject forward on St. Andrew's Day. For various reasons it has seemed good to transfer the day of intercession for missions from the festival of St. Andrew to another time of the year — a transference which will probably change, at least in this place, the character of the celebration. I have, therefore, thought that it might be suitable briefly to sum up the methods by which it has been endeavored to carry out the designs of our Church in these opportunities.

It appeared to me that the principle that "the field is the world" required a yet further exemplification than could be given to it by the ordinary appeals of Churchmen from the pulpit. Accordingly it was determined, after ascertaining that such procedure was in entire accordance with the laws of this Church and realm, to invite others than those of our own ministry or communion to take their part in showing that they, too, joined, on various grounds, in this common work of ours, and that, at least in this place, the heathen world should not be scandalized by the echoes of a disunited Christendom.

The first who undertook this office was a German scholar of world-wide renown,[1] who, beyond any other

---

[1] Professor Max Müller.

living man, has deeply studied the various religions and languages of mankind, and was sure to speak of them with that union of reverence and truthfulness which in itself is a model to all teachers of the heathen everywhere. In this spirit he spoke on the missionary aspect of the various religions of the world; and when, at a later date in this very year, he further developed the same truths from a somewhat different point of view in the ancient Chapter House adjoining this Abbey, the permission to him so to lecture within those venerable walls was granted at my special request, and with my full sympathy and responsibility, because I felt that he was still carrying out the same principles, namely, that through the whole field of the world, wherever we can find one sacred spot in the soil of the human heart, there the seed of religion, which is the Word of God, may be sown, and may yield fruit, some thirty-fold, some sixty-fold, some a hundred-fold.

The next who was invited to take this duty was one who, occupying one of the highest positions of education in a sister Church,[1] was known as combining, in no ordinary degree, the eloquence of the Christian preacher, with the depth of the Christian philosopher. He also, in tones which I would we could oftener hear within . these walls, dwelt in the most touching, and at the same time most convincing, strain, on the universal character of the Christian religion.

The third was far different from either of the two who had preceded him. He was a man great, not in speech, but in action; venerable, not from office, but from years; the patriarch of British missionaries,[2] the near kinsman of the famous explorer who lay beneath

---

[1] The Very Rev. John Caird, D.D., Principal of the University of Glasgow.

[2] The Rev. Dr. Moffat, father-in-law of Dr. Livingstone.

his feet, and partaker with him in the labor of evangelizing the tribes of Africa. He, though born and bred
in another communion and ministry than ours, and
showing in his simple style how little he had partaken
of the larger knowledge or culture of the seats of learning, yet bore not the less a powerful testimony to the
height and breadth of the missionary sphere.

For the fourth teacher in this succession there would
have been, but for the imperative duties required by
the like celebration in his own communion beyond the
border,[1] one whom the late Chief Ruler of India had
designated as, amongst all living names, the one that
had carried most weight amongst the Hindoo and Mohammedan nations of our vast empire, as a faithful
pastor and a wise and considerate teacher. Though he
belonged in his later years to a communion which had
broken off from its parent stock, yet his generous spirit
eagerly welcomed the call made to him, and, but for the
accidental circumstance to which I have referred, would
gladly have responded to it.

His place was filled by a representative preacher from
the Church of Ireland [2] — divided from our own through
causes over which it had no control, divided in its constitution, in its forms of worship, and in its national
character;. but not therefore the less entitled to take
its share with the scholars and the preachers of other
countries and other Churches in a work that seemed
especially to befit the Communion that had produced
such mighty missionaries as the Evangelizers in early
times of Scotland, of Switzerland, and of Western Germany.

The fifth was a distinguished scholar and pastor of
our own English Nonconformists,[3] who, by his gracious

---

[1] The Rev. Dr. Duff. [2] Archdeacon Reichel.
[3] The Rev. Dr. Stoughton.

and loving spirit, has perhaps done as much as any one in our distracted time could effect to reconcile the differences which divide our Churches. He, with his large historical knowledge and capacious sympathies, was able to illustrate this spirit and to confirm our work by showing the unity amidst diversity of the various types of Christian biography in the field of missionary labor.

And now on this, the last St. Andrew's Day on which the cause of missions will be pleaded in this place, it has seemed a not unsuitable occasion to invite the chief ecclesiastical head of the Church of Scotland, who is also the chief theological professor in that ancient university which bears the name of the Apostle from whom this day is called, to bear his witness in proclaiming that the world, and every part of the world, is the field on which Christianity must thrive and triumph. He has taught us, as no one else has yet taught us, the quiet strength and the temperate light which lay within our own Church of England, in the distinguished succession of philosophic and apostolic divines who glorified the seventeenth century in this country. He has taught his own Church the greatness of its position as the Church, not of a sect, but of a nation — as the Church which of all ecclesiastical institutions in the northern kingdom is most emphatically the refuge of learning, of culture, and of freedom. And if this occasion should assist in binding more closely together the two nations whose union has been cemented after so many years of bloodshed and dissension, not only by law, but by the dearest and nearest affections; if it should tend to a closer sympathy between two sister Churches, which have the same purpose of civilizing and enlightening the national elements with which they are connected, it will be carrying out the principle on which the Church and Realm of England have always

recognized the Church of Scotland, the principle that
all who call themselves Christians shall pursue the
unity of the Spirit in the bond of peace and in righteousness of life. Let us trust that on this the last of
our missionary services on St. Andrew's Day, we shall
be taught to carry away the vital principle of the Gospel from which all missions spring; let us trust that
some reason may be given for the hope that, whoever
else goes astray to the right hand or to the left, we may
truly find in the life of our Divine Master those words
of eternal life, of which the most learned historian of
Christianity has said in the most solemn passage of his
work, that "these, and these alone, are the primal, in-
defeasible truths of Christianity which shall not pass
away"—and which, in proportion as we reach to a
more practical use of those undying truths, shall trans-
form and purify the whole field of the world.

THE DISTRESS OF PARIS.

February, 1871, before the Lord Mayor of London.

How doth the city sit solitary, that was full of people! how is she become as a widow! she that was great among the nations, and princess among the provinces.

Arise, cry out in the night: in the beginning of the watches pour out thine heart like water before the face of the Lord: lift up thy hands towards Him for the life of thy young children, that faint for hunger in the top of every street.

Remember, O Lord, what is come upon us: consider, and behold our reproach. — LAMENTATIONS i. 1; ii. 19; v. 1.

THE full instruction of this sacred book, the Lamentations of the Prophet Jeremiah, can be understood only by considering the previous position of the Prophet himself. We dwelt last Sunday on the joyous, hopeful, confident tone of the Prophet Isaiah. The language of the prophecies of Jeremiah is just the reverse. He lived at a time when his country was reaping the bitter fruits of former corruption and sin. The throne of Judah had long been occupied by Princes unworthy of that great position. The priests and prophets fed the people with falsehoods, and the people loved to have it so. Jerusalem had become the seat of selfish luxury and of extravagant superstition. The Temple had become a den of robbers. Jeremiah almost alone of his countrymen saw things as they really were; he was the messenger of unwelcome truth, without illusion and without deception; for forty years, day by day, he delivered his testimony against king and priests and prophets, like a pillar of iron, like a wall of brass, solitary, fearless, undismayed.[1] And when the judgments closed around himself and his people, he alone had the courage to counsel submission to a fate which seemed inevitable. Not from indifference to his country, but from a deeper insight into its higher destiny, he advised the concessions which others despised. Unlike the ordinary leaders of political or religious parties, he had the wisdom to surrender a part for the sake of the whole, to concede the loss of the short to-day for the sake of gaining the long to-morrow.

At last, however, the end came; at last the queenly city fell; at last the cup of misery was drunk to the dregs. Then the whole tone of the Prophet changes. His exhortations, his invectives, his counsels of moderation and of prudence are suspended. One only feeling takes possession of his mind. " After the captivity of Judah, and the desolation of Jerusalem," so we are told in one [2] of the oldest of Jewish traditions, " Jeremiah sate down and wept, and lamented his lamentation over Jerusalem." A rocky cave outside the walls is still shown as that in which the Prophet buried himself in his passionate grief. His awestruck figure, his attitude of hopeless sorrow, remain forever enshrined in the genius of Michael Angelo. His words themselves are preserved to us in the Book of the Lamentations. There we see how his agony was allowed free course. Here and there he still dwells for a moment on the sins and follies of his people; here and there for a moment he cries for vengeance on their enemies. But for the most part these thoughts are gone. What fills his mind is the ruin of the royal city, the black and ghastly forms of the once polished and luxurious

[1] Jer. i. 17, 18; iii. iv.; v. 30; vii. 11.
[2] The Preface to Lamentations, in the Septuagint version.

nobles wasted into skeletons, the high-born women in their crimson robes vainly striving to eke out from the foul heaps of filth the failing supply of food; above all the little children, with their parched tongues, fainting in the streets, asking for bread, crying to their mothers for corn and wine.[1]

The Book, from beginning to end, is a heart-rending picture of calamities which have only to be compared with the actual experience of like events in succeeding ages, to make us feel the literal truth of every part. It is the one Book which the Bible contains filled from first to last with the almost unalloyed expression of unrestrained anguish, and utter, inconsolable desolation.

From this Book of Lamentations, thus placed among the sacred Scriptures, what do we learn?

First, there is the general principle which it involves, old indeed as the heart of man, but sometimes forgotten, and always needing to be re-enforced, that over and above, and beyond, and beside, and across all other calls and claims on our thoughts, is the cry of suffering humanity. However much Jeremiah had to say and to think of the sins of his people, and the superstitions of their prophets, or of the great prospects of the future kingdom of God; however much he had dwelt on these things in former times, yet now, in the presence of this overwhelming sorrow, they were put aside, they were almost, if not altogether, forgotten. He who had been regarded by his countrymen as a traitor, was once more drawn into the closest sympathy with them. He who had been excommunicated by the priests and prophets of his Church was again one with them through the constraining bonds of their common woe. The Book of Lamentations is the standing testimony

---

[1] Lam. i. 1; ii. 9, 11, 12, 19; iv. 4, 5, 7, 8.

to the absorbing, predominant sacredness of human suffering. "Death quits all scores" — misery makes companions of the most widely estranged. The soul, the intellect, the spirit, are indeed higher than the body. But there are times when physical distress has the first and deepest claim — when the homely maxim of St. James takes precedence of all philosophy and all theology. "If thy brother or thy sister be naked, or in lack of daily food, and one of you saith unto them, Go in peace, be ye warmed, and filled, — and yet ye give them not the things needful to the body, what doth it profit?"[1] On such occasions, the mere supply of outward wants, the simplest attention to the call of humanity, becomes a solemn, religious obligation, the first, second, and third duty of every Christian. It breaks down partitions, it opens all hearts, it finds its way through all Churches, it unites all nations. One touch of sorrow and pain, like one touch of nature, makes the whole world kin.

And if this be the general lesson of the Book of Lamentations, who can doubt its special application to the subject which to-day fills our thoughts? Here again, as in the time of the Prophet, such a spectacle is presented to us as at once arrests all the various conflicting emotions and opinions which the events of the last six months have inevitably produced amongst us. Whatever we may any of us have felt on the origin of this dreadful war, however much we may have condemned its authors, however bitterly we may have mourned over the means, on one side or the other, by which it has been prolonged and carried on — all these thoughts now sink to the second place; we think, we dream only or chiefly of the overwhelming misery of the two millions of human beings, exposed to want,

[1] James ii. 16.

to cold, to discomfort of every kind, increasing in intensity till it reaches famine, starvation, and death. My brethren, such a spectacle so produced has not been within the experience of this generation, in some respects not within the experience of any generation of modern history. There have been great national visitations, like the Irish Famine of 1846, like the Cotton Famine of our Northern districts in 1862; there have been also sieges both in ancient and modern times in which greater miseries have been endured. But a siege on so vast a scale has never been seen before in the world's annals — a distress at once so widely spread and so suddenly revealed has never been, before this, disclosed to mortal eyes. In the presence of such a misfortune, it is, I will not say the chief duty, it is the chief consolation of the bystanders, to do what in them lies to lighten it. It draws us out of ourselves. It compels us to feel that we too are part of the great human family. It invites us, it cries to us, to come to the rescue.

There are two special calls which this vast disclosure of misery makes upon us. One is of a more remote but of a more permanent kind — the other, more immediate and pressing. Let us speak of the more remote reflection first.

It is now nearly thirty years ago that a great academical audience was thrilled by the moving description which one of the wisest and best of England's teachers [1] gave of the siege of Genoa during the last great European war. It was told with the view of fixing public attention upon the cruel necessities imposed on armies and on nations by the present condition of the laws of war; and the speaker urged, with an impressive earnestness, which none who heard it can

[1] Arnold's *Lectures on Modern History*, pp. 168–72.

ever forget, that great cities should no longer be turned
into fortresses, and that, whatever have been the hor-
rors of war in past times, they might for the future be
relieved of this terrible aggravation. We may be
thankful that in this country the calamities which Paris
has been called upon to endure can never be witnessed;
for in England no large city can be converted into a
besieged camp, no vast population is enclosed within a
circle of forts which could compel us to suffer, or our
enemies to inflict, what became inevitable in France
from the moment that its capital was invested. It may
be that in the conflict of fierce passions, even when
peace is concluded, the hope, the desire to avert such
miseries for the future may wax feeble, and that no
voice of Christian minister or wise philanthropist will
be strong enough to root out for ever this special cause
of human suffering. Yet it may be worth while to
remind ourselves and others of the cause of its existence. It is something even in the way of consolation
to remember that this particular form of suffering
ought to have been avoidable, that it is not even one of
the necessary consequences of invasion or defence, but
is the result of an exceptional, abnormal state of
things; brought about by a policy which, whatever
incidental occasions it may have furnished for the display of noble endurance, yet was founded on expecta-
tions and calculations confessedly erroneous. May the
widely ramifying miseries which have sprung from this
single root of bitterness, induce those whose high concern it is at least to reconsider the whole question
involved; may God in His mercy give to them the
mind to know, and the will to act, for the alleviation
at least of this one evil in the times that are yet to
come!

But, as I said before, it is not of evils or remedies in

the far future, or even in the nearer future, that I have
chiefly to speak. It is of a want, pressing, immediate,
close at hand; it is the want not of a month hence, but
of this week; not of to-morrow, but of to-day. Now
is the time, and ours is the privilege, to unite with the
two contending nations to do what neither of them can
do alone, or even together, for the deliverance from
sickness, from poverty, from famine, of the crowds of
sufferers who, within a day's journey (or what used to
be a day's journey) from our doors, are pining and perishing for lack of food.

Let us think for a moment of the scene of these
unnamed, unnumbered woes — Paris, the capital of
France. Let us for once speak of that great city not
in its frivolous but in its nobler aspects; not as the
Babylon which made the nations drunk with the cup of
her sorceries, but as the Athens of modern refinement,
the clear luminous eye of Europe; not as the Lucifer
who made the nations tremble, and scattered terror
and desolation over the earth, but as the bright star of
the morning which has heralded the dawn of many a
glorious day in the progress of humanity; not as the
city of despotic rule, or of reigns of terror, incredulity,
and fanaticism, of the massacre of St. Bartholomew
and the massacres of September, but as the city of
heroic virtues all its own, of saintly and illustrious
names, which are the glory of all lands, whose praise is
in all the churches — St. Louis and Gerson, Coligny
and Duplessis-Mornay, Descartes and Cuvier, L'Hôpital
and D'Aguesseau, Bossuet and Fénelon, Pascal and
Racine, and (coming down almost to our own day,
though still speaking only of the dead) Adolphe Monod
and Athanase Coquerel, Lacordaire and Montalembert.
Let us think of all that, in these and many more of its
sons, it has embraced of whatever is gracious and gen-

erous, benignant and chivalrous, in former ages and in the present; enlivening, illuminating, engaging, attracting the best affections round the noblest of human pursuits. Let us think of it as the nurse of some of the tenderest feelings of the human heart, now so sorely wrung; of children towards their aged parents, of sons towards their mothers; as the second home, may we not say, to many an English and to many an American household, bound up with the dear memories of our own past years, with the thought of happy days and delightful converse, of friends whose faces recall the glad recollections of times which now seem parted from us as if by a chasm of ages, or whom we thankfully remember to have been snatched away from the evil to come. Let us enfold these thoughts in the familiar framework and form of that beautiful city; its encircling hills, its abounding river, its glorious quays, its brilliant streets, its world-historic squares, its spacious palaces, its venerable churches, its magnificent museums, its lengthened avenues, its lovely gardens — the glory of the world's greatness, the focus of the gayety of the human heart, the joy of the whole earth.

These are the scenes where death, they tell us, is now busy, these are the homes where want and misery has taken the place of splendor and plenty, where, as in Jerusalem, the young children faint for hunger in the top of every silent street. "How doth the city sit solitary that was full of people! how is she become as a widow! she that was great among the nations, and princess among the provinces." "How is the gold become dim, and the most fine gold changed!" "They that did feed delicately are desolate in the streets." "They that be slain with the sword are better than they that be slain with hunger: for they pine away, stricken through for want of the fruits of the field."

" The elders have ceased from the gate, the young men from their music; the joy of their heart is ceased; the dance is turned into mourning. For this their heart is faint; for these things their eyes are dim." "Remember, O Lord, what is come upon them; consider, and behold their reproach." In these sacred words I have described the misery which can be described by none other so well. None other so fitly belong to a catastrophe so awful.

We judge not the vanquished. We judge not the victors. We would remember that those on whom the tower in Siloam fell were not sinners above the rest of· mankind. We would remember that the successful nation has itself greatly suffered, and would, had the tide of war not been driven back from its borders, have suffered yet more deeply. Neither do we dwell on the prospect of what has been wrought for the future of France and Paris by this fiery baptism, — what purification, what regeneration, in ways till now unheard of, towards ends till now undreamed of!

These are not the thoughts which should now fill our minds. We are with Jeremiah on the rocky mount, weeping over Jerusalem, not with Jeremiah denouncing, prophesying, warning, condemning, judging the nations. We are called simply to assist in a great calamity, which, by God's good providence, we are specially enabled to remedy. That close neighborhood of England to France which has in former ages led to many a bitter rivalry, to many a cruel war, to many a threat of invasion, is now turned for us and for them into a blessed opportunity for charity, for beneficence, for healing many a worn-out frame, for soothing many a stricken heart, for saving many a precious life. To no other nation in Europe has the task been so visibly assigned by the finger of God as it is to us. To none other has such an occasion been afforded of showing that Christian charity is above difference of race and creed, above divergent judgments and clashing sympathies. To us, with our abundant wealth, with our untouched stores, with our ports close at hand, to us it has been permitted, in the most literal sense, to love our neighbor — our great, our suffering neighbor — as ourselves. To us even the all-powerful conquerors, in this dread emergency, appeal to aid them in their truly chivalrous and generous mission of dividing with their enemies the sustenance which they can ill spare. To us, with a yet more urgent entreaty, the thousands of sufferers themselves cry for assistance : the widow and the orphan, left without the hand which should have worked for their support ; the sickly and the weakly, to whom even the delicacies of life are necessaries ; the lower ranks of the middle classes, whose frugality had hitherto enabled them to struggle against the bitter poverty which has come in upon them like an overwhelming flood ; the little babes, whose innocent joyousness might yet have cheered many a desolate home, but whose tender lives fade away like flowers amidst the chilling cold, and biting hunger, and wasting miseries of this terrible winter.

I venture on no details, for none are known. I use no elaborate arguments, for none are needed. It is enough that a great neighboring nation is perishing within sight of our shores. It is enough that the wisdom and the necessity of supplying their wants is recognized by all those who have the best means of knowing. It is enough that this vast metropolis, and this whole nation, through its Government, its municipalities, its Churches, and its sects, responds to the call. It is enough that London — if any city in the world, the sister city of the capital which is thus afflicted — has come forward to head this enterprise of mercy ; and that in this historic church,

where lie mingled together the illustrious dust of Frenchmen and of Englishmen, should be fitly made this first
appeal. Give what you can now, for the time is short,
and the labor is long, and the need is urgent, and the
work is great.

THE CHRISTIAN RULE OF SPEECH.

July 4, 1869 (the anniversary of the Declaration of American Independence).

I say unto you, That whosoever is angry with his brother without a cause shall be in danger of the judgment: and whosoever shall say to his brother, Raca! shall be in danger of the council: but whosoever shall say, Thou fool! shall be in danger of hell fire. — MATTHEW v. 22.

THE Gospel of this day (the sixth Sunday after Trinity) requires first to be explained, and then to be applied to individuals, to Churches, and to nations.

I. It contains certain allusions to the Jewish language and customs which need to be brought out in order to be understood. The phrases "Raca," "council," "judgment" — the words which are translated "Thou fool," and "hell fire" — all imply some thoughts and usages which were familiar at that time, but which we have lost.

Our Lord is speaking of the sin of thoughts and words, as separate from acts, of anger. There is first the causeless anger. No doubt there is such a thing as righteous indignation, just anger: our Lord Himself showed it; no character is perfect without it. But there is such a thing as anger merely for anger's sake; readiness to take affront; rudeness, because we do not take the trouble to be civil; irritation, because we allow every thing to irritate us. We sometimes think it no matter whether we quarrel or not. It does matter a great deal. Never quarrel, if you can possibly help it.

374

This is the first thing which our Saviour urges. It is not enough to keep from striking a man dead; we must keep ourselves from those quarrels which lead to murder. "Whosoever shall be angry with his brother without a cause shall be in danger of the judgment"—that is, although it may not be a very great fault, yet it is a fault, a fault fully as worthy of condemnation as many of those acts which are condemned by the judgment of the courts of justice when they sentence a man to a month's imprisonment or to a pecuniary fine for some assault or theft.

But besides the feeling of anger, there is the still further mischief of angry words; and of these our Lord takes two instances. One is "Raca." That is a Syriac word, meaning "empty," "shallow," "thoughtless," such an expression of contempt as is often used in common conversation, and which leaves a rankling sore behind, because it is contemptuous. "Whoever uses such a word," he says, "ought to feel that he deserves such a severe condemnation as would be pronounced by the highest court of appeal in the whole country— by the great council or Sanhedrim itself." It is another step in the scale of offences; and though it is quite true that no council, civil or ecclesiastical, can take cognizance of mere expressions, though the law of England has long since ceased to regard words as treasonable, yet, in the judgment of God, and in the court of conscience, these light and contemptuous phrases have a significance which does injury both to those who utter them, and to those who hear them.[1]

There is yet another form of angry words that is still more mischievous. There are some words which not merely express general contempt, but gather into them-

[1] This is well put in Professor Maurice's *Kingdom of Christ*, vol. ii. p. 322.

selves an intensity of virulence, from being associated
with political or religious passions, and thus convey
a bitterness of meaning far beyond their own. Such a
word was that which in our English version is translated "Thou fool." It may be interesting to those who
can follow the original to know that this is not, as is
often supposed, a Greek word, nor does it perhaps mean
"fool." It is a Hebrew or Syriac word, *moreh,* like the
other word *raca;* and though it probably gains an
additional strength of meaning from its likeness to the
Greek word *morè* ("fool"), its own proper signification
is "rebel" or "heretic," one who wilfully breaks the
laws of his Church or country—one who would presume to teach his own teachers. It is the same word
which Moses (Num. xx. 10) uses to the Israelites:
"How now, ye '*rebels*'?"[1] It was, according to the
Jewish tradition, for using this offensive word to God's
people that he was forbidden to enter the promised
land. And, accordingly, it is this which our Lord visits
with His severest condemnation. He says that though
it is beyond the reach of any earthly tribunal, though
it is a word used by religious men and grave authorities in their own defence, yet it deserves as much shame
and reproach as belongs to those whose carcases were

---

[1] This meaning of the word, and the mistake of the usual version of
the New Testament, was first brought before me in a tract by Professor
F. W. Newman. It is also noticed by Dean Alford, as one out of two
or three interpretations. This is confirmed by Mr. Deutsch, who adds
this important comment : — " ' The word *morè,*' says the Midrash, ' has
many meanings. It means " rebel ;" it means " fool," for thus they call
a fool in the sea towns (*i.e.* the Greek colonies). It means such as
would presume to teach their own teachers. It means throwers of poi-
soned arrows, calumny, etc.' "

I am further indebted to the learning of Mr. Deutsch for a parallel
in the Talmud to the whole passage : — " He who calls his neighbor a
slave shall be anathematized ; he who calls him a bastard shall receive
forty stripes ; he who calls him *rasha* (wicked) shall answer for it to the
offended one in his own person (*i.e.* the law has nothing to do with an
intangible offence)."

thrown out into the valley of Hinnom — Ge-henna, as it was called — where they were burned up in the fires which consumed all the offal of the city. (This is the meaning of the words which we translate in this place "hell fire." It is the fire, the funeral pile, the burning furnaces of that dark valley, the Smithfield, the slaughter-house, the draught-house of Jerusalem.) It is like that other saying: "Salt is good; but if the salt has lost its savor, it is good for nothing but to be trodden under foot of man." All such words may have had a grave religious use once, but when used for mere polemical or revengeful purposes, they are as irreligious and as profane as the common cursing and swearing which belongs not to the city of Zion, but to the valley of Gehenna.

II. This is the original meaning of the passage. Now let us turn to its general application. It teaches us, like all other parts of our Lord's teaching, that not the outward act, but the inward spirit, is that which God judges. But it also calls our special attention to the mischief and the sin of our *words*. This is what He said on another occasion: " By thy words thou shalt be justified, and by thy words thou shalt be condemned:" and it is what His apostle St. James insists upon as the distinguishing mark between true and false religion — the power of governing the tongue. Considering the vast number of words that issue from our lips, considering how much of our life is carried on in talking, speaking, preaching, writing, reading, listening — this is a truth which cannot be too much insisted on. No doubt there is a precision in words which is pedantic; but all honor and praise to those who, consciously or unconsciously, obey their Lord's command, and try to measure their language, to define what they mean to themselves, to avoid phrases without meaning, or which

may injure and hurt the interests and feelings of others.
No doubt there are cases where, like our Lord Himself,
we are bound to use strong words against folly and sin.
But there are some whose lips act not as a fence to
their tongues, but as a mere opening, through which
flows an unceasing cataract of words — good, bad, light,
heavy, wise, foolish — without care or thought of who
may hear or of what may follow.   There are also some
whose pens are dipped in gall, who seem to delight in
saying what will vex or annoy their neighbors; who
have a cynical sneer, a scornful jest, a bitter insult for
every one whom they meet.   Their whole conversation
is one long repetition of " Raca, Raca."   Truly they
are in danger of condemnation of the council — not of
any earthly council, but of the council of all good and
wise men everywhere, of the council of the calm, and
just, and holy, of those who know, with our own
Hooker, that "the time will come when three words
spoken in charity will be worth more than ten thousand
words of disdainful scorn."

But there is yet a still more special application.   The
judgment of our Lord is yet more penetrating.   There
are many men who, whilst they avoid the common profane terms of abuse and contempt, yet think it even a
duty to use those words of bitter inextinguishable
hatred which have come down to us, like the Hebrew
word *moreh*, charged with the passions and prejudices
of a thousand generations — those names which having
been invented long ago by political or religious ani-
mosity, perhaps almost with an innocent intention, convey now a depth of offensiveness which no other words
from the mouth of men could convey.   I hardly venture
in this sacred place to call up the black catalogue of
such names before you, yet from places as sacred as
this they have unhappily been often heard.   They are

legion. On one side they are "heretic, schismatic, rationalist, infidel, deist, socinian, atheist;" on the other they are "papist, antichrist, Babylon, idolater, blasphemer, traitor;" on one side or on the other they are followed by a brood of other like names. They are one and all repetitions of the same old word, "rebel," "heretic," expressed by the Hebrew word *moreh*—they combine within themselves, as did that word, the intense virulence, both of the Jewish and of the Gentile race; they have one and all been applied in their day to the best and wisest of men; and they are one and all good for nothing but to be thrown into the valley of Hinnom, and burnt up with the filth and offal, and offscourings of dead abuses, and worn-out hatreds, and extinct controversies. Even though, like the word *moreh* itself, they may once have come out of Scripture, and from the pure fountain of life, they have now become full of fire and brimstone; they are as worthless, as mischievous, as polluting, as the coarse oaths and scurrilous epithets which are used by the less refined in their daily quarrels and wrangles in taverns and in fish-markets.

These thoughts are unhappily never out of place. Everywhere there will be some who are tempted to use these or like words against their neighbors; everywhere there will be those who in sermons, or in newspapers, or in speeches, if not in common conversation, think it a sacred duty to use them. And thus our Lord's warning needs to be everywhere lifted up. We have given up the ancient practice of killing our neighbors by slow torture in deep dungeons, or of carrying out our quarrels with murderous weapons. Feudal vengeance and the barbarous custom of duelling are both abandoned. The more necessary is it that we should be reminded that this is not enough, unless we restrain our tongues from those fierce words of scorn which duelling at least attempted to control; the more do we need to be reminded that not only is every duellist a murderer, but he who says to his brother "Raca," that is, who uses those insulting words which set the human heart on fire, and leave a blister there forever.

And again, we have given up the practice of killing our neighbors by fire, and sword, and rack, and scourge, for holding different opinions from ourselves. So much the more necessary is it for us to remember that this is not enough, unless we restrain our tongues from those biting and burning words which show that we nourish in our hearts the same feelings of undying wrath that our ruder forefathers expressed by carrying fagots to the stake, or tearing the flesh from the bones of our victims. So much the more do we need to be reminded that not only the old Inquisitors or the old Puritans were persecutors, but all who say to their brethren, *Moreh*, that is, "rebel," "heretic," that is, who use those anathemas and furious words of ancient hereditary reproach, which are meant to break up Christian union, and destroy Christian fellowship.

These expressions are beyond the reach of earthly tribunals of judgment and of council; but not the less are they doomed to that extremity of condemnation of which the valley of Hinnom was the type and symbol. They belong to that mass of worthless chaff, and of stinging briers and brambles, which will be burned up at last, as we hope, in a fire unquenchable.

III. This warning, spoken first against the language of individuals, is also needed for the language of Churches and nations. It is needed for them even more, because the interests at issue are greater; because also their temptation to indulge in these words is stronger. Look at the Churches of Christendom. How many a solemn document has issued from press or pulpit, which is, after all, nothing but a long reverberation of *Morch, morch,* "Thou fool! thou rebel!" Look at the anathemas hurled in former times by East against West, and by West against East, by Presbyterians against Prelates, and by Prelates against schismatics. Listen to their echoes in our own times — fainter, let us hope, but still coming of the same stock, springing out of the same bottomless pit. Look, too, at the contemptuous insolence with which nations have invented words of reproval for hostile or oppressed or subject nations; words which stick in the memory when the occasion, the excuse for them has long ceased; fountains of bitterness, which from generation to generation keep alive the sense of soreness and revenge, and stimulate to deeds of bloodshed and war.

What is the check to all this? It is contained in one word, which occurs throughout this passage — "Thy brother." Each man, in common life, has a brotherly, family relation to his neighbor, even to his enemy, which ought to make him feel and practise towards him something of a brother's respect, something of a brother's consideration. Each Church and nation — at least of Christendom — has a brotherly, sisterly relationship with all other Churches and nations; flesh of the same flesh, bone of the same bone, called by the same sacred name; which ought at least to induce courtesy, sympathy, fear to give offence, wish to bury the past, determination never to quarrel, hope to avoid irritating words, as well as irritating acts, and malignant names, which are but covers of malignant deeds.

There are many cases to which these remarks might specially apply. There is one immediately at hand. This day is the Fourth of July. It is the anniversary of the Declaration of American Independence — the

anniversary of the breach between the mother and the
daughter country. On such a day may we not feel
that our Lord's warnings have a peculiar significance
and force? The sons of that great Republic are, indeed,
our brothers — brothers in a sense in which no other
two great nations on the face of this earth are brothers
and sisters to each other; speaking the same language,
inheriting the same traditions, descended from the same
ancestors, intwined with the same dearest relationships,
rejoicing in the same history, in the same faith, in the
same hopes.

Both, no doubt, of these two mighty brothers have,
like the actual brothers of an actual family, had their
temper tried or their passions roused, sometimes the
elder by the younger, sometimes the younger by the
elder; but not the less are the ancient bonds of union
indissoluble, not the less of them are the poet's words
true : —

> No distance breaks the tie of blood;
>   Brothers are brothers evermore;
> Nor wrong, nor wrath of deadliest mood,
>   That magic may o'erpower.[1]

And how specially true is it of these brothers that hard
words may kill, and gentle words save, the peace and
life between them! How deeply was that first breach
widened on the first anniversary by the bitter recriminations of king and statesmen, of the mother country
and of the daughter colony! How fiercely were the
words tossed to and fro across the Atlantic — "Raca"
on one side, and "Moreh" on the other; "tyrant" from
the one, and "rebel" from the other! Yet how speedily,
how easily was that wound closed! how soon did the
Declaration of Independence become the name for the
peaceful birth of a new and glorious nation! how soon

---

[1] Keble's *Christian Year*, 2d Sunday after Trinity.

did the minister of the young Republic pay respectful homage, and receive respectful recognition, in the court of the ancient sovereign! What American is there who is not now proud of that history, which he then spurned behind him? What Englishman is there who is not now proud of the once dreaded name of Washington?

So, as years roll on, may all those fierce watchwords of party strife and national hatred perish and cease to be! So may each succeeding generation learn to leave those ancient curses to consume away in the fires of the dark valley whence they came, among the offal and carrion from which they originally sprang!

Woe on either side to those who revive those relics of barbarous days, those signals of strife and bitterness! Blessings on those peacemakers who, from either side, by gentle phrase, by conciliating temper, by determination not to give or take offence, by rigid abstinence from insulting words, as from something altogether unholy and accursed, bind together the two nations in one communion and fellowship of good deeds, great thoughts, and undying hopes of a yet more blessed future for both, in the far distant history of which this day was the first inauguration — when neither distance of space nor wrath of man shall put asunder those whom God, by speech, by blood, by the wonders of Science, and by the grace of Religion, has joined together.

THE CRUSADE OF CHARITY.

June 6, 1866, at the first annual service for the Bishop of London's Fund.[1]

Build Thou the walls of Jerusalem. — PSALM li. 18.

WE are met together to consecrate a great religious effort. Let us for a moment look at such religious efforts and consecrations in former times. They will teach us what is meant by enthusiasm in a holy cause. These walls themselves speak to us of it in language not to be mistaken. Had we been present here at such a meeting as this in the twelfth or thirteenth century, every one would have known what had called us to-

---

[1] *Prayer before the Sermon.* — O Lord, raise up, we pray Thee, Thy power and come among us, and with great might succor us; that whereas through our sins and wickedness we are sore let and hindered in running the race that is set before us, we may daily increase and go forwards in the knowledge and faith of Thee and of Thy Son, by the Holy Spirit: so that as well by these Thy ministers, as by them amongst whom they minister, Thy holy Name may be forever glorified, and Thy blessed Kingdom enlarged. Grant unto them grace and wisdom to hold up the weak, heal the sick, bind up the broken, bring again the outcasts, seek the lost, in this vast city, scattered abroad as sheep without a shepherd. Put it into the hearts of those whom Thou hast blessed with wealth and power, as they have freely received, freely to give of their abundance. Take away from us all hatred and prejudice, and whatever else may hinder us from godly union and concord in all good works; that as there is but one Body, and one Spirit, and one hope of our calling, one Lord, one faith, one baptism, one God and Father of us all, so we may henceforth be all of one heart and one soul, united in one holy bond of Truth and Peace, and Faith and Charity; through Jesus Christ our Lord. Amen.

Service for the Day. — First Lesson, Isa. lxi. Second Lesson, St. John x. 1-16. Anthem, "Hallelujah Chorus." Introit, "Jerusalem the Golden." Epistle, 1 St. John iv. 7-21. Gospel, St. Luke xvi. 19-31.

384

gether. . The object which then occupied the whole
religious world was one which admitted of no mistake,
and no wavering allegiance. We should have been
inaugurating one of the mighty efforts for the redemption of the Holy City from the hands of the Saracens.
To this work the first Crusading king was devoted
almost on the day of his coronation in this place. Into
this work two of the princes who here lie close to each
other flung themselves no less eagerly. Another ex-
pired almost beneath this roof, with the expression on
his lips of the long-cherished hope that he should die.
in Jerusalem. Another, his still more stirring son, the
conqueror of Agincourt, as he lay on his deathbed, and
heard the chanting of the penitential Psalm, bade them
halt at the words, "Build Thou the walls of Jerusalem,"
and with the dying wish that he could have fulfilled
that prayer, as once he had hoped, passed away from
the earth. The venerable ancestress of the House of
Tudor, no less saintly than wise, carried on the strain,
and breathed the last sigh of those inspiring times, when
she declared that if the Christian princes would again
combine in one final effort, she would attend the army
in the humblest and meanest of all capacities. So general, so ardent, was that great enthusiasm. All shared
in it. Even those that remained aloof dared not condemn it. Even the second founder of this noble edifice
was hardly excused by all his splendid works for his
unwillingness to join in the universal effort. Princes,
nobles, peasants, women, soldiers, clergy, even little
children caught the grand contagion. None liked to
be behindhand. It was discreditable, it was unortho-
dox, it was unworthy, it was cowardly to hang back.
Many motives, worldly, superstitious, religious, — ex-
citement, romance, love of adventure, — mingled in the
persuasion that drew them on. Still the thing itself was,

as we say, in the air; there was a fixed belief that to join
in the attempt was the Will of God, and for that Will
they were prepared to spend fortune and life, in the full
conviction that in so doing they were doing the best for
themselves, for the world, and for God.

This enthusiasm has long since passed away. The
Crusader sleeps on his marble tomb, and no successors
have risen to follow in his train. It may even be said
that the effort itself was founded on a mistake, and was
for an object which has come to naught. But I have
called your attention to it, because it exactly exemplifies
what sort of passion and energy that is which is needed
to accomplish mighty works; and because, as we think
of it, the question irresistibly rises in our minds, Is
there no new Crusade which we can preach, and you
can fight, now that the old Crusades are dead and
gone? Is there no New Jerusalem to be built again,
its waste city raised up, its desolations of many generations repaired?

Yes; there is assuredly the vast Christian effort, of
which one part at least has called us here together.
The Crusade of the nineteenth century is not less holy,
not less stirring, than that of the thirteenth. The
Jerusalem for which we must live and die is that which
lies all around us in this enormous city, ground down
by evils as gigantic and as terrible as ever were the
oppressors under whom the Syrian Jerusalem groaned,
but to be raised, repaired, restored, enlarged. Look
to the Gospel and Epistle of this week; the Gospel
which proclaims the rich man's duties, the Epistle in
which the beloved disciple entreats us "to love one
another:" "If God so loved us, we ought also to love
one another." These are the war-cries of our Crusade;
this is the enthusiasm which we are to enkindle. To
love, that is, to make the best and the most of every

human soul, to make this the chief object of our political, ecclesiastical, and social life, — this is what we have to proclaim. To hang back from this war of charity, this chivalric attack of beneficence, on sin, and ignorance, and selfishness, and misery, and want, is as heretical, as discreditable — may I say, as unworthy of a nobleman, or a gentleman, or a Christian? — as ever was thought the conduct of recreant knight, or selfish prince, or worldly merchant, who refused to take the Red Cross under Richard or Saint Louis.

The object surely is ten thousand times greater. It is not, as then, for the mere name of Christ, or for the outward sepulchre of Christ, but for the very work and command of Christ Himself that we are now called to fight. In a certain limited sense He was with the old Crusaders, as He was with the ancient Jews. But in the call to universal charity, in the call to build up the ruins of human society, to repair the breaches, and guard against the decay, of ages, we are in the most absolute and literal sense obeying the summons which He made to His first disciples, and which is of the very essence of His character. It is for the sake of raising, recovering, purifying, sanctifying, humanizing those very souls for which He died, that we are called to make a new effort, to receive a new commandment, to sound a new Crusade, to awaken a new devotion.

And that devotion, let us be sure, is there to arouse, if we know how to find it, and how to employ it. Persuade by your success, by your sincere and enlightened zeal, the powerful, the intelligent, the wealthy classes of this metropolis and of this country, that any good work in which you are engaged is one of pure, unmixed usefulness ; and then, depend upon it, the spirit of the Crusaders will once more rise in the hearts of us their descendants ; the generosity of the ancient princes and prelates of the Middle Ages will revive, as it actually has revived in the minds of at least two illustrious and munificent individuals of our own day, who have had the discernment to see their object clear before them, and the grace to accomplish it by their ample means; and this spirit will spread with a force as much more mighty, an effect as much more visible, as the resources of our age are vaster than those of five centuries past, as the victories of zeal according to knowledge, and faith working by love, ought to be greater than of zeal almost without knowledge, and faith almost without charity.

If henceforth it could become the rule of English life that all should devote at least a tenth of their income to the good of others in any form that seems best to the mind of each, what a revolution might be effected in the condition of the poor, what an alleviation of human suffering, what a blessed change in the prospects of Christianity itself!

So much for the general call of our age. Let me state some of the reasons why, in this call, the work of the evangelization of London, for which we are now met together, may justly take a chief place; why it is, humanly speaking, full of the promise of the utmost good, with the slightest admixture of evil.

First, whatever it may effect, it professes no other object than to promote the welfare of the people of London. It attacks no one, it attacks nothing, except sin and ignorance. · It is not intended to exclude any, but to include all. It represents no party in the Church of England, but the Church of England itself. Whatever the Church of England is, that also in its measure is the Bishop of London's Fund. It holds out its resources to all within the Church who choose to use them. It does not throw over this or that person,

this or that party, because they happen for the moment
to be unpopular. It has the courage rather to support
them, even at the cost of temporary sacrifice. No
forms of Christian belief within our pale, however
extreme, are exempted from a share in its aid, if only
they are combined with active usefulness in the Lord's
vineyard. The name of "the Bishop of London's
Fund" is itself a guaranty for its true character. It
owes its origin to the unwearying charity and energy
with which, at the cost of ease and health, your present
Chief Pastor has thrown himself into this and every
other movement for the welfare of his great diocese.
But it takes its permanent stand on that diocese itself.
Each of the leading sees of the English Church has,
no doubt, its own historical influences which may trans-
form its occupant into something beyond himself. But
of all these influences, though some may be more
elevating, others more magnificent, others more restraining, others more enlightening, others more poetic,
none can be more inspiring of large beneficence, of
practical sense, of wide impartiality, of lofty designs,
than those which belong to the see of this immense
metropolis. Here, if in any see in Christendom, the
magnitude of the task may well humble the proudest,
the vainest of men; before its multiplicity of conflicting views and interests the narrowest may become wide;
the very thought of presiding over the greatest city
which this earth contains, with all its world-wide power
and wealth, might well raise the most prosaic and most
worldly of men above the petty struggles of the moment in Church and State, into the atmosphere of those
deeds and thoughts which belong not to party, but to
mankind, the love of human souls, and the fear of God
Most High. Other sees may lose their significance, but
the see of London never, so long as England remains a

nation.   In the result of this effort, the Church of England is on its trial, failing with its failure, triumphant
in its success.

Secondly, the work before us belongs exactly to that
kind of duty in which the teaching of the Gospel and
the circumstances of our time coincide with the utmost
force.

The sin which Christ most frequently denounces (with
one exception, of which we are not now speaking) is the
sin of doing nothing. It is the sin of the rich man of this
week's Gospel, of whom no ill is recorded, except that a
poor man lay at his gate, and received no comfort or
sympathy. It is the sin to which the easy, the wealthy,
the prosperous, are constantly tempted. It is the sin
— or the virtue, as we sometimes call it — of letting
well alone, of not meddling in other men's matters, of
trusting that Providence will find a way for escape.
That old maxim of ecclesiastical wisdom, " to let things
go as they are going," has a kind of prudence of this
world, of prudence in one sense, but in all higher senses
a rashness how portentous! To let things go as they
are going; to let this vast population go on increasing,
multiplying, with no restraining, regenerating influences,
till it becomes uncontrollable, unmanageable, illimitable,
as the sea in its strength, as the fire in its fury; to let
this huge train of human society, with all its precious
freight of human lives and souls, rush on towards the
chasm which lies before it; to let it pass, because perchance it will last our day, because we have not taken
the trouble to look ahead, or go forwards with the signal of danger, or repair the broken line which it has to
traverse; — this neglect, this indifference is, as we say,
only negligence, only indolence, only want of fore-
thought. But oh! with what tremendous consequences,
with what crash of hopes and lives, even in the smaller

spheres of human duty! with what still greater crashes, sooner or later, in the history of nations! All honor to any one who has the courage at least to look the peril in the face; to wave the danger-flag; to discard that old maxim, of which I just now spoke, so popular in the days of old; to "go before his flock," in the true spirit of the Good Shepherd, if with no other purpose, at least to show what is to be done, what to be feared, what to be hoped.

Truly, in this matter of the neglect of the moral condition of our humbler population, as in the matter of the neglect of the material resources of our country, we may listen to that warning voice which was raised but the other day in the great Council of the nation, reminding us of the sacrifices we are bound to make for the sake of posterity; reminding us of the immense debt we owe to posterity, which it is our bounden duty to repay. "In the name of that dutiful concern for posterity which has been strong in every nation that ever did any thing great, and which has never left the mind of any such nation until it was already falling into decrepitude,"[1] our philosophic statesman called upon us to husband our natural resources, that we might still bequeath to the coming generations the gifts which former generations have bequeathed to us. In the name of that same dutiful concern for posterity, the Christian Evangelist may well labor to see that we do what in us lies to diminish that festering mass of barbarism, and irreligion, and ignorance, against which the most heroic virtue of after times will else contend in vain, — may well labor to be the unseen, unknown yet not unremembered, benefactor of ages yet unborn. It is not too late now: it may be too late a few years hence.

[1] Speech of Mr. J. S. Mill, on the Malt Duty, April 17, 1866.

And thirdly, how is this good work so auspiciously, so opportunely begun, to be carried on ?

It must be carried on, like all good works in this complicated age of ours, not by solitary efforts, not by the Red-Cross knight pricking forth alone in quest of adventure, but by organization, by co-operation, by discipline, by comprehension of all the gifts you can command. There should be a place for every one who is ready to work in the army of God. " The enthusiasm should not be allowed to die out in any one for want of the occupation best calculated to keep it alive." This work should be the natural outlet for all the pent-up energies of our multifarious age. All the random enterprise, honest doubt, imperfect faith, eccentric activity, eager zeal, homely sense, ardent aspirations of the rising generation should here find that they have their proper work to do under their willing leaders. Let one, if he can, win souls by his ritual ; another, if he can, by his schools ; another by his preaching and teaching ; another by his provident clubs or his lectures ; another by his personal intercourse from house to house ; let one throw himself into the force of the everlasting Gospel of Jesus Christ in its original fulness and freshness ; let another, if he finds it more easy, work it out in its later dogmatic manifestations. " There are diversities of gifts, but the same Spirit . . . differences of administration, but the same Lord . . . diversities of operations, but it is the same God which worketh all in all." Here, it may be, a sudden, strong inroad is to be made to clear out one of those nests of corruption which infect a whole neighborhood ; there, we see the beneficent effect of the better dwellings and purer habits to which modern philanthropy at last has turned its serious attention ; here (which, I am told, is now the special need and opportunity) districts, separated from the overgrown parishes of which they form a part, are to be turned into separate, and, as it is hoped in time, self-supporting spheres of pastoral ministration. Only in all let us bear in mind the end for which we labor; the end for which the walls of Jerusalem are to be built up; the end for which, in simpler and more Christian language, "he who loves God is to love his brother also." It is to make the people of London better than they are now. It is to make them more temperate, more pure, more truthful, more devout. In comparison of this all our appliances are merely as means to ends. Ritual, preaching, schools, church-going, chapel-going, Religion itself, are but so many means which God in His infinite mercy has given to bring men nearer to Himself, by making them like to Himself in holiness, goodness, and truth. Individuals, households, streets, reclaimed from vice and sin, and living justly, soberly, and reverently, in the fear of God and in charity with their neighbors — these are the one convincing proof of the reality of your mission, of the efficiency of your work. For the sake of making men good — it is a homely phrase, but it is no less certainly true — Christ lived, died, and rose again. For the sake of making men good, we must not disdain, after His example, and in His Spirit, to spend, and to be spent. Choose for this end, let this Fund choose for this end, whatever means, after mature experience, are thought best to secure it. But in God's name, in the name of Christ our Saviour, remember that this is our end, and that unless we in some measure accomplish it, the Church and the world alike will believe that we have spent our time for naught. Be this your boast, be this your joy, that you have toiled not for exalting yourselves or your party, or even your Church; but for making men like Christ, and earth like heaven;

for making these hundreds and thousands of forgotten
souls worthy of Christian England, manly, upright, citizens, alike of the earthly and of the heavenly city.

And for this object we have a peculiar advantage,
and a peculiar reward. It is the peculiar honor and
privilege of our Established Church, that, whatever its
defects, it has this one advantage, possessed by none
of the unendowed priesthoods and ministries of other
Churches and sects, that it can preach the Gospel to
the poor, literally, without money and without price.
You depend on no voluntary contributions from them;
you have not to obtain, as others have, the hard-won
savings of those amongst whom you minister for your
own maintenance; you are "independent" in the best
sense of the word. This Fund, if it enables you to do
nothing else, enables you, in the true spirit of the
Church of England, to go to those from whom you
have nothing to gain, and who can owe nothing to
you, except their own selves. Oh, value this privilege
rightly! value it as the greatest of ancient philosophers, the greatest of Christian Apostles, declare that
they valued it! It is the only solution, in our complicated society, of that difficult problem on which they
so touchingly dwell, how to combine the purity and the
delicacy of the relation between teacher and taught,
with the honest hire of which every laborer is worthy,
with the freedom from mere worldly care, which for
every high calling is so indispensable.

And it is also the peculiar reward of your labors that
you have to deal with classes so little known, yet so
deeply interesting, as the vast population of the poor
of England. We are sometimes told of the romance of
missionary enterprise, the charm which leads adventurous spirits across the sea, to preach the Gospel to distant and heathen races of mankind. Not for a moment

would I disparage such a soaring ambition as this. The lonely death of a lonely missionary preacher, unknown and unrequited, amongst the savages of Australia has, believe me, moved the admiring envy of one of the calmest and most philosophic of modern inquirers. Yet surely there is a romance and charm at least as powerful, in purifying and elevating the future hope of our own country, the sturdy race of our own flesh and blood, the deep substratum, from which the heart of our nation is formed, out of which rise, from time to time, even the nobles and teachers of our land. To explore that unknown region (I will not say, as some would say, of heathen darkness, but) of twilight dawn or of fading day; to track the strange, mysterious, inextricable traditions of dim religious belief floating in those unsophisticated classes; to ascertain for ourselves by hearing and seeing what is the real unfeigned creed of the great mass of the people of England; to catch the growth of new thoughts, new customs, new habits in the dark corners and dusky outskirts of our primeval barbarism; to watch the strivings of the Holy Spirit of God, with groanings that seek in vain for articulate utterance, yet intercede not in vain before God and man, as they make themselves felt in the natural conscience and the domestic affections even of the worst of men, against all the force of outward degradation and of inward temptation — surely this is a voyage of discovery, which, to the mere intellectual seeker after truth, much more to the Evangelist of Christ, has all the charm of an entrance into a new world, of a passage beyond the pillars of Hercules, into a region, rich in virgin soil, and unexhausted mines of knowledge and experience.

And not merely the interest, but the instruction of such an enterprise ought to be its own sufficient reward.

In that simple, undefined religious belief of the poor, defying all the untoward conditions of their outward life; in that instinct of immortality, proof against all the trials, and sufferings, and oppressions of their hard lot; in that deep unfathomable sense, which neither vice nor ignorance can eradicate, of a Supreme Judge, and of an all-merciful Saviour; what an encouragement to our wavering faith, what a rebuke to our artificial systems, what a light shining in a dark place to cheer us onwards! In their simple, honest, truthful questions, in their keen insight into the difficulties which have perplexed the learned of all ages, what a warning to us to deal with them in all sincerity, what a straight and easy clew to guide us through all the labyrinths of the half-informed and the ill-educated to the simplicity of true wisdom, which is the simplicity that is in Christ!

This, then, is your Crusade. This is that warfare of Christian Love, to which in the Holy Communion of this day you pledge yourselves by your sacramental oath of allegiance to your heavenly Captain. The work will be slow and gradual. But it will not, it cannot, like those old Crusades, die and be forgotten, except through our own fault. They ceased with the change of times and modes of thought. But "the poor," the suffering, ignorant poor of London will, I fear, "be always with us," as long as London lasts; and the summons to assist them will, I trust, become louder and louder as England rises more and more to the sense of her lofty calling. As often as you see, or as any of us see, the helmet of Agincourt, the helmet of that last of the Crusaders, — a Crusader in heart, if not in act, — towering above our heads in the far vista of this sacred edifice, let it remind you of those dying words of his which I have chosen for my text. "Build Thou the walls of Jerusalem." To his mind, doubtless, they conveyed the sense of an expiring effort, which was come too late to accomplish its object. To our minds, translated into true Christian language, they ought to convey the sense of an effort but just begun, of a prayer which depends on this generation for its fulfilment, of a trumpet-call which speaks not of that which is ready to wax old and vanish away, but of that which is full of life, and energy, and hope.

The heavenly Jerusalem cannot be built in a day, but it can be built stone by stone, and tower by tower, even in the midst of Babylon, wherever there is a good pastor to lead, and a faithful clergy to follow, and a gallant laity to advise and assist, and a noble people to edify and enlighten. And if we sometimes dream of more zealous faith or of fairer prospects in other ages or other lands, or of an ideal standard which seems never to be reached, yet here 'and not there, now and not then, with the resources of the present, not of the past or of the future, our lot is cast. Be our words those of the inspired genius of the painter [1] and poet, whose illusions were sometimes more solid than other men's realities —

> And did those Feet in ancient time
>   Walk upon England's mountains green,
> And was the holy Lamb of God
>   On England's pleasant pastures seen?
>
> And did the Countenance Divine
>   Shine forth upon our clouded " heights,"
> And was Jerusalem builded here,
>   Among those dark Satanic " streets? "
>
> Bring me my bow of burning gold,
>   Bring me my arrows of desire;
> Bring me my spear — O clouds unfold,
>   Bring me my chariot of fire!

[1] Blake.

I will not cease from mental fight,
  Nor shall my sword sleep in my hand,
Till we have built Jerusalem
  In England's green and pleasant land.

THE GREEK MASSACRE.

May 15, 1870, being the day after the arrival in England of the remains of Edward Herbert and Frederick Vyner, murdered in Greece with Edward Lloyd and Count de Boyl on April 21, 1870.

Thy way is in the sea, and Thy paths in the great waters, and Thy footsteps are not known.

Thou leddest Thy people like sheep by the hand of Moses and Aaron. — PSALM lxxvii. 19, 20.

THIS Psalm,[1] sung in this morning's service, is one of which we know not the exact origin, but which almost for that very reason appeals more deeply to the heart of all ages. It describes a soul torn by some deep grief, some trial which could not be unravelled or explained, some calamity which cut off all the ordinary means of consolation.

The Psalmist cannot sleep for the visions of distress

[1] PSALM LXXVII.

I.

"I will cry unto God with my voice,
    even unto God will I cry, and He shall hearken unto me."
In the time of my trouble I sought the Lord,
    I stretched out my hand and ceased not in the night season,
        my soul refused comfort:
        "when I think upon God I am in heaviness,
    I muse in mine heart and my spirit waxeth faint!"

Thou didst hold fast mine eyelids,
    I was troubled and spake nothing,
I considered the days of old,
    and the years that are past:
"let me call to remembrance my song in the night,
    and commune with mine heart!"—
and my spirit inquired thus within itself: —

that haunt him — "Thou hast held mine eyes waking."
He cannot find words to express his anxiety — "I am
so troubled that I cannot speak." In the long restless
night "he stretches out his hand, and cries in vain for
help." Like Jacob, when they brought to him his
son's coat rent and stained with blood, "he refused"
(the same words are used) "he refused to be comforted."

It almost seems as if there were something hard and

"Will the Lord absent Himself forever,
        and will He be no more entreated?
is His mercy clean gone forever,
        and His promise come utterly to an end for evermore?
hath God forgotten to be gracious,
        will He shut up His lovingkindness in displeasure?"

Then said I: — "this is my affliction,
        even during the years of the right hand of the Most Highest
I will think of the works of Jehovah,
        yea, I will call to mind Thy wonders of old time,
I will sing also of all Thy works,
        and my talking shall be of Thy doings."

II.

Thy way, O God, is holy;
        who is so great a god as our God?
Thou art the God that doeth wonders,
        and hast declared Thy power among the nations;
Thou didst mightily deliver Thy people,
        even the sons of Jacob and Joseph.

The waters saw Thee, O God, the waters saw Thee and were afraid;
        the depths also were troubled;
the clouds poured out water, the air thundered,
        and Thine arrows went abroad;
the voice of Thy thunder was heard in the whirlwind, lightnings
                shone upon the world;
        the earth was moved and shook withal.

Thy way was in the sea,
        and Thy paths in the great waters,
    and Thy footsteps were not known, —
Thou leddest Thy people like sheep
        by the hand of Moses and Aaron.

The Psalms, chronologically arranged, by Four Friends.

cruel in the fate that has overtaken him — an iron law which has crushed him, a relentless Nemesis that has struck him down; — "Will the Lord absent Himself forever, and will He be no more entreated? Is His mercy clean gone forever, and hath His promise come utterly to an end for evermore? Hath God forgotten to be gracious, and will He shut up His lovingkindness in displeasure?"

Such despairing, overwhelming thoughts have, no doubt, in every age and in every country, fallen upon the heart of many a son and daughter of man. Let us see to what quarters the Psalmist turns for consolation. It is, perhaps, somewhat unexpected, yet not on that account the less capable of being used by us. He goes out of himself altogether; he goes out of his own time and circumstances; he looks upon himself as part of a vaster, deeper system. "I have considered the days of old — the years that are past — the years of the right hand of the Most Highest. I call to mind His wonders of old time. I meditate on all His works, and commune with myself on His doings." He goes back to the earlier history of his race. He draws his comfort, not from the thought of his individual condition, but from his identification with the joys and sorrows of a great and mighty people. He summons before his imagination, by a vivid effort, the scene of that famous night when the Jewish nation was delivered from Egypt in the passage of the Red Sea. He puts it before himself and before us in an aspect which, true as it doubtless was, escapes us in the more measured and tranquil march of the Mosaic narrative. He speaks of it as effected not to the sound of trumpet and timbrel, not in the clearness and calmness of daylight, nor in the broad and ample spaces left by the receding walls of water, but in the depth of midnight, amidst the roar

of the hurricane which caused the sea to go back, with
the army pressing close behind, and the driving spray
on either side, amidst a gloom lit up only by the glare
of the lurid lightning, as the Lord looked out from the
thick darkness of the cloud, along a mysterious and
unknown pathway over which the returning waves
relentlessly broke, and which no after age has been able
to discover with certainty. " The waters saw Thee, O
God, the waters saw Thee and were troubled; yea, the
depths also were troubled and shuddered. The clouds
also poured out water: the skies thundered: Thy light-
ning-arrows went abroad: the voice of Thy thunders
rolled along in the whirlwind: the lightnings glared
upon the earth: the earth trembled and shook. *Thy
way was in the sea, and Thy paths in the great waters, and
Thy footsteps were not known.*" Such was the surprise,
such the mystery, such the terror, such the uncertainty;
and yet in the midst of all this, a solemn deliverance was
wrought. In one brief abrupt conclusive sentence, the
Psalmist sums it up, as sufficient for them, as sufficient for himself. Through this dark and terrible night,
through that deep and awful baptism, through that long
and perilous way, " *Thou leddest Thy people like sheep
by the hand of Moses and Aaron.*" The watchful Shepherd was there, through unknown ways, guiding them,
by the hand of the two faithful brothers, leading them,
as a later prophet [1] expresses it, " through the deep, as
a horse in the wilderness, that they should not stumble;
as a beast goeth down into the valley, the Spirit of the
Lord caused him to rest: so didst Thou lead Thy
people, to make Thyself a glorious name."

This peculiar source of the consolation of the Psalmist
is indeed applicable to many earthly griefs; of some
griefs it is almost the only thing to be said. There

---

[1] Isa. lxiii. 13, 14.

may be calamities so strange, so bewildering, so entangled with the mistakes of men, and the chances of accident, that they seem to send us back at once for our only comfort to the wide system of the universe of which they are part, and of which God is the centre.

There is a striking passage in which a great philosopher, the famous Bishop Berkeley, describes the thought which occurred to him of the inscrutable schemes of Providence, as he saw in St. Paul's Cathedral a fly moving on one of the pillars. "It requires," he says, "some comprehension in the eye of an intelligent spectator to take in at one view the various parts of the building, in order to observe their symmetry and design. But to the fly, whose prospect was confined to a little part of one of the stones of a single pillar, the joint beauty of the whole or the distinct use of its parts were inconspicuous. To that limited view, the small irregularities on the surface of the hewn stone seemed to be so many deformed rocks and precipices." That fly on the pillar, whether of that Cathedral of which the philosopher spoke or of this Abbey in which we are assembled, is the likeness of each human being as he creeps along the vast pillars which support the universe. The sorrow which appears to us nothing but a yawning chasm or hideous precipice may turn out to be but the joining or cement which binds together the fragments of our existence into a solid whole. That dark and crooked path in which we have to grope our way in doubt and fear, may be but the curve which, in the full daylight of a brighter world, will appear to be the necessary finish of some choice ornament, the inevitable span of some majestic arch.

Again, there are calamities where, as in the case of the Psalmist, we derive a certain comfort, not to be despised (for it comes from Him who has made us), from feeling that not only the events of the world, but ourselves, in our own individual being and circles, are, in a still closer sense, parts of a larger whole. It may be that we are enabled to feel the consolation of being one of a wide family or race, which is bowed down with us in our sorrows, which makes our sorrows its own, as we make theirs ours. It may be, that we have a grief which by its very suddenness and severity strikes the hard cold heart of the outer world and neighborhood, and brings out from their unknown depths those springs of natural affection which it is the very object, if one may say so, of such startling, inexplicable dispensations to evoke and make manifest. It may even be that our grief is one in which a whole nation joins; in which the hearts of a mighty people are moved with us, "as the trees of the forest are moved with the wind;" in which the whole community suddenly finds itself, under the inspiration of deep and strong emotion, one heart and one soul, drawn together as one family, mourning for its children, as "Rachel" on her rocky hill was "weeping for her children, and refused to be comforted because they were not." Then it is that the fountains of the great deep of the human heart are broken up, and hundreds and thousands may feel together, and, by the mysterious sympathy of a common grief, comfort those whom they have never seen; and the iron hand of sorrow holds the golden key by which the secret affinities and hidden charities of mankind are unlocked and poured forth.

It is from the consciousness that such an event has occurred in our history within the last few weeks, and that on this day and to-morrow it will be present, in its most affecting form, to hundreds of our countrymen, that I have ventured, in this the centre of English life, to touch on a chord, else perhaps too private and too sacred to be stirred, and to give to the services of this day a funereal character which else they could hardly have worn.

On this day have been deposited, in their respective homes, the loved remains of two of our unfortunate countrymen, whose untimely and tragic fate in Greece has roused the pity, the indignation, and the sympathy of Europe. One, the third, rests still in that fated land. The fourth victim reposes in his own not less famous country beside the Arno.

This is not the place to dwell on any of the circumstances of that dreadful week. Others, doubtless, will draw the just conclusion — calmly, wisely, faithfully — which, perchance, even out of this frightful calamity, will bring good to the world. On this day, and in this place, we are not on the seat of judgment. We are rather at the grave and gate of death, which is the gate of Heaven. Let us, for a few moments, for ourselves, and for those here or far away, whose mourning we have made our own, draw from this event the lessons which the Psalmist's words suggest.

Surely to us, as to him, such sorrows as this bring the thought that there is a wider, higher world, of which this little round of life is but a part. "Lord, if Thou hadst been here my brother had not died." So Martha and so Mary, each with their different characters, exclaimed in the bitterness of grief, at the thought of the unexplained delay which, as it seemed, had cost that precious life. "If thou hadst been here, if this or that had been otherwise, if this had but been foreseen, arranged, prevented — all might yet have been well." So, again and again we think; yet let us rise into a loftier region. It is our main comfort. "I am the Resurrection and the Life," was the answer. Far above, where Christ sitteth at the right hand of God;

far above, where all secondary laws resolve themselves
into the primary Source of Being, "Our Father which
is in heaven;" thither let us ascend.   Let us remember
the "years of the right hand of the Most Highest."
From how much evil to come in this life, into what
blessedness in the Better Land, they may have been
taken, how and why it was expedient for them and for
us that they should have gone away — we know not
now, but we shall know hereafter.

Again, let us take comfort in the thought that the
very greatness and suddenness of the grief which gathers
the sympathy of so many round the hearts of a few, has
in itself an exalting, elevating, transfiguring consequence.   Over those graves we seem to see lamenting
the forms of Two, may we not say of Three, ancient
nations.   The stern anger and bitter grief of Two, the
yet more bitter shame of the Third, will forever invest
the names of those who have been thus loved and lost
with a tragic solemnity which, if not the best balm to
the broken heart, yet has, in spite of ourselves, a healing, soothing, invigorating effect.   The ghastly visions
of those nights and days will fade away, and in their
place will come the remembrance that with those famous "old poetic mountains," with those scenes of sur-
passing grandeur which almost to the last moment
moved the admiration and cheered the spirits of the
suffering captives themselves, their memories will
henceforth be indissolubly blended; that the hills and
valleys, the very sound of whose names now awakens
a shudder, will, in after years, come back to us again
charged with a new and peculiar pathos as the everlasting monuments of the beloved and lamented Englishmen whose last days were spent beneath their graceful
and majestic heights, and in their deep romantic dells.
The mountains of Gilboa, the high places where the

beauty of Israel fell, were forever enshrined in the chant of David over his lost friend.[1] So may the old immortal names of Athens, Thebes, and Marathon, bitter as they now seem, become at last even sweet to the memory by association with those who there met their end with a courage unpremeditated, unpretending, but not the less worthy of the deeds of the great old days which once ennobled those ancient scenes.

And finally, in the recollection of the suddenness, the untimeliness of the stroke, is there not this last thought for all of us — Where, how, when, did that stroke find them? Where, how, when, will it find us? That uncertainty of death which we all know, but which we all find so difficult to remember — what is the lesson which it ought to teach us? It is that old familiar word which our Master taught — " Watch, for ye know not the hour." Watch; be watchful; keep your conscience clear, your judgment calm, your presence of mind steady, your faith cheerful and strong, for the last dread emergency which will tax every faculty whenever it shall come. It is only these sudden wrenches from the bloom and fulness of life that bring before us that truth so well set forth by one who formerly occupied this place [2] —

> Thou inevitable day,
> When a voice to me shall say —
> " Thou must rise and come away;
>
> All thine other journeys past,
> Gird thee, and make ready fast,
> For thy longest and thy last " —
>
> Day deep-hidden from our sight
> In impenetrable night,
> Who may guess of thee aright?
>
> .   .   .   .   .

---

[1] 2 Sam. i. 19, 21.   [2] " The Day of Death," by Archbishop Trench.

> Shall I lay my drooping head
> On some loved lap, round my bed
> Prayers be made and tears be shed?
>
> Or at distance from mine own,
> Name and kin alike unknown,
> Make my solitary moan?

Suddenly, like thunder in a clear sky, in the midst of innocent enjoyment, came the blow which thus has ended. We know the verse of the poet which tells how "fierce" is the "light that beats upon a throne," revealing every speck and spot in the character that, by its conspicuous eminence, is thus exposed to the public gaze. Something, too, of that "fierce light" belongs to the sudden test and trial of characters involved in some great catastrophe, which for the time makes even the inmost souls and simplest words of those concerned the property, as it were, of the world. Such is the disclosure of the noble bearing of these our countrymen, in the days of their last trial, in the touching letters which last reached us from those distant shores.

Happy, thrice happy, may any one be, who can hope that, in the like unexpected call, in the like agony of conflicting fears, he might show the same grand forgetfulness of self, the same gallant resolve, not once only, but twice and thrice repeated, to save the lives of others by the sacrifice of his own; the same calm collected judgment that nothing should be done even for the preservation of life that was not in itself just and reasonable; the same simple Christian trust in God's goodness; the same modest yet proud hope, in the prospect of the coming end, to die bravely as Englishmen should do. Those affecting lines, that last and latest request for the sending of a Bible, for the prayers of a friend, will be read by hundreds as though they had lost a brother, will be cherished by those who possess them, as though they had gained a king's treasure.

They have died as Englishmen and as Christians should die; they have been mourned for, as England alone can mourn for her children.

The mortal tabernacles of those two blameless, gentle spirits are now on the native soil where they desired to rest — "lovely and pleasant in their lives, and in their deaths not divided." Their souls are with Him who gave them. The way was dark and terrible. The footsteps of the merciful God were hard to trace. Yet through the deep waters He led them, we may humbly hope, to the haven where they would be. "God be with us," was the short all-embracing prayer which closes one of those brief heart-rending letters, written but two days before the close. That prayer, we may sincerely trust, was heard. Yea, though they walked through the valley of the darkest shadow of death, we need fear no evil for them, for He was with them — His rod and His staff comforted them, as they comfort us. He led them to the still waters."[1] All is over now. He led them to the long last home, where there shall be no more parting, and where "the former things are passed away."[2]

[1] Psalm xxiii. 2, 4.   [2] Rev. xxi. 4.

Lange's Commentary,

CRITICAL, DOCTRINAL, AND HOMILETICAL.

TRANSLATED, ENLARGED, AND EDITED

BY

PHILIP SCHAFF, D.D.,

PROFESSOR IN THE UNION THEOLOGICAL SEMINARY.

This is the most comprehensive and exhaustive Commentary on the whole Bible ever published in this or any other country.

The German work, on which the English edition is based, is the product of about twenty distinguished Biblical scholars, of Germany, Holland, and Switzerland, and enjoys a high reputation and popularity wherever German theology is studied.

The American edition is not a mere translation (although embracing the whole of the German), but, to a large extent, an *original* work ; about one-third of the matter being added, and the whole adapted to the wants of the English and American student. Its popularity and sale has been lately increasing in Great Britain.

The press has been almost unanimous in its commendation of LANGE'S COMMENTARY. It is generally regarded as being, on the whole, the most useful Commentary, especially for ministers and theological students—in which they are more likely to find what they desire than in any other. It is a complete treasury of Biblical knowledge, brought down to the latest date. It gives the results of careful, scholarly research ; yet in a form sufficiently popular for the use of intelligent laymen. The Homiletical department contains the best thoughts of the great divines and pulpit orators of all ages, on the texts explained, and supplies rich suggestions for sermons and Bible lectures.

The following are some of the chief merits of this Commentary :

1. *It is orthodox and sound*, without being sectarian or denominational. It fairly represents the exegetical and doctrinal *consensus* of evangelical divines of the present age, and yet ignores none of the just claims of liberal scientific criticism.

2. *It is comprehensive and complete*—giving in beautiful order the authorized English version with emendations, a digest of the Critical Apparatus, Exegetical Explanations, Doctrinal and Ethical Inferences and Reflections, and Homiletical and Practical Hints and Applications.

3. *It is the product of fifty American (besides twenty European) Scholars*, from the leading denominations and Theological institutions of the country. Professors in the Theological Seminaries of New York, Princeton, Andover, New Haven, Hartford, Cambridge, Rochester, Philadelphia, Cincinnati, Alleghany, Chicago, Madison, and other places, representing the Presbyterian, Episcopal, Congregational, Baptist, Methodist, Lutheran, and Reformed Churches, have contributed to this Commentary, and enriched it with the results of their special studies. It may, therefore, claim a national character more than any other work of the kind ever published in this country.

8vo, per vol., in sheep, $6.50 ; in half calf, $7.50 ; cloth, $5.00.

CHARLES SCRIBNER'S SONS,

743 AND 745 BROADWAY, NEW YORK

Epochs of Modern History.

Each 1 vol. 16mo., with Outline Maps.   Price per volume, in cloth, $1.00.

EACH VOLUME COMPLETE IN ITSELF AND SOLD SEPARATELY.

EDITED BY EDWARD E. MORRIS, M.A.

The ERA of the PROTESTANT REVOLUTION.   By F. SEEBOHM, Author of "The Oxford Reformers—Colet, Erasmus, More."

The CRUSADES. By the Rev. G. W. Cox, M.A., Author of the "History of Greece."

The THIRTY YEARS' WAR, 1618—1648. By SAMUEL RAWSON GARDINER.

The HOUSES of LANCASTER and YORK; with the CONQUEST and LOSS of FRANCE. By JAMES GAIRDNER, of the Public Record Office.

The FRENCH REVOLUTION and FIRST EMPIRE; an Historical Sketch. By WM. O'CONNOR MORRIS, with an Appendix by Hon. ANDREW D. WHITE, Prest. of Cornell University.

The AGE OF ELIZABETH. By the Rev. M. CREIGHTON, M.A.

The PURITAN REVOLUTION. By J. LANGTON SANFORD.

The FALL of the STUARTS; and WESTERN EUROPE from 1678 to 1697 By the Rev. EDWARD HALE, M.A., Assist. Master at Eton.

The EARLY PLANTAGENETS and their relation to the HISTORY of EUROP— the foundation and growth of CONSTITUTIONAL GOVERNMENT. By the R WM. STUBBS, M.A., etc., Regius Professor of Modern History in the University Oxford.

The BEGINNING of the MIDDLE AGES; CHARLES the GREAT and ALFRED; the HISTORY of ENGLAND in its connection with that of EUROPE in the NINTH CENTURY. By the Very Rev R. W. CHURCH, M.A., Dean of St. Paul's.

The AGE of ANNE. By Edward E. MORRIS, M.A., Editor of the Series.

The NORMAN KINGS and the FEUDAL SYSTEM. By the Rev. A. H. JOHNSON, M.A. EDWARD III. By the Rev. W. WARBURTON, M.A., late Her Majesty's Senior Inspector of Schools.

FREDERICK the GREAT and the SEVEN YEARS' WAR. By F. W. LONGMAN, of Ballic College, Oxford.

The above 13 Volumes in Roxburg Style. Leather Labels and Gilt Top. Pu up in a handsome Box. Sold only in Sets. Price per Set, $13.00.

• The above book for sale by all booksellers, or will be sent, post or express charges paid, upon receipt of the price by the publishers,

CHARLES SCRIBNER'S SONS,

743 AND 745 BROADWAY, NEW YORK

www.ingramcontent.com/pod-product-compliance
Lightning Source LLC
Chambersburg PA
CBHW021328110726
47900CB00005B/1391